NOW YOU CAN ENSURE
THAT EATING LITE
MEANS EATING RIGHT . . .

. . . with the only complete guide available that helps you count calories and check the fat, cholesterol, and sodium content for hundreds of lite products—from breads and butter to cooking oils, soups, frozen entrees, desserts, and much, much more.

It's the essential reference to carry with you when you shop, so you can be sure you're getting the most wholesome—and most delicious—lite foods available today!

**THE COMPLETE "LITE" FOODS
CALORIE,
FAT,
CHOLESTEROL,
AND SODIUM
COUNTER—
your key to lighter, healthier eating**

THE
COMPLETE

"LITE"
FOODS

Calorie, Fat,
Cholesterol,
and Sodium Counter

DENSIE WEBB, Ph.D., R.D.

BANTAM BOOKS
NEW YORK • TORONTO • LONDON • SYDNEY • AUCKLAND

THE COMPLETE "LITE" FOODS CALORIE, FAT, CHOLESTEROL,
AND SODIUM COUNTER

A Bantam Book/May 1990

*The Healthy Choice label on page 18 and 19 was used with permission of
ConAgra® Frozen Foods, 1989.*

ISBN 0-553-28471-1

Bantam Books are published by Bantam Books, a division of Bantam
Doubleday Dell Publishing Group, Inc. Its trademark, consisting of the
words "Bantam Books" and the portrayal of a rooster, is Registered in U.S.
Patent and Trademark Office and in other countries. Marca Registrada,
Bantam Books, 666 Fifth Avenue, New York, New York 10103.

PRINTED IN THE UNITED STATES OF AMERICA

OPM   0 9 8 7 6 5 4 3 2 1

Contents

Abbreviations used in this book

CAL — calories
FAT — fat
CHOL — cholesterol
SOD — sodium
(G) — grams
(mg) — milligrams
sl — slice
pc — piece
oz — ounces
tsp — teaspoon
na — not available
fl — fluid
T — tablespoon
% — percentage

Introduction

There used to be a time when "dietetic" foods were the only "light" foods available and even the choices of those were few. Today, however, we can choose from "light" or "lite,"* reduced-calorie, low-calorie, low-cholesterol, reduced-cholesterol, cholesterol-free, low-sodium, very low sodium, and salt-free foods—the list of terms that indicate a food is "lite" in a particular ingredient seems endless.

Who started it all? The grandfather of lite foods is arguably the Stouffer's Company of Solon, Ohio. They introduced their Lean Cuisine line in 1981 with ten entrees, and the lite race was officially on. Today, Stouffer's has thirty-one Lean Cuisine entrees, four Lean Cuisine French bread pizzas, and no fewer than eight major competitors, companies who make lite versions of everything from chicken chow mein to chicken enchiladas. Swanson's straitlaced three-compartment meat loaf dinners have been joined by; light stuffed sole with Newburg sauce and light chicken burritos.

The light explosion started with a few lite entrees, but today we have lite ketchup to go with our lite french fries, lite syrup to pour over lite pancakes, and lite margarine to spread on our lite bread. We can even have lite instant gourmet coffees to accompany our lite cheesecake, and lite beer to quench our thirst after eating lite potato chips. There's no denying that today, lite food is one of the fastest-growing parts of the American food industry. The NutraSweet Company, makers of the artificial sweetener aspartame, estimates that over 1,200 products—most of which are lite or low-calorie foods—contain the sweetener.

*(For the purposes of this book we will be using the word "lite" when referring to "light" or "lite" foods.)

The demand for more lite products doesn't appear to be waning either. According to the Calorie Control Council, a group representing the lite food industry, 57 percent of adult women and 45 percent of adult men use low-calorie or lite foods and beverages—that's about 93 million Americans. As long as the demand exists, companies will continue to supply new and more innovative lite products.

Although lite foods generally appeal to people trying to reduce or maintain their weight, they also attract people concerned about eating too much fat, a risk factor for heart disease and a possible risk factor for cancer; too much cholesterol, a risk factor for heart disease; and too much sodium, a potential risk factor for high blood pressure. However, knowing which of the lite foods are truly lite in calories, fat, cholesterol, or sodium is a major obstacle in making the most healthful food choices.

The idea of producing lite foods was ingenious. Unfortunately, ingenuity has jumped far ahead of government regulations. The result? There is no standard definition for what constitutes a lite product. Is it lite in calories, fat, sodium, or cholesterol? Or, is it simply lite in color, texture, or taste? As it currently stands—with a few important exceptions (see Chapter 3)—the words "light" or "lite" on a food label can mean almost anything. And as the number of products claiming to be lite increases, so does the difficulty in interpreting what lite on the label really means. It is therefore important to always remember the Golden Lite Rule: *Never assume, when a label says light/lite, that the food inside is low in calories, fat, sodium, or cholesterol.* Quite often, lite products are lite in one ingredient, cholesterol, for example, yet still very high in another unwanted ingredient, such as fat. The fat may be from vegetable oils—such as corn oil, soybean oil, or safflower oil—which contain no cholesterol, but at the same time provide the same number of calories as cholesterol-containing lard or butter.

It is estimated that the "lite" food market will climb to more than $41 billion by 1990. As products claiming to be light appear, you, the buyer, will be faced wtih even more on-the-spot purchasing decisions. The complete ''Lite'' Food Calorie, Fat, Cholesterol, and Sodium Counter is a brand-name product guide to the lite and not-so-lite foods on supermarket shelves. The food listings in Chapter 4 provide all the information needed to help you make those on-the-spot purchasing decisions and to decide if a product is truly lite.

1

The Lite Food Health Link

From lite sausage to lite ice cream, it seems as though we have a lite alternative to virtually every food choice today. This huge selection of lite foods should, in theory, make it easier for us to lose weight, reduce our cholesterol, and lower our blood pressure. But how helpful are these products in helping us achieve our health goals? Not very, if government statistics are any indication. It's a paradox that although the number of lite foods on the market continues to increase, the average caloric consumption in the United States rose from about 3,200 calories per day in 1975 to 3,600 per day in 1985. In addition, our fat intake hovers around 40% of the total calories we eat each day, despite the fact that major health organizations like the American Heart Association and the National Cancer Institute tell us it's healthiest to keep fat to 30 percent or less of the day's total calorie intake. And all indications are that as a country, we're getting fatter. Not only do extra pounds slow you down, but they increase your risk of developing heart disease, hypertension, diabetes, and some types of cancer.

Several national organizations have issued dietary guidelines that they say can, if followed, reduce our risk of developing such killer diseases. The organizations' recommendations vary slightly, but they all essentially urge us to follow the same general rules.

1. Eat a variety of foods. No one type of food should be overemphasized or eliminated from your diet.

1

2. Maintain a desirable weight. The more overweight you are, the greater your chances of suffering side effects of excess pounds.

3. Avoid too much fat, saturated fat, and cholesterol. Total fat in your diet should be kept to 30 percent of your total day's calories or less. (See Chapter 3 on how to do it.) Research shows that calorie for calorie, fat may actually be more fattening than carbohydrates or protein. So cutting back on fat is not only good for your heart, it's the best way to knock off extra pounds. Saturated fat in your diet from animal foods like fatty meats and whole milk dairy products can raise your blood cholesterol. It should be no more than ⅓ of the total fat calories. And cholesterol intake should be kept to no more than 300 milligrams per day.

4. Avoid too much sugar. Keep your sugar intake to no more than 10 percent of your daily calories. Sugar offers no nutrients, only calories. And if eaten too often, it causes cavities.

5. Eat food high in fiber and complex carbohydrates. This includes plenty of fresh fruits and vegetables and whole grain breads and cereal. Most experts recommend you get 20 to 35 grams of fiber per day. To put this into perspective, a 1-ounce serving of a high-fiber cereal such as Kellogg's All-Bran provides 10 grams of fiber.

6. Avoid too much sodium. 1,100 to 3,300 milligrams of sodium a day is considered a safe and adequate intake. Most nutritionists consider 2,000 milligrams per day to be a mild sodium-restricted diet. The majority of packaged foods provide sodium information on the label.

Obviously, foods lighter in calories, fat, cholesterol, or sodium can help us follow these healthful dietary guidelines. So, with all the so-called "lite" foods available, why are so many of us still suffering from obesity, high blood pressure, and high blood cholesterol? The "mis-use" of lite foods may play a role. We usually assume that a food labeled as light, low, or reduced must be low in fat, cholesterol, and/ or sodium. Unfortunately, the world of lite foods is far more complicated than that. There are no fewer than twenty labeling terms to persuade you that a food is lite in at least one ingredient. Some of these terms have clearly defined meanings; others do not. (See Chapter 3 for meanings of lite terms.) But buying foods labeled as light/lite and assuming that they will help you lose weight or lower your blood cholesterol is a big mistake. Many so-called light/lite foods are no lighter in fat, calories, or sodium than their "regular" counterparts. A few, believe it or not, are actually higher in calories, fat, or sodium. Another lite mistake is to assume that the term "dietetic" means low-calorie. This book is filled with examples of so-called "dietetic" foods that have just as many calories and just as much fat as their regular counterparts. Some Estee and Featherweight products, for example, carry the term "dietetic" on the label but are low only in sodium, not fat or calories.

Do nutritionists recommend lite foods? Yes, if they are truly lite and only if they are a part of an overall well-balanced diet. Nutritionists prefer that you eat more foods that are naturally lite such as fruits and vegetables, and starchy foods such as breads, potatoes, and pastas unadulterated with butter, cream, or cheese.

Do lite foods help in weight loss, cholesterol lowering, and blood pressure reduction? Aside from government survey statistics of calorie intake, no studies have specifically examined the intake of lite foods and their impact on weight, cholesterol, or blood pressure. It makes sense, however, that if you eat foods truly lite in calories, fat, cholesterol, and sodium, you can reap the benefits a healthier diet can provide.

Does using artificial sweeteners help weight loss? Researchers have investigated whether or not using artificial sweeteners can help you lose weight, but the results are mixed. It seems that when a person eats artificially sweetened foods unknowingly, under controlled research conditions, he eats fewer calories. But in real life we know when we're eating artificially sweetened foods. And, unfortunately, some people use artificial sweeteners as justification for overindulgence in other high-calorie foods.

Are some of the lite foods better than others? Absolutely. They vary greatly in taste as well as nutrition. Taste is an individual matter, but the nutritional differences between lite foods is what this book is all about. Some brands tend to be truer to the lite label than others. For example, all ten entrees with the Healthy Choice label are low in calories, fat, cholesterol, and sodium. But not all brands follow suit.

Though a particular brand may tend to be too high in fat or calories to be truly lite, the brand may have one product that is an outstanding example of what a lite product should be. So, even if some products a company makes are high in fat, it doesn't mean every product they make should automatically be rejected. For example, the fat in Weight Watchers frozen entrees range from a low, low 7 percent of calories to a whopping 56 percent of calories from fat. Le Menu LightStyle entrees, on the other hand, all fall within the healthful range of 14 to 29 percent calories from fat.

Lite Food of the Future

The world of lite foods may soon be further complicated by the introduction of a completely new food ingredient—fat substitutes. There are two "fake fats" currently pending approval by the Food and Drug Administration (FDA). Simplesse is a fat-free, cholesterol-free, low-calorie (1 to 2 calories per gram) fat substitute made by the NutraSweet Company. Olestra, also known as sucrose polyester, is a fat-free, cholesterol-free, and calorie-free fat substitute made by Proctor & Gamble. Considering that 37 to 40 percent of the calories most Americans eat come from fat, these fat substitutes may potentially have a much greater impact on our dietary habits than the artificial sweeteners have had.

Surrounded by a lot of hoopla, Simplesse was introduced in early

1988. The NutraSweet Company originally intended to bring the product to market without seeking the Food and Drug Administration's approval. The company said that because Simplesse is made of naturally occurring protein in eggs and milk, it was exempt from all the usual regulatory red tape. The FDA, however, was ''unhappy'' with NutraSweet's decision and promised an investigation. To avoid starting off on the wrong foot with the FDA, NutraSweet submitted research which the company says proves Simplesse's safety. NutraSweet is now awaiting FDA approval before making the product available.

Even if Simplesse is approved by the FDA, its ability to reduce the calorie content of your favorite foods is somewhat limited. Although Simplesse could be used in dairy products like ice cream, spreads, cheeses, sour cream, and dips as well as oil-based products like salad dressings, margarine, and mayonnaise, products with Simplesse cannot be used in baking or frying. The reason is that Simplesse is a protein and heat will cause it to congeal—similar to an egg cooking. The chart below shows the calorie savings that manuacturers of Simplesse say you can expect.

Calorie Comparison of Traditional vs. Simplesse Products		
PRODUCT	TRADITIONAL calories	SIMPLESSE calories
Cream Cheese (1 oz)	100	45
Mayonnaise	100	30
Premium Ice Cream (4 oz)	280	130
Salad Dressing (1 T)	90	20
Sour Cream	25	10

Olestra, on the other hand, is a synthetic compound developed in the laboratory. It is not used by the body, so it is calorie-free, and unlike Simplesse it can be used in cooking, frying, and baking. Some consumer activist groups, such as the Center for Science in the Public

Interest (CSPI) in Washington, D.C., are concerned about olestra's safety, claiming it increases the risk of cancer, liver damage, and leukemia. Proctor & Gamble has submitted more than 11,000 pages of research data to the FDA to prove the product's safety. However, a new study to examine its safety has begun and it may be years before olestra is on the market.

If approved, olestra would initially be used in frying oils, substituting as much as 35 percent of the oil in products available for consumers, and as much as 75 percent in oils available for use by restaurants and fast food chains. How many fat calories would olestra actually save? Proctor & Gamble says that a single meal consisting of sautéed flounder, french fries, and a brownie, in which an olestra-containing oil was used, would save approximately 8.5 grams of fat or 77 calories. Obviously, olestra alone won't cure America's weight problem, but the two "fake fats" plus more artificial sweeteners waiting in the wings could change the way we eat and introduce a new era of "fake foods."

Because the FDA has yet to approve either "fake fat," this book lists no products containing either Simplesse or olestra.

New artificial sweeteners also awaiting approval include sucralose by Pfizer Inc. and alitame by Johnson & Johnson. In addition, General Foods recently received a patent for its own sweetener. As more artificial sweeteners become available, each with its own advantages and disadvantages, the variety of lite products will no doubt expand.

2

What Makes a Lite Food Lite

Before you use the information in this book, you might find it helpful to know how a food is transformed from a dieter's nightmare to a dieter's dream. What do the manufacturers do to lighten food? There are generally five ways to make a food lighter than its original version.

1) Provide smaller portion sizes. This is one to be aware of. Some so-called lite products actually contain about the same calories per ounce than their regular versions, but by making a serving weigh less, the product suddenly contains fewer calories and less fat per serving and is then labeled as lite. Uncovering this sly maneuver may take some detective work on your part and a pocket calculator at the supermarket.

There is, however, a positive side to this tactic. You'll probably only eat one serving of the food regardless of how much it weighs, so they've cut the calories for you. For example, you make a sandwich with two slices of bread, no matter how much the slices weigh. If the slices are smaller and have fewer calories, it's an automatic calorie saver. Nutritionists call this practice "portion control."

2) Eliminate or reduce fats. Because fats are the most concentrated source of calories (9 calories per gram compared to 4 calories per gram for carbohydrates or protein) cutting back the fat in a food is one of the best ways to reduce calories. Since no "fake fats" are available yet, reduced-calorie bulking agents like polydextrose are put in the place of fat. Polydextrose has a similar texture to fat but 90 percent fewer calories. Other replacements like maltodextrin can replace as much as 50 percent of the fat in salad dressings and frozen desserts.

3) Use sugar substitutes. Sugar substitutes contain virtually no calories. So, by substituting artificial sweeteners such as aspartame (brand names NutraSweet and Equal) or saccharin for sugar, you save about 16 calories for every teaspoon of sugar replaced with an artificial sweetener. The newest calorie-free sweetener to join the ranks is acesulfame-K (brand name Sunette and Sweet One). To date, it is available in individual packets and in a few products like puddings, chewing gum, and instant beverages. The manufacturer, Hoechst Celanese Corporation, is awaiting approval for the sweetener's use in soft drinks and baked goods.

4) Substitute other low-calorie ingredients for standard ingredients. Vegetables may be used instead of meat, as in vegetable lasagna; low-fat cheese substituted for high-fat cheese on a pizza; low-fat or fat-free yogurt for whole milk dairy products; skim milk for whole milk; butter flavor used in place of real butter; calorie-free gums and thickeners added for bulk in salad dressings; and breading can be reduced in breaded chicken or fish products.

5) Use different preparation methods that require lower calorie ingredients. Bake frozen french fries instead of frying them, for example. The amount of cooking oils used to cook lite foods often differs from that used to prepare standard foods. In sodium-reduced products, less salt and more herbs and spices are used in preparation.

Reading the Label

A trip through the supermarket aisles can be a harrowing experience for the shopper looking to buy truly lite products, i.e., foods that are lower in calories, fat, cholesterol, and sodium. The number of selections is dizzying. By latest count there are no fewer than 200 lite frozen entrees on the market. Looking for one that contains fewer than 300 calories? That's easy. But wait, it's also high in fat and sodium. Okay, here's one that's low in fat and sodium, but hold on, it's pretty high in cholesterol.

Because of the lack of control over the use of the terms "light" and "lite," it's a labeling free-for-all. One misleading example: Wesson's Light and Natural vegetable oil. Is it lite in calories? No, it contains the same 117 calories per tablespoon as any other vegetable oil. Is it lite in sodium? It's sodium-free, but again, so are all vegetable oils. Lite in cholesterol? Same story—all vegetable oils are cholesterol-free. So what is it lite in? Color. It's lighter in color than the original Wesson cooking oil. In all fairness to the manufacturer, the label doesn't claim that the product is lite in calories, or anything else for that matter. But for most of us the term "lite" or "light" connotes something more healthful than the usual product, and we buy it.

Ironically, it was found in putting together this book that many lite products labeled as low in fat are high in sodium, as much as ten times higher than the regular version. For example, one tablespoon of regular Wishbone blue cheese dressing has 70 calories and 150 milligrams of sodium. On the other hand, one tablespoon of Wishbone Lite blue cheese dressing has 40 calories and 200 milligrams of sodium. You save 30 calories, but you gain 50 milligrams of sodium. The same is true of cheeses. Natural Swiss cheese contains about 74 milligrams of sodium per ounce, compared to processed Swiss cheese slices which contain about 350 milligrams of sodium per ounce. This may not present a problem if you and your family don't suffer from high blood pressure. But frequently, people who are overweight and trying to lose weight also suffer from high blood pressure.

Not all manufacturers use lite labeling casually. Some products labeled as lite truly are. There are particular brands that are generally light in both fat and sodium. Health Valley is such a brand. But it doesn't have low-fat products across the board. Products like no-salt chips are virtually salt free, but still contain 56 percent of calories from fat.

Lite Ingredients

A product typically considered a healthful alternative doesn't necessarily remain so when used as an ingredient in a processed food. Tofu,
for example, is considered a healthful protein-containing alternative to
meat. True, it is cholesterol-free and very low in saturated fats (the
kind that raise blood cholesterol). It is not, however, low in total fat. It
contains over 50 percent of its calories from fat. When it becomes part
of the frozen dessert Tofutti, it's no lower in fat than many other high-
fat frozen desserts. Is it more healthful? Well, it's more healthful than
ice cream, because it contains no cholesterol or saturated fats as ice
cream does, but you'll get no calorie or fat savings from eating Tofutti
instead of ice cream. Tofutti does, however, make Lite-lite Tofutti, an
excellent lite product (see page 271).

Another ingredient that can lead you astray is chicken. Chicken in
its purest form, stripped of skin and broiled or baked, is an excellent
diet food. It can, however, provide more fat calories than a sirloin
steak if it's doused in creamy sauces, wrapped in ham, or covered in
melted cheese. Tyson, for example, makes several chicken entrees
including such gourmet delights as Chicken Kiev and Chicken Peking.
They are not marketed as lite products, but you may think they're lite
because they contain chicken. However, of the nineteen Tyson Gourmet
entrees, only one made its way into this book as a Lite Surprise (page
435). The rest are too high in fat and/or sodium to be considered lite
products.

Skim milk is an ingredient that may also give the impression that a
low-fat product waits inside the package. But high-fat ingredients such
as cream may also be a part of the ingredient list. Check carefully
before you buy.

An important fat tip: Don't be fooled into believing that a cholesterol-
free claim on the label means low-fat as well—it doesn't. When a
manufacturer substitutes a vegetable oil such as soybean, safflower,
or corn oil for butter or lard, a product becomes cholesterol-free, but
it still contains the same amount of fat and the same number of
calories, if no other substitutions are made.

3

Lite Labeling Language

Simply knowing that the meaning of the word "lite" on food labels can be misleading is not enough. But armed with some basic information about reading food package labels, you will learn to discover if a food is indeed lite. The best place to start is with labeling terms. Some, such as those for sodium-reduced foods, are well defined and strictly regulated by the Food and Drug Administration. Others, including light, lite, and extra light have no definitions, although the FDA "encourages" manufacturers to use them responsibly.

Legal Lite Labeling Terms

The Food and Drug Administration has legally defined the following food labeling terms:

Low Calorie—The food contains 40 calories of fewer per serving and fewer than .4 calories per gram. The number of calories must be stated on the label.

Reduced Calorie—Foods must contain at least one third fewer calories than the original version or the food it most closely resembles.

Sodium-Free—Foods that contain less than 5 milligrams of sodium per serving.

Very Low Sodium—Foods that contain 35 milligrams of sodium or less per serving.

Reduced Sodium—Foods processed so that the usual sodium is reduced by 75 percent.

Unsalted, salt-free, or no salt added—All mean that the product which is normally processed with salt is processed without salt. Such a product is not necessarily low in sodium, as the food may be naturally high in sodium.

Although the FDA does not require that nutrition labeling include sodium content, several companies provide the information.

Legally Defined, But Often Misleading Terms

Dietetic, diet, or dietary—These terms mean that at least one ingredient, often sodium, has been changed, substituted, or restricted in the product. They do not necessarily mean the food is low in calories. In fact, many "dietetic" foods are lower only in sodium, not in fat or calories.

Sugar-free or sugarless—Foods that do not contain sucrose (table sugar), but may include other calorie-containing sweeteners such as honey, corn syrup, or sorbitol. Sugar-free gum, for example, says in the fine print on the package that it is "not noncaloric," meaning that although the gum contains no sucrose, it does have calories from other sweeteners. These terms also describe foods that contain artificial sweeteners like saccharin or aspartame.

Legally Meaningless Terms

Light, lite, or lightly—With the few exceptions mentioned on page 14, these terms have no legal definitions. They can mean lite in color, lite in sodium, lite in taste or texture, or lite in calories. The FDA asks that if a manufacturer calls a product "lite" and claims it is useful in reducing calories, that it meet the requirements for the term "low calories or reduced calories." But this request often falls on deaf ears.

Organic—This term used on a food label indicates that no synthetic pesticides, fungicides, or fertilizers were used in growing the food. But there are no federal laws regulating its use. The term does not indicate that the product is lower in calories, fat, cholesterol, or sodium than its nonorganically grown counterpart.

Natural—It sounds good but it means absolutely nothing. A manufacturer can use this term on any product without having to justify its use.

Lower Salt—Even with five strictly defined terms indicating the amount of sodium in foods, someone has come up with a variation that has no legal definition and therefore can mean whatever a manufacturer chooses.

Proposed Labeling Terms

These are terms that have been proposed by the Food and Drug Administration and by Congress, but are not yet required. Some products that fit in the proposed guidelines use them anyway. In fact, the following cholesterol terms are used in Chapter 4:

Cholesterol-Free—Product must contain less than 2 milligrams cholesterol per serving.

Low-Cholesterol—Food contains between 2 and 20 milligrams cholesterol per serving.

Cholesterol-Reduced—The cholesterol content of a food must be reduced by at least 75 percent as compared to the original product.

Legislation is being proposed for the third time in three years to define lite labeling terms and require food companies to comply. If passed, the FDA would require products claiming to be lite to fit the following definition:

Light or lite—A food using either of these terms would have to have at least one third fewer calories, at least one third less sodium, or at least one third less fat than the regular product. The label would also specify how many fewer calories, how much less sodium, or how much less fat the product has than its regular counterpart.

The United States Department of Agriculture (USDA), separate from the FDA, has jurisdiction over the labeling of meat products. This agency has its own legal definitions for labeling meats.

Lite—When referring to franks and bologna, the term is legally defined to mean the fat has been reduced by 25 percent.

Light, lite, lightly, or leaner—In meat products other than franks or bologna these terms may refer to calories, fat, sodium, or breading (as in breaded fish fillets) if reduced by at least 25 percent of the original amount.

Lean or low-fat—No more than 10 percent fat by weight (not by calories).

Extra lean—No more than 5 percent fat by weight (not by calories).

Because the USDA lean terms are defined as fat by weight rather than fat by calories, they can be deceptive. Products that claim to be 90 percent fat-free (or 10 percent fat by weight), for example, may contain as much as 50 percent calories from fat. Better to stick with your own fat calculations (see Chapter 3) than to rely on ''low-fat'' claims on the package label.

Labeling Fine Points

The key to any of the regulated labeling terms is the phrase ''per serving.'' A serving can be whatever the manufacturer wants it to be. If the label says a ½ teaspoon serving of a product is low sodium, but a typical serving is closer to 1 tablespoon, the sodium listed on the label then increases sixfold and in reality the product loses its "low sodium" claim.

Some consumer and industry groups have petitioned the FDA to define the term lite for specific products. That is, just as mayonnaise, ice cream, and sour cream have to meet certain ingredient requirements or "standards of identity" before they can be identified as such, proposed lite products would also be subject to certain formulas. Among the new lite products being proposed are lite eggnog, lite ice cream, and light sour cream. As it now stands, a product which deviates from the standards of identity (the formulas) set by the government has to call itself "imitation" or "substitute." Obviously, the term "imitation ice cream" is much less appealing than "light ice cream."

Another point to consider: Light*er* does not necessarily mean lite. Cheeses, for example, are naturally high-fat foods (about 75 percent calories from fat). Some lite cheeses on the market are indeed lower in fat, and as such are preferable alternatives to regular cheese. However, they still contain more than 30 percent calories as fat (and usually more sodium than the natural version). In Chapter 4 of the lite food listings, no cheese is singled out as a "Lite Pick" (a food that is low in calories, fat, sodium, and cholesterol) but there are some excellent alternatives to higher-fat natural and regular processed cheeses.

Reading the Labels

The amount of information a product label provides varies greatly. At the very least it should tell you the serving size as well as the number of servings per container, the calories, protein, carbohydrates, fat, and the percentages of the U.S. Recommended Daily Allowances (USRDA) of certain vitamins and minerals which one serving of the product contains.

Most food products do not provide cholesterol information on their labels. Where such information is provided it is included in the listings in Chapter 4. However, many food companies are now analyzing their products for cholesterol content, and you can expect to see more food packages offering cholesterol information in the future. Another trend in food labeling is to provide detailed information about the type of fat in the product, i.e., saturated vs. unsaturated fats. It's now known that saturated fats—the kind found in fatty meats, whole milk dairy products, and tropical oils such as coconut, palm, and palm kernel—are powerful raisers of blood cholesterol, more so than the cholesterol in the foods you eat. So it's important to know not just the total fat you're eating but the type of fat as well. Very few products currently reveal such detailed information, but no doubt there will be more in the future.

Another aspect of labeling unique to lite foods is a caloric comparison of the regular and lite versions. A few products such as Aunt Jemima's light syrup provide this type of information on the package. The company does not, however, provide comparisons to *their* regular products. Often the lite version is compared to a standard value found in nutrition books.

The label on page 18 is an excellent example of a food label of the future, and provides all the information you need to know.

Counting all Calories

Calories, as well as all nutrition information on a label, should be listed per serving. Be sure to check the serving size and the number of servings per package. Some frozen foods contain two servings per package and the serving size may be too small to accurately reflect the number of calories you will consume. However, calorie content alone doesn't tell the whole story.

Ferreting out the Fat

Most food labels do not tell you how many of the calories come from fat, only the number of grams of fat. The sample label is an exception. It is possible, however, for you to figure it out for yourself. Fat on the label is listed in grams (28 grams = 1 ounce) and 1 gram of fat equals 9 calories. Use the following formula to determine if the food falls within the healthy range of 30 percent or less calories as fat. If you always choose foods with 30 percent of less calories from fat you will not exceed the healthful limit.

$$\frac{\text{Grams of fat per serving} \times 9}{\text{Total calories per serving}}$$

Here's an example using the sample label to show you how that company arrived at 15 percent calories from fat.

$$\frac{5 \times 9}{290} = \frac{45}{290} = 15\%$$

However, the percentage method doesn't always accurately reflect your total fat intake. For example, a food that has only 30 calories and 2 grams of fat also has a seemingly unhealthful 60 percent calories from fat. Though the percentage is high, the actual fat measured in grams is low. You'll find several foods that fall into this category in the listings in Chapter 4. As long as your average intake is 30 percent or less, occasionally eating foods that are higher than the limit won't ruin your healthy eating plan.

There is another quick method for estimating the fat content of a food—it should contain no more than 3 grams of fat per 100 calories. Again, using the sample label, the dinner has 290 calories. Let's say it's an even 300. To fall within the 3 grams per 100 calories guideline, it should have no more than 9 grams of fat. This product has only 5 grams, so it's well within the fat limits. The chart below serves as a quick reference guide to use in the supermarket for other foods.

If one serving provides:	It should contain no more than:
50 calories	1.5 grams of fat
100 calories	3 grams of fat
150 calories	5 grams of fat
200 calories	6 grams of fat
250 calories	8 grams of fat
300 calories	9 grams of fat
350 calories	11.5 grams of fat
400 calories	12 grams of fat
450 calories	15 grams of fat

ORIENTAL PEPPER

Healthy Choice ® Dinners are delicious combinations of lean† meats, delicate sauces and wholesome fruits and vegetables. These dinners can be part of a diet that meets the recommendations of the National Cholesterol Education Program for persons with high blood cholesterol who should limit their intake of saturated fat and cholesterol.

The program recommends reducing saturated fat and cholesterol intake as a primary means of reducing high blood cholesterol levels, thereby reducing the risk of heart disease. Reducing sodium intake may help control high blood pressure, which can also reduce the risk of heart disease.††

Nutrient	National Cholesterol* Education Program Recommendations (Daily Avg.)	Healthy Choice Oriental Pepper Steak
Total Fat	Less than 30% of Calories	18% of Calories
Saturated Fat	Less than 10% of Calories	8% of Calories
Polyunsaturated Fat	Up to 10% of Calories	1% of Calories
Cholesterol	Less than 300mg	60mg

Nutrient	Estimated Level**	Healthy Choice Oriental Pepper Steak
Sodium	2,200mg (Daily Midpoint)	510mg

**Midpoint of the 1,100mg to 3,300mg range estimated by the National Academy of Sciences to be a safe and adequate dietary intake for adults.

The National Cholesterol Education Program which is coordinated by the National Heart, Lung, and Blood Institute, does not endorse any particular product.

NUTRITIONAL INFORMATION PER SERVING
Serving size: 11 oz.
Servings per container: 1

Calories	290	Polyunsaturated Fat	less than 1g
Protein	23g	Saturated Fat	3g
Carbohydrate	35g	Cholesterol	60mg
Fat	6g	Sodium	510mg
Percent of Calories from Fat	**18%**	Potassium	400mg

PERCENTAGE OF U.S. RECOMMENDED DAILY ALLOWANCE (U.S. RDA)

Protein	35	Riboflavin	15
Vitamin A	10	Niacin	10
Vitamin C	160	Calcium	4
Thiamine	10	Iron	10

††This dinner is not a remedy or cure for heart disease, and is only one part of a daily regimen for healthful living.

CHOICE®

ROL* • LOW SODIUM MEAL

STEAK DINNER

290 CALORIES

HEATING INSTRUCTIONS:

MICROWAVE OVEN: Microwave ovens vary, heating time may require adjustment. These heating instructions were developed for use in 600 to 700 watt ovens.
- Remove dinner from carton.
- Cut and remove film cover from fruit compartment only.
- Cut a small slit in center of film over main entree.
- Heat on HIGH 6 minutes or until hot, rotating dinner once.
- Let stand in microwave oven 1 to 2 minutes.
- Stir main entree before serving.

When heating TWO dinners, follow instructions above, heating approximately 12 minutes or until hot, rotating once.

CONVENTIONAL OVEN: Preheating of oven is not necessary.
- Remove dinner from carton.
- Cut and remove film cover from fruit compartment only.
- Cut a small slit in center of film over main entree.
- Heat at 350°F on COOKIE SHEET in center of oven 30 to 35 minutes or until hot.
- Remove dinner from oven on COOKIE SHEET.
- Let stand 1 to 2 minutes before serving.

NOTE: When removing cover, be careful to avoid steam burns. Do not prepare in toaster oven.

For information on Healthy Choice, call Monday–Friday 10:00 A.M.–7:00 P.M. (Central Time Zone), 1-800-323-9980.

INGREDIENTS: BEEF SIRLOIN, BEEF BROTH, BROCCOLI, APPLES, COOKED RICE, WATER, GREEN PEPPERS, SUGAR, WATER CHESTNUTS, SOY SAUCE, MODIFIED FOOD STARCH, CARROTS, RAISINS, TOMATO PASTE, FLAVORING, BUTTER, SALT, SOYBEAN OIL, SPICES, CORN SYRUP SOLIDS, MILK AND CREAM SOLIDS, WHEY, CARAMEL COLOR.

IMPORTANT: Keep solidly frozen until ready to use. If contents become thawed, use immediately. **DO NOT REFREEZE.**

DIET EXCHANGES PER SERVING:
2½ Lean Meat • 1 Bread • 1 Vegetable • 1 Fruit

Exchange calculations based on **Exchange Lists for Meal Planning** © 1986, American Diabetes Association Inc. and the American Dietetic Association.

 Frozen Foods
Omaha, Nebraska 68102

0 50100 45957 4

A third way to keep fat in check in your diet is to keep a running tally of your daily fat intake in grams and, using the chart below, determine if you're within the healthful range of 30 percent or less of total daily calories from fat.

If your total daily calories are:	Then eat no more than:
1000	33 grams of fat
1200	40 grams of fat
1500	50 grams of fat
1800	60 grams of fat
2100	70 grams of fat
2400	80 grams of fat
2700	90 grams of fat

Cutting Cholesterol

As already mentioned, not all food labels provide cholesterol information. If it is given, keep in mind that the current recommendations are to keep cholesterol intake at less than 300 milligrams a day. This is especially important for people who have high blood cholesterol levels. The sample dinner contains 65 milligrams, low enough to allow freedom of choice for the rest of the day's meals.

Sodium

Sodium content is found on most nutrition labels and is given in milligrams per serving. The safe and adequate daily dietary intake for sodium is 1,100 to 3,300 milligrams. The five sodium-related labeling terms defined earlier will help you to choose foods lower in sodium.

The sample label is atypical in that it compares the product's nutrition with healthful recommendations set forth by the National Cholesterol Education Program in Washington, D.C., right on the label. Don't expect to see such information on most food labels today, but hopefully, this practice will become the wave of the future.

Lite Ratings

Product Information Sources

The nutrition information for the products in this book was obtained either from the manufacturer upon request or from the food label. Keep in mind that because food manufacturers are constantly reevaluating and updating their products' labels, you may find discrepancies between the information here and the nutrition labeling on the product you buy at the supermarket. Food manufacturers may also reformulate a product and in the process change its nutritional content. Another cause for discrepancy may come in rounding off numbers. Food and Drug Administration labeling laws permit rounding to the nearest 5 or 10, depending upon the nutrient. As a result, the actual nutritional analysis (which may be given here) could be different than what appears on the product label. Because products are constantly being discontinued, some products listed may no longer be available.

How Comparisons Were Made

Where possible, each "lite" product is compared to its regular version. If the same company does not make a regular version, the product was compared to a similar product from another company, or to product values found in other sources (see Appendix B). For each product the comparison is given under the section labeled "Comments." For example:

Diet Coke

COMMENTS: 132 fewer calories and 6 less milligrams sodium than 12 ounces regular Coca-Cola Classic. Sweetened with aspartame.

Comparisons of products lacking serving size information was not possible. For example, if one cookie is the serving size, but no information is available about the weight of the cookie, an accurate comparison was not possible and only the rating (as described below) and general comments are given.

Products with 20 percent of calories from fat are designated as very low in fat—40 percent or more calories from fat is very high in fat. However, if a product has 40 percent or more calories from fat but has only 2 grams of fat or less, it is not considered very high in fat and an appropriate comment is made.

Lite Ratings

Ratings were done independently of the product comparison, i.e., each food was rated as lite in fat, cholesterol, or sodium, and ratings did not depend on how much lighter the food was than the regular version. Products rated as lite in fat, sodium, *and* cholesterol are marked "Lite Picks." The rating symbols are as follows:

○	**Low fat**	30% or less calories from fat
◇	**Cholesterol-free**	2 milligrams or less cholesterol
◇◇	**Low cholesterol**	20 milligrams or less cholesterol
◇◇◇	**Reduced cholesterol**	25% less cholesterol than the original version
□	**Sodium-free**	less than 5 milligrams sodium
□□	**Very low sodium**	35 milligrams or less sodium
□□□	**Low sodium**	140 milligrams or less sodium
□□□□	**Reduced sodium**	75% less sodium than the original version
□□□□□	**Unsalted**	processed without salt

Lite entrees have their own rating system described in that section. Remember, some products lite in sodium and cholesterol, for example, but not in fat are not designated as Lite Picks. If you're interested in foods lite in one or more items, but not necessarily all three, look for the rating symbols next to each entry.

Cholesterol information is estimated for some products. For example a company may not have analyzed their frozen juice bar for cholesterol, but if the ingredient list shows nothing but fruit and sugar, it was given a cholesterol-free (◇) rating.

BAKED GOODS

PRODUCT	SERV	CAL	FAT (G)	% cal from fat	CHOL (mg)	SOD (mg)
Biscuits (Weight Watchers, Country Style Buttermilk)	1 pc	50	.5	9	na	220

○

COMMENTS: 15 fewer calories, 3 grams less fat than 1 regular buttermilk biscuit, but 15 milligrams *more* sodium. Very low in fat.

PRODUCT	SERV	CAL	FAT (G)	% cal from fat	CHOL (mg)	SOD (mg)
Bread, Italian (Arnold Bakery, Light)	1 sl	40	0	0	0	90

LITE PICK ○◇□□□

COMMENTS: 26 fewer calories, 2 grams less fat, 7 milligrams less sodium than 1 slice Arnold Francisco Italian Bread. Fat free.

PRODUCT	SERV	CAL	FAT (G)	% cal from fat	CHOL (mg)	SOD (mg)
Bread, oatmeal (Arnold Bakery, Light)	1 sl	40	0	0	0	100

LITE PICK ○◇□□□

COMMENTS: 50 fewer calories, 2 grams less fat, 66 milligrams less sodium than 1 slice regular Arnold Branola Style Country Oat Bread. Fat free.

PRODUCT	SERV	CAL	FAT (G)	% cal from fat	CHOL (mg)	SOD (mg)
Bread, raisin (Weight Watchers, Light Cinnamon Raisin)	1 sl	60	1	15	na	85

○□□□

COMMENTS: 10 fewer calories, 9 milligrams less sodium than 1 slice regular raisin bread. Very low in fat.

PRODUCT	SERV	CAL	FAT (G)	% cal from fat	CHOL (mg)	SOD (mg)
Bread, rye (Arnold Bakery, Light Soft)	1 sl	40	<1	<23	0	100

LITE PICK ○◇□□□

COMMENTS: 10 fewer calories, 70 milligrams less sodium than 1 slice regular Arnold Rye.

PRODUCT	SERV	CAL	FAT (G)	% cal from fat	CHOL (mg)	SOD (mg)
Bread, wheat (Arnold Bakery, Light Golden)	1 sl	40	<1	<23	0	80

○◇□□□

COMMENTS: 8 fewer calories, 18 milligrams less sodium than 1 slice regular Arnold Stone Ground 100% Whole Wheat Bread.

PRODUCT	SERV	CAL	FAT (G)	% cal from fat	CHOL (mg)	SOD (mg)
Bread, wheat (Home Pride, Butter Top Light)	1 sl	40	<1	<23	5	130

LITE PICK ○◇◇□□□

COMMENTS: 30 fewer calories, 10 milligrams less sodium than 1 slice regular Home Pride Butter Top wheat bread.

PRODUCT	SERV	CAL	FAT (G)	% cal from fat	CHOL (mg)	SOD (mg)
Bread, wheat (Roman Meal, Light Wheat)	1 sl	40	<1	<11	na	53

LITE PICK ○□□

COMMENTS: 30 fewer calories, 87 milligrams less sodium than 1 slice regular Roman Meal Wheat bread. Very low in fat.

PRODUCT	SERV	CAL	FAT (G)	% cal from fat	CHOL (mg)	SOD (mg)
Bread, wheat (Thomas', Protogen Lite)	1 sl	40	1	23	0	750

LITE PICK ○◇□□□

COMMENTS: 21 fewer calories, 54 milligrams less sodium than 1 slice regular white bread.

PRODUCT	SERV	CAL	FAT (G)	% cal from fat	CHOL (mg)	SOD (mg)
Bread, wheat (Wonder, Light)	1 sl	40	<1	<23	0	120

LITE PICK ○◇□□□

COMMENTS: 30 fewer calories, 20 milligrams less sodium than 1 slice regular Wonder 100% whole wheat bread.

PRODUCT	SERV	CAL	FAT (G)	% cal from fat	CHOL (mg)	SOD (mg)
Bread, white (Arnold Bakery, Light Premium)	1 sl	40	0	0	0	90

LITE PICK ○◇□□□

COMMENTS: 25 fewer calories, 1 gram less fat, 3 milligrams less cholesterol, 13 milligrams less sodium than 1 slice regular Arnold Brick Oven White Bread. Fat free.

PRODUCT	SERV	CAL	FAT (G)	% cal from fat	CHOL (mg)	SOD (mg)
Bread, white (Home Pride, Butter Top Light)	1 sl	40	<1	<23	5	130

LITE PICK ○◇◇□□□

COMMENTS: 30 fewer calories, 10 milligrams less sodium than 1 slice regular Home Pride Butter Top white bread.

PRODUCT	SERV	CAL	FAT (G)	% cal from fat	CHOL (mg)	SOD (mg)
Bread (Weight Watchers, thick sliced, all flavors)	1 sl	40	0	0	na	95

LITE PICK ○□□□

COMMENTS: 24 fewer calories, 1 gram less fat, 34 milligrams less sodium than 1 slice regular white bread. Fat free.

PRODUCT	SERV	CAL	FAT (G)	% cal from fat	CHOL (mg)	SOD (mg)
Bread (Weight Watchers, thin sliced, all flavors)	1 sl	40	1	23	na	95

LITE PICK ○□□□

COMMENTS: 24 fewer calories, 28 milligrams less sodium than 1 slice regular white bread.

PRODUCT	SERV	CAL	FAT (G)	% cal from fat	CHOL (mg)	SOD (mg)
Bread, white						
(Wonder, Light)	1 sl	40	<1	<23	0	110

LITE PICK ○◇□□□

COMMENTS: 30 fewer calories, 30 milligrams less sodium than 1 slice regular Wonder white bread.

PRODUCT	SERV	CAL	FAT (G)	% cal from fat	CHOL (mg)	SOD (mg)
Cookies						
(Estee, all varieties)	1 pc	30	1	30	0	0

○◇□

COMMENTS: Lighter in sodium than regular plain variety cookies, but not lighter in calories or fat. Sweetened with fructose syrup.

PRODUCT	SERV	CAL	FAT (G)	% cal from fat	CHOL (mg)	SOD (mg)
Cookies						
(Estee, Assorted Wafers, Creme-filled)	1 pc	30	2	60	0	5

◇□□

COMMENTS: No weight information is available so there is no direct comparison here, but a serving size would probably be more than 1 wafer because wafers are very small. The percentage of calories from fat is deceiving; with 2 grams fat per piece, it is actually a low fat product. Sweetened with sorbitol.

PRODUCT	SERV	CAL	FAT (G)	% cal from fat	CHOL (mg)	SOD (mg)

Cookies
(Estee, Snack
Wafers, Chocolate
Coated)

	1 pc	120	7	53	<5	10

◇◇□□

COMMENTS: No weight information is available so there is no direct comparison here, but these are light only in sodium and are very high in fat. Sweetened with sorbitol.

PRODUCT	SERV	CAL	FAT (G)	% cal from fat	CHOL (mg)	SOD (mg)

Cookies
(Estee, Snack
Wafers, chocolate,
vanilla, strawberry)

	1 pc	80	4	45	0	5

◇□□

COMMENTS: No weight information is available so there is no direct comparison here, but these are light in sodium and cholesterol, not calories, and are very high in fat. Sweetened with sorbitol.

PRODUCT	SERV	CAL	FAT (G)	% cal from fat	CHOL (mg)	SOD (mg)

Cookies
(Featherweight,
Chocolate Chip)

	1 pc	45	2	40	na	0

□

COMMENTS: No weight information is available so there is no direct comparison here, but these are light in sodium. The percentage of calories from fat is deceiving; with 2 grams fat per piece, it is actually a low fat product. Sweetened with fructose.

PRODUCT	SERV	CAL	FAT (G)	% cal from fat	CHOL (mg)	SOD (mg)
Cookies (Featherweight, Double Chocolate Chip)	1 pc	45	2	40	0	0

☐

COMMENTS: No weight information is available so there is no direct comparison here, but these are light in sodium. The percentage of calories from fat is deceiving; with only 2 grams fat per piece, it is actually a low fat product. Sweetened with fructose.

PRODUCT	SERV	CAL	FAT (G)	% cal from fat	CHOL (mg)	SOD (mg)
Cookies (Featherweight, Lemon)	1 pc	45	2	40	0	0

☐

COMMENTS: No weight information is available so there is no direct comparison here, but these are light in sodium. The percentage of calories from fat is deceiving; with only 2 grams fat per piece, it is actually a low fat product. Sweetened with fructose.

PRODUCT	SERV	CAL	FAT (G)	% cal from fat	CHOL (mg)	SOD (mg)
Cookies (Featherweight, Oatmeal Raisin)	1 pc	45	2	40	0	0

☐

COMMENTS: No weight information is available so there is no direct comparison here, but these are light in sodium. The percentage of calories from fat is deceiving; with only 2 grams fat per piece, it is actually a low fat product. Sweetened with fructose.

PRODUCT	SERV	CAL	FAT (G)	% cal from fat	CHOL (mg)	SOD (mg)
Cookies (Featherweight, Peanut Butter)	1 pc	40	2	45	0	10

□□

COMMENTS: No weight information is available so there is no direct comparison here, but these are light in sodium. The percentage of calories from fat is deceiving; with only 2 grams of fat per piece, it is actually a low fat product. Sweetened with fructose.

PRODUCT	SERV	CAL	FAT (G)	% cal from fat	CHOL (mg)	SOD (mg)
Cookies (Featherweight, Vanilla)	1 pc	45	2	40	0	0

□

COMMENTS: No weight information is available so there is no direct comparison here, but these are light in sodium. The percentage of calories from fat is deceiving; with only 2 grams of fat per piece, it is actually a low fat product. Sweetened with fructose.

PRODUCT	SERV	CAL	FAT (G)	% cal from fat	CHOL (mg)	SOD (mg)
Cookies (Featherweight, Wafers, Chocolate Creme)	1 pc	20	1	45	0	0

☐

COMMENTS: No weight information is available so there is no direct comparison here, but these are light in sodium. The percentage of calories from fat is deceiving; with only 1 gram of fat per piece, it is actually a low fat product. Sweetened with sorbitol.

PRODUCT	SERV	CAL	FAT (G)	% cal from fat	CHOL (mg)	SOD (mg)
Cookies (Featherweight, Wafers, Peanut Butter Creme)	1 pc	25	1	36	0	0

☐

COMMENTS: No weight information is available so there is no direct comparison here, but these are light in sodium. The percentage of calories from fat is deceiving; with only 1 gram of fat per piece, it is actually a low fat product. Sweetened with sorbitol.

PRODUCT	SERV	CAL	FAT (G)	% cal from fat	CHOL (mg)	SOD (mg)
Cookies (Featherweight, Wafers, Strawberry Creme)	1 pc	20	1	45	0	0

☐

COMMENTS: No weight information is available so there is no direct comparison here, but these are light in sodium. The percentage of calories from fat is deceiving; with only 1 gram of fat per piece, it is actually a low fat product. Sweetened with sorbitol.

PRODUCT	SERV	CAL	FAT (G)	% cal from fat	CHOL (mg)	SOD (mg)
Cookies (Featherweight, Wafers, Vanilla Creme)	1 pc	20	1	45	0	0

☐

COMMENTS: No weight information is available so there is no direct comparison here, but these are light in sodium. The percentage of calories from fat is deceiving; with only 1 gram of fat per piece, it is actually a low fat product. Sweetened with sorbitol.

BEVERAGES

PRODUCT	SERV	CAL	FAT (G)	% cal from fat	CHOL (mg)	SOD (mg)
Beer (BUD Light)	12 oz	108	0	0	0	na

LITE PICK ○◇

COMMENTS: 36 fewer calories than regular 12 ounces Budweiser beer.

PRODUCT	SERV	CAL	FAT (G)	% cal from fat	CHOL (mg)	SOD (mg)
Beer (Coors, Light 3.2%)	12 oz	98	0	0	0	10

○◇□□

COMMENTS: 21 fewer calories than regular 12 ounces Coors 3.2% beer.

PRODUCT	SERV	CAL	FAT (G)	% cal from fat	CHOL (mg)	SOD (mg)
Beer						
(Coors, Light)	12 oz	100	0	0	0	10
LITE PICK ○◇□□						

COMMENTS: 33 fewer calories than regular 12 ounces Coors beer.

PRODUCT	SERV	CAL	FAT (G)	% cal from fat	CHOL (mg)	SOD (mg)
Beer						
(HJ, Light 3.2%)	12 oz	125	0	0	0	1
NO LITE BARGAIN ○◇□□						

COMMENTS: 6 calories *more* than regular 12 ounces HJ 3.2% beer.

PRODUCT	SERV	CAL	FAT (G)	% cal from fat	CHOL (mg)	SOD (mg)
Beer						
(HJ, Light)	12 oz	134	0	0	0	10
○◇□□						

COMMENTS: 24 fewer calories than regular 12 ounces HJ beer.

PRODUCT	SERV	CAL	FAT (G)	% cal from fat	CHOL (mg)	SOD (mg)
Beer						
(Michelob, Light)	12 oz	134	0	0	0	na
○◇						

COMMENTS: 22 fewer calories than regular 12 ounces Michelob beer.

PRODUCT	SERV	CAL	FAT (G)	% cal from fat	CHOL (mg)	SOD (mg)
Cocoa mix (Alba, Hot Cocoa Mix, Chocolate Marshmallow)	1 packet	60	0	0	na	160

○

COMMENTS: 60 fewer calories, 10 milligrams less sodium than regular Ovaltine Hot'n Rich Cocoa Mix (both are Heinz products). Sweetened with aspartame.

PRODUCT	SERV	CAL	FAT (G)	% cal from fat	CHOL (mg)	SOD (mg)
Cocoa mix (Alba, Hot Cocoa Mix, Milk Chocolate)	1	60	0	0	na	160

○

COMMENTS: 60 fewer calories, 10 milligrams less sodium than regular Ovaltine Hot'n Rich Cocoa Mix (both are Heinz products). Sweetened with aspartame.

PRODUCT	SERV	CAL	FAT (G)	% cal from fat	CHOL (mg)	SOD (mg)
Cocoa mix (Alba, Hot Cocoa Mix, Mocha)	1	60	0	0	na	160

○

COMMENTS: 60 fewer calories, 10 milligrams less sodium than regular Ovaltine Hot'n Rich Cocoa Mix (both are Heinz products). Sweetened with aspartame.

PRODUCT	SERV	CAL	FAT (G)	% cal from fat	CHOL (mg)	SOD (mg)
Cocoa mix (Featherweight, Hot Cocoa Mix)	6 oz	40	0	0	na	54

O□□□

COMMENTS: 43 fewer calories, 62 milligrams less sodium than 6 ounces regular hot cocoa mix made with water. Sweetened with aspartame.

PRODUCT	SERV	CAL	FAT (G)	% cal from fat	CHOL (mg)	SOD (mg)
Cocoa mix (Ovaltine, 50-Calorie)	1 packet	50	2	36	na	145

COMMENTS: 70 fewer calories, 25 milligrams less sodium than 1 packet regular Ovaltine Hot'n Rich cocoa mix. The percentage of calories from fat is deceiving; with only 2 grams of fat per packet, it is actually a low fat product. Sweetened with saccharin.

PRODUCT	SERV	CAL	FAT (G)	% cal from fat	CHOL (mg)	SOD (mg)
Cocoa mix (Ovaltine, Sugar Free)	1 packet	40	1	23	na	160

O

COMMENTS: 80 fewer calories, 10 milligrams less sodium than 1 packet regular Ovaltine Hot'n Rich cocoa mix. Sweetened with aspartame.

PRODUCT	SERV	CAL	FAT (G)	% cal from fat	CHOL (mg)	SOD (mg)
Cocoa mix (Swiss Miss, Lite)	1 packet	50	<1	<18	na	170

○

COMMENTS: 60 fewer calories, 2 grams less fat than 1 packet regular Swiss Miss Hot Cocoa mix. Very low in fat. Sweetened with aspartame.

PRODUCT	SERV	CAL	FAT (G)	% cal from fat	CHOL (mg)	SOD (mg)
Cocoa mix (Swiss Miss, Sugar Free Milk Chocolate)	1 packet	50	1	18	na	170

○

COMMENTS: 60 fewer calories, 2 grams less fat than 1 packet regular Swiss Miss Hot Cocoa mix. Very low in fat.

PRODUCT	SERV	CAL	FAT (G)	% cal from fat	CHOL (mg)	SOD (mg)
Cocoa mix (Swiss Miss, Sugar Free Milk Chocolate with Marshmallow Flavor)	1 packet	50	<1	<18	na	190

○

COMMENTS: 60 fewer calories, 2 grams less fat but 40 milligrams *more* sodium than 1 packet regular Swiss Miss Hot Cocoa with marshmallows. Very low in fat. Sweetened with aspartame.

PRODUCT	SERV	CAL	FAT (G)	% cal from fat	CHOL (mg)	SOD (mg)
Cocoa mix (Weight Watchers, Hot Cocoa mix, Chocolate Marshmallow/Milk Chocolate)	1 packet	60	0	0	na	160

○

COMMENTS: 55 fewer calories, 2 grams less fat than 1 ounce regular hot cocoa mix made with water, but 19 milligrams *more* sodium. Sweetened with aspartame.

PRODUCT	SERV	CAL	FAT (G)	% cal from fat	CHOL (mg)	SOD (mg)
Coffee (General Foods, Sugar Free International Coffees, Café Amaretto)	6 oz	35	3	77	0	20

◇□□

COMMENTS: 15 fewer calories than regular Café Amaretto, but 1 gram *more* fat! Most of the calories come from fat. Sweetened with aspartame.

PRODUCT	SERV	CAL	FAT (G)	% cal from fat	CHOL (mg)	SOD (mg)

Coffee
(General Foods,
Sugar Free
International Coffees,

Café Francais)	6 oz	35	2	51	0	20

◇□□

COMMENTS: 15 fewer calories, 1 gram less fat, 5 milligrams less sodium than regular Café Francais. Most of the calories come from fat but with only 2 grams of fat per serving, it is actually a low fat product. Sweetened with aspartame.

PRODUCT	SERV	CAL	FAT (G)	% cal from fat	CHOL (mg)	SOD (mg)

Coffee
(General Foods,
Sugar Free
International Coffees,

Café Irish Creme)	6 oz	30	2	60	0	15

◇□□

COMMENTS: 30 fewer calories, 1 gram less fat, 5 milligrams less sodium than regular Café Irish Creme. Most of the calories come from fat but with only 2 grams of fat per serving, it is actually a low fat product. Sweetened with aspartame.

PRODUCT	SERV	CAL	FAT (G)	% cal from fat	CHOL (mg)	SOD (mg)
Coffee (General Foods, Sugar Free International Coffees, Café Irish Mocha Mint)	6 oz	25	2	72	0	20

◇□□

COMMENTS: 25 fewer calories than regular Café Irish Mocha Mint. Most of the calories come from fat but with only 2 grams of fat per serving, it is actually a low fat product. Sweetened with aspartame.

PRODUCT	SERV	CAL	FAT (G)	% cal from fat	CHOL (mg)	SOD (mg)
Coffee (General Foods, Sugar Free International Coffees, Café Orange Cappuccino)	6 oz	30	2	60	0	60

◇□□□

COMMENTS: 30 fewer calories, 45 milligrams less sodium than regular Café Orange Cappuccino. Most of the calories come from fat but with only 2 grams of fat per serving, it is actually a low fat product. Sweetened with aspartame.

PRODUCT	SERV	CAL	FAT (G)	% cal from fat	CHOL (mg)	SOD (mg)
Coffee (General Foods, Sugar Free International Coffees, Café Vienna)	6 oz	30	2	60	0	95

◇□□□

COMMENTS: 30 fewer calories, 10 milligrams less sodium than regular Café Vienna. Most calories come from fat but with only 2 grams of fat per serving, it is actually a low fat product. Sweetened with aspartame.

PRODUCT	SERV	CAL	FAT (G)	% cal from fat	CHOL (mg)	SOD (mg)
Coffee (General Foods, Sugar Free International Coffees, Suisse Mocha)	6 oz	30	2	60	0	20

◇□□

COMMENTS: 20 fewer calories, 5 milligrams less sodium than regular Suisse Mocha. Most of the calories come from fat but with only 2 grams of fat per serving, it is actually a low fat product. Sweetened with aspartame.

PRODUCT	SERV	CAL	FAT (G)	% cal from fat	CHOL (mg)	SOD (mg)
Drink mix (Country Time, Sugar Free, all flavors)	8 oz	4	0	0	0	0

LITE PICK ○◇□

COMMENTS: 76 fewer calories than 8 ounces regular Country Time. Sweetened with aspartame.

PRODUCT	SERV	CAL	FAT (G)	% cal from fat	CHOL (mg)	SOD (mg)
Drink mix (Crystal Light, Sugar Free, all flavors)	8 oz	4	0	0	0	0

LITE PICK ○◇□

COMMENTS: No direct comparison, but a calorie savings similar to Country Time Sugar Free Drink Mix. Sweetened with aspartame.

PRODUCT	SERV	CAL	FAT (G)	% cal from fat	CHOL (mg)	SOD (mg)
Drink mix (Kool-Aid, Sugar Free, all flavors)	8 oz	4	0	0	0	0

LITE PICK ○◇□

COMMENTS: 76 fewer calories than regular presweetened Kool-Aid made with sugar. Sweetened with aspartame.

PRODUCT	SERV	CAL	FAT (G)	% cal from fat	CHOL (mg)	SOD (mg)
Drink mix (Tang, Sugar Free Breakfast Crystals)	6 oz	6	0	0	0	0

LITE PICK ○◇□

COMMENTS: 84 fewer calories than 6 ounces regular Tang. Sweetened with aspartame.

PRODUCT	SERV	CAL	FAT (G)	% cal from fat	CHOL (mg)	SOD (mg)
Juice drink (Hawaiian Punch, Lite Fruit Juicy Red)	6 oz	60	0	0	0	30

LITE PICK ○◇□□

COMMENTS: 30 fewer calories than 6 ounces regular Hawaiian Punch, but 10 milligrams *more* sodium.

PRODUCT	SERV	CAL	FAT (G)	% cal from fat	CHOL (mg)	SOD (mg)
Juice drink (Light n' Juicy, Grape)	6 oz	13	0	0	na	18

LITE PICK ○◇□□

COMMENTS: 76 fewer calories than 6 ounces regular grape drink, but 18 milligrams *more* sodium. Sweetened with aspartame.

PRODUCT	SERV	CAL	FAT (G)	% cal from fat	CHOL (mg)	SOD (mg)

Juice drink
(Light n' Juicy, Lemonade)

| | 6 oz | 16 | 0 | 0 | na | 17 |

LITE PICK ○◇□□

COMMENTS: 73 fewer calories, 13 milligrams less sodium than 6 ounces regular lemonade drink. Sweetened with aspartame.

PRODUCT	SERV	CAL	FAT (G)	% cal from fat	CHOL (mg)	SOD (mg)

Juice drink
(Light n' Juicy, Orange)

| | 6 oz | 14 | 0 | 0 | na | 17 |

LITE PICK ○◇□□

COMMENTS: 78 fewer calories, 41 milligrams less sodium than 6 ounces regular orange juice drink. Sweetened with aspartame.

PRODUCT	SERV	CAL	FAT (G)	% cal from fat	CHOL (mg)	SOD (mg)

Juice drink
(Light n' Juicy, Punch)

| | 6 oz | 14 | 0 | 0 | na | 17 |

LITE PICK ○◇□□

COMMENTS: 85 fewer calories, 10 milligrams less sodium than 6 ounces regular fruit punch. Sweetened with aspartame.

PRODUCT	SERV	CAL	FAT (G)	% cal from fat	CHOL (mg)	SOD (mg)
Juice drink (Ocean Spray, Low Calorie Cranapple)	6 oz	40	0	0	0	<10

LITE PICK ○◇□□

COMMENTS: 90 fewer calories than 6 ounces regular Ocean Spray Cranapple Juice Drink. Sweetened with fructose and saccharin.

PRODUCT	SERV	CAL	FAT (G)	% cal from fat	CHOL (mg)	SOD (mg)
Juice drink (Ocean Spray, Low Calorie Cranberry Juice Cocktail)	6 oz	40	0	0	0	<10

LITE PICK ○◇□□

COMMENTS: 70 fewer calories than 6 ounces regular Ocean Spray Cranberry Juice Cocktail. Sweetened with fructose and saccharin.

PRODUCT	SERV	CAL	FAT (G)	% cal from fat	CHOL (mg)	SOD (mg)
Juice drink (Ocean Spray, Low Calorie CranRaspberry)	6 oz	40	0	0	0	<10

LITE PICK ○◇□□

COMMENTS: 70 fewer calories than 6 ounces regular Ocean Spray CranRaspberry Juice Drink. Sweetened with fructose and saccharin.

PRODUCT	SERV	CAL	FAT (G)	% cal from fat	CHOL (mg)	SOD (mg)
Juice drink (Welch's, Frozen Fruit Juice Cocktail, No Sugar Added, Cranberry)	6 oz	40	0	0	0	5

LITE PICK ○◇□□

COMMENTS: 60 fewer calories than 6 ounces regular Welch's Cranberry Juice Cocktail, but 5 milligrams *more* sodium. Sweetened with aspartame.

PRODUCT	SERV	CAL	FAT (G)	% cal from fat	CHOL (mg)	SOD (mg)
Juice drink (Welch's, Frozen Fruit Juice Cocktail, No Sugar Added, Grape)	6 oz	40	0	0	0	5

LITE PICK ○◇□□

COMMENTS: 70 fewer calories than 6 ounces regular Welch's Grape Juice Cocktail, but 5 milligrams *more* sodium. Sweetened with aspartame.

PRODUCT	SERV	CAL	FAT (G)	% cal from fat	CHOL (mg)	SOD (mg)
Juice drink (Welch's, Frozen Fruit Juice Cocktail, No Sugar Added, Apple-White Grape)	6 oz	40	0	0	0	5

LITE PICK ○◇□□

COMMENTS: 80 fewer calories than 6 ounces regular Welch's Orchard Frozen Apple Grape Cocktail, but 5 milligrams *more* sodium. Sweetened with aspartame.

PRODUCT	SERV	CAL	FAT (G)	% cal from fat	CHOL (mg)	SOD (mg)
Juice, tomato (Featherweight, Low Sodium)	6 oz	35	0	0	0	10

○□□

COMMENTS: 507 milligrams less sodium than 6 ounces regular tomato juice, but 4 *more* calories.

PRODUCT	SERV	CAL	FAT (G)	% cal from fat	CHOL (mg)	SOD (mg)
Seltzer (Crystal Geyser, Light Seltzer with Natural Fruit Flavors)	10 oz	108	0	0	na	<10

NO LITE BARGAIN ○◇□□

COMMENTS: 108 calories *more* than calorie-free plain seltzer. Sweetened with fructose syrup and juice concentrate.

PRODUCT	SERV	CAL	FAT (G)	% cal from fat	CHOL (mg)	SOD (mg)
Shake mix (Alba 77, Fit 'n Frosty, Chocolate Double Fudge)	1 packet	70	1	13	na	170

○

COMMENTS: No direct comparison, but this is very low in fat. Sweetened with aspartame.

PRODUCT	SERV	CAL	FAT (G)	% cal from fat	CHOL (mg)	SOD (mg)
Shake mix (Alba 77, Fit 'n Frosty, Chocolate Marshmallow)	1 packet	70	1	13	na	250

○

COMMENTS: No direct comparison, but this is very low in fat. Sweetened with aspartame.

PRODUCT	SERV	CAL	FAT (G)	% cal from fat	CHOL (mg)	SOD (mg)
Shake mix (Alba 77, Fit 'n Frosty, Chocolate)	1 packet	70	1	13	na	210

○

COMMENTS: No direct comparison, but this is very low in fat. Sweetened with aspartame.

PRODUCT	SERV	CAL	FAT (G)	% cal from fat	CHOL (mg)	SOD (mg)
Shake mix (Alba 77, Fit 'n Frosty, Strawberry)	1 packet	70	0	0	na	150

○

COMMENTS: No direct comparison, but this is fat free. Sweetened with aspartame.

PRODUCT	SERV	CAL	FAT (G)	% cal from fat	CHOL (mg)	SOD (mg)
Shake mix (Alba 77, Fit 'n Frosty, Vanilla)	1 packet	70	0	0	na	150

○

COMMENTS: No direct comparison, but this is fat free. Sweetened with aspartame.

PRODUCT	SERV	CAL	FAT (G)	% cal from fat	CHOL (mg)	SOD (mg)
Shake mix (Weight Watchers, Chocolate Fudge)	1 packet	70	1	13	na	170

○

COMMENTS: No direct comparison, but this is very low in fat. Sweetened with aspartame.

PRODUCT	SERV	CAL	FAT (G)	% cal from fat	CHOL (mg)	SOD (mg)
Shake mix (Weight Watchers, Orange Sherbet)	1 packet	70	0	0	na	210

○

COMMENTS: No direct comparison, but this is fat free. Sweetened with aspartame.

PRODUCT	SERV	CAL	FAT (G)	% cal from fat	CHOL (mg)	SOD (mg)
Soft drink (Diet Coke, all varieties)	12 oz	1.4	0	0	0	8

LITE PICK ○◇□□

COMMENTS: 132 fewer calories, 6 milligrams less sodium than 12 ounces regular Coca-Cola Classic. Sweetened with aspartame.

PRODUCT	SERV	CAL	FAT (G)	% cal from fat	CHOL (mg)	SOD (mg)
Soft drink (Fresca, Diet)	12 oz	4.2	0	0	0	0

○◇□

COMMENTS: No direct comparison, but calorie savings similar to other diet soft drinks. Sweetened with aspartame.

PRODUCT	SERV	CAL	FAT (G)	% cal from fat	CHOL (mg)	SOD (mg)
Soft drink (Diet Minute Maid, Lemon Lime)	12 oz	19.4	0	0	0	8

LITE PICK ○◇□□

COMMENTS: 123 fewer calories than 12 ounces regular Minute Maid Lemon Lime. Sweetened with aspartame.

PRODUCT	SERV	CAL	FAT (G)	% cal from fat	CHOL (mg)	SOD (mg)
Soft drink (Diet Minute Maid, Orange)	12 oz	16	0	0	0	0

LITE PICK ○◇□

COMMENTS: 158 fewer calories than 12 ounces regular Minute Maid Orange. Sweetened with aspartame.

PRODUCT	SERV	CAL	FAT (G)	% cal from fat	CHOL (mg)	SOD (mg)
Soft drink (Diet Pepsi Free)	12 oz	1	0	0	0	2.4

LITE PICK ○◇□

COMMENTS: 159 fewer calories than 12 ounces regular Pepsi. Sweetened with aspartame and caffeine free.

PRODUCT	SERV	CAL	FAT (G)	% cal from fat	CHOL (mg)	SOD (mg)
Soft drink (Diet Pepsi)	12 oz	1	0	0	0	2.4

LITE PICK ○◇□

COMMENTS: 159 fewer calories than 12 ounces regular Pepsi. Sweetened with aspartame.

PRODUCT	SERV	CAL	FAT (G)	% cal from fat	CHOL (mg)	SOD (mg)
Soft drink (Diet Slice, Apple)	12 oz	20	0	0	0	5

LITE PICK ○◇□□

COMMENTS: 176 fewer calories than 12 ounces regular apple Slice. Sweetened with aspartame.

PRODUCT	SERV	CAL	FAT (G)	% cal from fat	CHOL (mg)	SOD (mg)
Soft drink (Diet Slice, Cherry Cola)	12 oz	20	0	0	0	5

LITE PICK ○◇□□

COMMENTS: 144 fewer calories than 12 ounces regular cherry cola Slice. Sweetened with aspartame.

PRODUCT	SERV	CAL	FAT (G)	% cal from fat	CHOL (mg)	SOD (mg)
Soft drink (Diet Slice, Lemon Lime)	12 oz	26	0	0	0	11

LITE PICK ○◇□□

COMMENTS: 126 fewer calories than 12 ounces regular Slice. Sweetened with aspartame.

PRODUCT	SERV	CAL	FAT (G)	% cal from fat	CHOL (mg)	SOD (mg)
Soft drink (Diet Slice, Mandarin Orange)	12 oz	19	0	0	0	22

LITE PICK ○◇□□

COMMENTS: 173 fewer calories than 12 ounces regular Slice Mandarin Orange. Sweetened with aspartame.

PRODUCT	SERV	CAL	FAT (G)	% cal from fat	CHOL (mg)	SOD (mg)
Soft drink (Diet Sprite)	12 oz	3.6	0	0	0	tr

LITE PICK ○◇□

COMMENTS: 13 fewer calories, 23 milligrams less sodium than 12 ounces regular Sprite. Sweetened with aspartame.

PRODUCT	SERV	CAL	FAT (G)	% cal from fat	CHOL (mg)	SOD (mg)
Soft drink (TAB, regular and caffeine-free)	12 oz	.8	0	0	0	8

LITE PICK ○◇□□

COMMENTS: 132 fewer calories, 6 milligrams less sodium than regular Coca-Cola Classic. Sweetened with aspartame and saccharin.

PRODUCT	SERV	CAL	FAT (G)	% cal from fat	CHOL (mg)	SOD (mg)
Tea mix (Crystal Light, Sugar Free Fruit Tea, all flavors)	8 oz	4	0	0	0	0

○◇□

COMMENTS: 4 calories *more* than plain tea, which has none. Sweetened with aspartame.

PRODUCT	SERV	CAL	FAT (G)	% cal from fat	CHOL (mg)	SOD (mg)
Tea mix (Nestea, Sugar Free)	8 oz	4	0	0	0	0

○◇□

COMMENTS: Has 4 calories; regular tea has none. Sweetened with aspartame.

PRODUCT	SERV	CAL	FAT (G)	% cal from fat	CHOL (mg)	SOD (mg)
Tea mix (Purepak Nestea, Sugar Free with Lemon)	8 oz	4	0	0	0	5

○◇□□

COMMENTS: This light version has 4 calories; regular tea has none. Sweetened with saccharin.

PRODUCT	SERV	CAL	FAT (G)	% cal from fat	CHOL (mg)	SOD (mg)
Yogurt drink (Dannon Dan'up, all flavors)	8 oz	190	4	19	10	110

LITE PICK ○◇◇□□□

COMMENTS: 10 fewer calories, 30 milligrams less sodium than 8 ounces Dannon Vanilla yogurt in a carton. Very low in fat.

PRODUCT	SERV	CAL	FAT (G)	% cal from fat	CHOL (mg)	SOD (mg)
Yogurt drink (Tuscan Liquid Low- Fat Yogurt Drink)	8 oz	180	2	10	na	150

○

COMMENTS: 16 fewer calories, 1 gram less fat, 1 milligram less cholesterol than 8 ounces Dannon Vanilla yogurt in a carton. Very low in fat.

Breakfast Meats

PRODUCT	SERV	CAL	FAT (G)	% cal from fat	CHOL (mg)	SOD (mg)
Bacon (Sizzlean, Breakfast Strips, Beef)	2 pc	70	5	64	na	480

NO LITE BARGAIN

COMMENTS: 1 gram less fat, but 252 milligrams *more* sodium than 2 pieces regular cooked bacon. Very high in fat.

PRODUCT	SERV	CAL	FAT (G)	% cal from fat	CHOL (mg)	SOD (mg)
Bacon (Sizzlean, Breakfast Strips, Brown Sugar Cured Pork)	2 pc	110	9	74	na	490

NO LITE BARGAIN

COMMENTS: 40 calories, 3 grams fat, 262 milligrams *more* sodium than 2 pieces of bacon. Very high in fat.

PRODUCT	SERV	CAL	FAT (G)	% cal from fat	CHOL (mg)	SOD (mg)
Bacon (Sizzlean, Breakfast Strips, Pork)	2 pc	90	8	80	na	530

NO LITE BARGAIN

COMMENTS: 20 calories, 2 grams fat, 302 milligrams *more* sodium than 2 pieces regular cooked bacon. Very high in fat.

PRODUCT	SERV	CAL	FAT (G)	% cal from fat	CHOL (mg)	SOD (mg)
Breakfast links (Jones Dairy Farm Light, Pork)	2 pc	140	11	71	na	440

◇◇

COMMENTS: 140 fewer calories, 16 grams less fat, 23 milligrams less cholesterol but 88 milligrams *more* sodium than 2 links regular Jones link sausage. Very high in fat and sodium.

PRODUCT	SERV	CAL	FAT (G)	% cal from fat	CHOL (mg)	SOD (mg)
Breakfast links (Jones Dairy Farm Golden Brown Light, Pork)	2 pc	120	10	75	30	260

COMMENTS: 160 fewer calories, 17 grams less fat, 18 milligrams less cholesterol, 92 milligrams less sodium than 2 links regular Jones link sausage, but still very high in fat.

PRODUCT	SERV	CAL	FAT (G)	% cal from fat	CHOL (mg)	SOD (mg)
Breakfast strips (Oscar Mayer, Lean n' Tasty, Beef)	1 pc	46	3.8	74	13	190

NO LITE BARGAIN ◇◇

COMMENTS: 10 *more* calories, 1/2 gram *more* fat, 8 milligrams *more* cholesterol, and 89 milligrams *more* sodium than a strip of bacon, but also weighs twice as much. Very high in fat.

PRODUCT	SERV	CAL	FAT (G)	% cal from fat	CHOL (mg)	SOD (mg)
Breakfast strips (Oscar Mayer, Lean n' Tasty, Pork)	1 pc	54	4.7	78	14	207

NO LITE BARGAIN ◇◇

COMMENTS: 18 *more* calories, 2 grams *more* fat, 9 milligrams *more* cholesterol, and 106 milligrams *more* sodium than a strip of bacon, but also weighs twice as much. Very high in fat.

PRODUCT	SERV	CAL	FAT (G)	% cal from fat	CHOL (mg)	SOD (mg)
Sausage (Eckrich, Lean Supreme Polska Kielbasa)	2 oz	144	12	75	na	448

COMMENTS: 46 fewer calories, 5 grams less fat, 92 milligrams less sodium than 2 ounces regular Hillshire Farm Polska Kielbasa, but still very high in fat and sodium.

PRODUCT	SERV	CAL	FAT (G)	% cal from fat	CHOL (mg)	SOD (mg)
Sausage (Eckrich, Lean Supreme Heat n' Serve Sausage Links)	2 pc	120	10	75	na	440

COMMENTS: 40 fewer calories, 4 grams less fat than two Eckrich original Smok-Y-Links, but 100 milligrams *more* sodium and still very high in fat.

PRODUCT	SERV	CAL	FAT (G)	% cal from fat	CHOL (mg)	SOD (mg)
Sausage (Eckrich, Lean Supreme Smoked Sausage, Beef)	2 oz	160	14	79	na	460

COMMENTS: 40 fewer calories, 4 grams less fat, 80 milligrams less sodium than 2 ounces regular Eckrich smoked beef sausage, but still very high in fat and sodium.

PRODUCT	SERV	CAL	FAT (G)	% cal from fat	CHOL (mg)	SOD (mg)
Sausage (Eckrich, Lean Supreme Smoked Sausage)	2 oz	140	12	77	na	460

COMMENTS: 60 fewer calories, 6 grams less fat, 80 milligrams less sodium than 2 ounces regular Eckrich smoked beef sausage, but still very high in fat and sodium.

PRODUCT	SERV	CAL	FAT (G)	% cal from fat	CHOL (mg)	SOD (mg)
Sausage (Hillshire Farm, Lite Smoked Sausage; Polska Kielbasa)	2 oz	160	13	73	na	na

COMMENTS: 30 fewer calories, 4 grams less fat than 2 ounces regular Hillshire Farm Polska Kielbasa, but still very high in fat.

CANDY

PRODUCT	SERV	CAL	FAT (G)	% cal from fat	CHOL (mg)	SOD (mg)
Candy, chocolate (Featherweight, Chocolate Almond Bar) ◇□□	1 pc	90	7	70	0	20

COMMENTS: Light only in sodium; 8% *more* calories from fat than a regular chocolate almond bar. Very high in fat. Sweetened with mannitol.

PRODUCT	SERV	CAL	FAT (G)	% cal from fat	CHOL (mg)	SOD (mg)
Candy, chocolate (Featherweight, Milk Chocolate Bar; Chocolate Crunch Bar) ◇□□	1 pc	80	6	68	0	20

COMMENTS: Light only in sodium; 23% *more* calories from fat than a regular chocolate crunch bar. Very high in fat. Sweetened with mannitol.

PRODUCT	SERV	CAL	FAT (G)	% cal from fat	CHOL (mg)	SOD (mg)
Candy, chocolate nougat (Whitman's Lite, Honey Nut Nougat)	2 pc	60	2	30	na	35

○□□

COMMENTS: No direct comparison. Lower in fat than most chocolate candies.

PRODUCT	SERV	CAL	FAT (G)	% cal from fat	CHOL (mg)	SOD (mg)
Candy, coconut (Whitman's Lite)	2 pc	60	3	45	na	25

□□

COMMENTS: No direct comparison, but provides the same percent of calories from fat as most regular chocolate candy.

PRODUCT	SERV	CAL	FAT (G)	% cal from fat	CHOL (mg)	SOD (mg)
Candy, fruit (Featherweight, Orchard Blend; Tropical Blend; Berry Patch Blend)	1 pc	12	0	0	0	0

○□

COMMENTS: No direct comparison, but although the Featherweight manufacturers list this as "low sodium," regular hard candy has little or no sodium.

PRODUCT	SERV	CAL	FAT (G)	% cal from fat	CHOL (mg)	SOD (mg)
Candy, hard						
(Estee)	2 pc	25	0	0	0	5

○◇□□

COMMENTS: No lighter in calories or sodium than regular hard candy. Sweetened with sorbitol.

PRODUCT	SERV	CAL	FAT (G)	% cal from fat	CHOL (mg)	SOD (mg)
Chocolate bar						
(Estee, Crunch)	2 sq	45	3	60	2	10

◇□□

COMMENTS: Only about 3 milligrams sodium less per ⅓ ounce square than the same amount of a regular chocolate crunch bar. Sweetened with sorbitol.

PRODUCT	SERV	CAL	FAT (G)	% cal from fat	CHOL (mg)	SOD (mg)
Chocolate-coated raisins	6 pc					
(Estee)	(¼ oz)	30	2	60	<1	10

NO LITE BARGAIN ◇□□

COMMENTS: The same calories as, and 1 gram fat and 9 milligrams *more* sodium than, ¼ ounce regular chocolate covered raisins. Sweetened with sorbitol.

PRODUCT	SERV	CAL	FAT (G)	% cal from fat	CHOL (mg)	SOD (mg)

Gum
(Bubble Yum,
Sugarless Bubble
Gum, all flavors)

	SERV	CAL	FAT (G)	% cal from fat	CHOL (mg)	SOD (mg)
	1 pc	20	0	0	0	0

○◇□

COMMENTS: 5 fewer calories than regular Bubble Yum. Sweetened with sorbitol and saccharin.

PRODUCT	SERV	CAL	FAT (G)	% cal from fat	CHOL (mg)	SOD (mg)

Gum
(Carefree Sugarless,
all flavors)

	SERV	CAL	FAT (G)	% cal from fat	CHOL (mg)	SOD (mg)
	1 pc	8	0	0	0	0

○◇□

COMMENTS: 2 fewer calories than regular Carefree gum. Sweetened with sorbitol and saccharin.

PRODUCT	SERV	CAL	FAT (G)	% cal from fat	CHOL (mg)	SOD (mg)

Gum
(Carefree Sugarless
Bubble Gum, all
flavors)

	SERV	CAL	FAT (G)	% cal from fat	CHOL (mg)	SOD (mg)
	1 pc	10	0	0	0	0

LITE PICK ○◇□

COMMENTS: 15 fewer calories than regular bubble gum. Sweetened with sorbitol and saccharin.

PRODUCT	SERV	CAL	FAT (G)	% cal from fat	CHOL (mg)	SOD (mg)
Gumdrops (Estee)	4	25	0	0	0	0

NO LITE BARGAIN ○◇□

COMMENTS: No lighter in sodium and 11 calories *more* than four regular gumdrops. Sweetened with sorbitol and hydrogenated starch hydrolysate.

PRODUCT	SERV	CAL	FAT (G)	% cal from fat	CHOL (mg)	SOD (mg)
Peanut brittle (Estee, sugar-free)	¼ oz	35	1	26	na	30

NO LITE BARGAIN ○□□

COMMENTS: 4 *more* calories, 28 milligrams *more* sodium than an equal amount of regular peanut brittle. Although it's low in fat and sodium, ¼ ounce may be too small a serving size. Sweetened with hydrogenated starch hydrolysate.

PRODUCT	SERV	CAL	FAT (G)	% cal from fat	CHOL (mg)	SOD (mg)
Peanut butter cups (Estee)	1 pc	45	3	60	<1	10

◇□□

COMMENTS: 47 fewer calories, 5 grams less fat, 45 milligrams less sodium than one regular peanut butter cup, but also less than half the size. Sweetened with sorbitol.

CONDIMENTS

PRODUCT	SERV	CAL	FAT (G)	% cal from fat	CHOL (mg)	SOD (mg)
Coating mix, seasoned (Featherweight, Chicken)	¼ pkg	18	0	0	0	30

LITE PICK ○□□

COMMENTS: 51 fewer calories, 3 grams less fat, 563 milligrams less sodium than ¼ package of regular coating mix for poultry.

PRODUCT	SERV	CAL	FAT (G)	% cal from fat	CHOL (mg)	SOD (mg)
Coating mix, seasoned (Featherweight, Fish)	¼ pkg	18	0	0	0	10

LITE PICK ○□□

COMMENTS: 52 fewer calories, 1 gram less fat, 400 milligrams less sodium than ¼ package of regular coating mix for fish.

PRODUCT	SERV	CAL	FAT (G)	% cal from fat	CHOL (mg)	SOD (mg)
Cooking spray (Mazola, No Stick)	2.5 second spray	6	1	100	0	0

COMMENTS: 116 calories fewer than 1 tablespoon oil.

PRODUCT	SERV	CAL	FAT (G)	% cal from fat	CHOL (mg)	SOD (mg)
Ketchup (Del Monte, No Salt added)	1 T	15	0	0	0	25

LITE PICK ○◇□□

COMMENTS: The same number of calories as and 144 milligrams less sodium per tablespoon than Del Monte's regular ketchup.

PRODUCT	SERV	CAL	FAT (G)	% cal from fat	CHOL (mg)	SOD (mg)
Ketchup (Estee)	1 T	6	0	0	0	20

LITE PICK ○◇□□

COMMENTS: 12 fewer calories and 136 milligrams less sodium than 1 tablespoon regular ketchup.

PRODUCT	SERV	CAL	FAT (G)	% cal from fat	CHOL (mg)	SOD (mg)

Ketchup
(Health Valley, No-Salt Catch-Up)

	1 T	16	<1	<56	0	70

◇□□□

COMMENTS: 86 milligrams less sodium than 1 tablespoon regular ketchup. The percentage of calories from fat is deceiving; with less than 1 gram fat per tablespoon, regular ketchup is actually a low-fat product.

PRODUCT	SERV	CAL	FAT (G)	% cal from fat	CHOL (mg)	SOD (mg)

Ketchup
(Heinz, Lite)

	1 T	8	0	0	0	110

LITE PICK ○◇□□□

COMMENTS: 10 fewer calories and 70 milligrams less sodium than 1 tablespoon regular Heinz ketchup.

PRODUCT	SERV	CAL	FAT (G)	% cal from fat	CHOL (mg)	SOD (mg)

Ketchup
(Heinz, Low Sodium Lite)

	1 T	8	0	0	0	90

LITE PICK ○◇□□□

COMMENTS: 10 fewer calories and 80 milligrams less sodium than 1 tablespoon regular Heinz ketchup. The same number of calories but 20 milligrams less sodium than 1 tablespoon Heinz Lite Ketchup.

PRODUCT	SERV	CAL	FAT (G)	% cal from fat	CHOL (mg)	SOD (mg)
Ketchup (Weight Watchers)	1 T	8	0	0	0	110

LITE PICK ○◇☐☐☐

COMMENTS: 8 fewer calories, 46 milligrams less sodium than 1 tablespoon regular ketchup.

PRODUCT	SERV	CAL	FAT (G)	% cal from fat	CHOL (mg)	SOD (mg)
Mustard (Featherweight, Low Sodium)	1 tsp	5	.3	54	na	1

☐

COMMENTS: 63 milligrams less sodium than 1 teaspoon regular mustard. The high percentage of fat is deceiving; with less than ½ gram of fat per teaspoon, mustard is actually a low-fat product.

PRODUCT	SERV	CAL	FAT (G)	% cal from fat	CHOL (mg)	SOD (mg)
Pickles (Featherweight, Low Sodium Dill, Whole)	1 pc	4	0	0	0	5

LITE PICK ○◇☐☐

COMMENTS: No direct comparison, but is much lower in sodium than regular pickles.

PRODUCT	SERV	CAL	FAT (G)	% cal from fat	CHOL (mg)	SOD (mg)
Pickles (Featherweight, Low Sodium Sweet, Sliced)	3-4 sl	24	0	0	0	5

LITE PICK ○◇□□

COMMENTS: Actually has 5 *more* calories, but 163 milligrams less sodium than 4 slices regular bread-and-butter pickles.

PRODUCT	SERV	CAL	FAT (G)	% cal from fat	CHOL (mg)	SOD (mg)
Pickles (Vlasic, Half-the-Salt Hamburger Dill Chips)	1 oz	2	0	0	0	175

○◇

COMMENTS: 200 milligrams less sodium than 1 ounce regular Vlasic Original Dills.

PRODUCT	SERV	CAL	FAT (G)	% cal from fat	CHOL (mg)	SOD (mg)
Pickles (Vlasic, Half-the-Salt Kosher Crunch Dills)	1 oz	4	0	0	0	125

LITE PICK ○◇□□□

COMMENTS: 85 milligrams less sodium than 1 ounce regular Vlasic Kosher Crunch Dills.

PRODUCT	SERV	CAL	FAT (G)	% cal from fat	CHOL (mg)	SOD (mg)
Pickles (Vlasic, Half-the-Salt Sweet Butter Chips)	1 oz	30	0	0	0	80

LITE PICK ○◇□□□

COMMENTS: 80 milligrams less sodium than 1 ounce regular Vlasic Sweet Butter Chips.

PRODUCT	SERV	CAL	FAT (G)	% cal from fat	CHOL (mg)	SOD (mg)
Pickles (Vlasic, Half-the-Salt Kosher Dill Spears)	1 oz	4	0	0	0	120

LITE PICK ○◇□□□

COMMENTS: 170 milligrams less sodium than 1 ounce regular Vlasic Kosher Deli Dills.

PRODUCT	SERV	CAL	FAT (G)	% cal from fat	CHOL (mg)	SOD (mg)
Salt Substitute (Estee, Salt-It)	1 tsp	0	0	0	0	2

LITE PICK ○◇□

COMMENTS: Virtually no sodium.

PRODUCT	SERV	CAL	FAT (G)	% cal from fat	CHOL (mg)	SOD (mg)
Salt substitute (Salt Sense)	1 tsp	0	0	0	0	1570

○◇

COMMENTS: 810 milligrams less sodium than a teaspoon of salt.

CRACKERS

PRODUCT	SERV	CAL	FAT (G)	% cal from fat	CHOL (mg)	SOD (mg)
Breadsticks (Barbara's Bakery, No Salt Added)	1 oz	120	3	23	0	1

LITE PICK ○◇□

COMMENTS: The same number of calories as Barbara's regular bread-sticks. No salt is added during processing.

PRODUCT	SERV	CAL	FAT (G)	% cal from fat	CHOL (mg)	SOD (mg)
Crackers, cheese (Estee, Cheddar)	½ oz	70	4	51	na	120

□□□

COMMENTS: 11 fewer calories, 1 gram less fat and 60 milligrams less sodium than regular cheese crackers.

PRODUCT	SERV	CAL	FAT (G)	% cal from fat	CHOL (mg)	SOD (mg)
Crackers, rice (Holgrain, Lite Thins Unsalted)	4 pc	40	0	0	0	1

○◇□

COMMENTS: 10 *more* calories but 10 milligrams less sodium, per 4 crackers, than 4 regular Holgrain salted rice crackers.

PRODUCT	SERV	CAL	FAT (G)	% cal from fat	CHOL (mg)	SOD (mg)
Crackers, rice (Holgrain, Lite Thins)	4 pc	30	0	0	0	11

○◇□□

COMMENTS: 11 calories *more* than 4 regular rice wafers.

PRODUCT	SERV	CAL	FAT (G)	% cal from fat	CHOL (mg)	SOD (mg)
Crackers, Ritz (Ritz, Low Salt)	4 pc	70	4	51	na	60

□□□

COMMENTS: The same number of calories as but 60 milligrams less sodium than 4 regular Ritz crackers.

PRODUCT	SERV	CAL	FAT (G)	% cal from fat	CHOL (mg)	SOD (mg)
Crackers, rye						
(Wasa Lite)	1 pc	25	0	0	0	40

LITE PICK ○◇□□□

COMMENTS: 20 fewer calories and 30 milligrams less sodium than 1 Wasa Hearty Rye Cracker, but only half as much weight.

PRODUCT	SERV	CAL	FAT (G)	% cal from fat	CHOL (mg)	SOD (mg)
Crackers, sesame						
(Estee)	½ oz	70	4	51	0	120

◇□□□

COMMENTS: About the same calories, fat, and cholesterol as, and only 8 milligrams less sodium than, ½ ounce regular sesame crackers.

PRODUCT	SERV	CAL	FAT (G)	% cal from fat	CHOL (mg)	SOD (mg)
Crackers, soda						
(Estee, Unsalted)	2 pc	30	1	30	<1	<5

○◇□

COMMENTS: 6 *more* calories and 175 milligrams less sodium than 2 regular saltines.

PRODUCT	SERV	CAL	FAT (G)	% cal from fat	CHOL (mg)	SOD (mg)
Crackers, soda (Premium Saltines, No Salt)	5	60	2	30	na	115

LITE PICK ○◇□□□

COMMENTS: The same number of calories as but 65 milligrams less sodium than five regular Premium Saltines.

PRODUCT	SERV	CAL	FAT (G)	% cal from fat	CHOL (mg)	SOD (mg)
Crackers, wheat (Estee, Six-Calorie Wafers)	1 pc	6	<1	na	<5	<5

◇◇□

COMMENTS: No direct comparison here. These are very thin wafers, each only about one half the weight of a soda cracker. However, there's a tremendous sodium savings over most regular wheat crackers.

PRODUCT	SERV	CAL	FAT (G)	% cal from fat	CHOL (mg)	SOD (mg)
Crackers, wheat (Triscuit, Low-Salt Wafers)	3 oz	60	2	30	na	35

○□□

COMMENTS: The same number of calories as and 55 milligrams less sodium than three regular Triscuits.

PRODUCT	SERV	CAL	FAT (G)	% cal from fat	CHOL (mg)	SOD (mg)
Crackers, wheat (Wheat Thins, Low Salt)	8 pc	70	3	39	na	60

□□□

COMMENTS: The same number of calories as but 60 milligrams less sodium, per 8 crackers, than regular Wheat Thins.

PRODUCT	SERV	CAL	FAT (G)	% cal from fat	CHOL (mg)	SOD (mg)
Crackers, whole wheat (Holgrain, Lite Thins, Unsalted)	4 pc	30	0	0	na	1

○□

COMMENTS: The same number of calories as, 17 milligrams less sodium than regular Holgrain whole wheat crackers.

PRODUCT	SERV	CAL	FAT (G)	% cal from fat	CHOL (mg)	SOD (mg)
Crackers, whole wheat (Holgrain, Lite Thins)	4 pc	30	0	0	0	18

LITE PICK ○◇□□

COMMENTS: 40 fewer calories, 3 grams less fat, 110 milligrams less sodium than 4 regular whole wheat crackers.

PRODUCT	SERV	CAL	FAT (G)	% cal from fat	CHOL (mg)	SOD (mg)
Crackers, soda (Uneeda Biscuits, Unsalted tops)	3 pc	60	2	30	na	100

LITE PICK ○□□□

COMMENTS: Ounce for ounce, fat and calories are the same, but saltine crackers have about 80% *more* sodium.

PRODUCT	SERV	CAL	FAT (G)	% cal from fat	CHOL (mg)	SOD (mg)
Crispbread (Weight Watchers, Crispbread, all flavors)	2 pc	30	0	0	na	55

○□□□

COMMENTS: No direct comparison, but has about the same number of calories and sodium as regular crispbreads. Fat free.

DAIRY PRODUCTS

PRODUCT	SERV	CAL	FAT (G)	% cal from fat	CHOL (mg)	SOD (mg)
Cheese (Cabot, Light Vitalait, all flavors)	1 oz	67	4	54	15	173

◇◇

COMMENTS: 39 fewer calories, 3 grams less fat, 13 milligrams less cholesterol, and 233 milligrams less sodium than 1 ounce regular process American cheese. Although lower in fat than most cheese, it's still very high in fat.

PRODUCT	SERV	CAL	FAT (G)	% cal from fat	CHOL (mg)	SOD (mg)
Cheese (Dorman's Lo-Chol Low Cholesterol, slices or chunk)	1 oz	70	5	64	3	190

◇◇

COMMENTS: 36 fewer calories, 4 grams less fat, 24 milligrams less cholesterol, and 216 milligrams less sodium than 1 ounce regular process American cheese. Very high in fat.

PRODUCT	SERV	CAL	FAT (G)	% cal from fat	CHOL (mg)	SOD (mg)
Cheese (Formagg, Pizza Topper, shredded)	1 oz	70	5	64	0	140

◇□□□

COMMENTS: A blend of white, cheddar, mozzarella, and parmesan-flavored Formagg. Very high in fat.

PRODUCT	SERV	CAL	FAT (G)	% cal from fat	CHOL (mg)	SOD (mg)
Cheese (Formagg, Salad Topper, shredded)	1 oz	75	5	60	0	180

◇

COMMENTS: A blend of cheddar, mozzarella, provolone, and parmesan-flavored Formagg. Very high in fat.

PRODUCT	SERV	CAL	FAT (G)	% cal from fat	CHOL (mg)	SOD (mg)
Cheese (Weight Watchers, Low Sodium Natural, stick)	1 oz	80	5	56	na	70

□□□

COMMENTS: 34 fewer calories, 4 grams less fat, 106 milligrams less sodium than 1 ounce regular cheddar cheese. Although lower in fat than most cheese, it's still very high in fat. One slice weighs one ounce.

PRODUCT	SERV	CAL	FAT (G)	% cal from fat	CHOL (mg)	SOD (mg)
Cheese (Weight Watchers, Natural, stick)	1 oz	80	5	56	na	150

COMMENTS: 34 fewer calories, 4 grams less fat, 26 milligrams less sodium than 1 ounce regular cheddar cheese. Although lower in fat than most cheese, it's still very high in fat. One slice weighs one ounce.

PRODUCT	SERV	CAL	FAT (G)	% cal from fat	CHOL (mg)	SOD (mg)
Cheese (Weight Watchers, Slices, Dijon)	1 oz	50	2	36	na	400

COMMENTS: 64 fewer calories, 7 grams less fat, 20 milligrams less cholesterol than 1 ounce regular cheddar cheese, but 224 milligrams *more* sodium. Although much lower in fat than most cheese, is high in sodium. One slice weighs one ounce.

PRODUCT	SERV	CAL	FAT (G)	% cal from fat	CHOL (mg)	SOD (mg)
Cheese (Weight Watchers, Slices, Regular)	1 oz	50	2	36	na	400

COMMENTS: 64 fewer calories, 7 grams less fat, 20 milligrams less cholesterol than 1 ounce regular cheddar cheese, but 224 milligrams *more* sodium. Each slice weighs 1 ounce and, although much lower in fat than most cheese, is high in sodium. One slice weighs one ounce.

PRODUCT	SERV	CAL	FAT (G)	% cal from fat	CHOL (mg)	SOD (mg)
Cheese, American (Formagg, Sliced American Flavor, white)	1 oz	67	5	67	0	307

◇

COMMENTS: 39 fewer calories, 4 grams less fat, 27 milligrams less cholesterol, 99 milligrams less sodium than 1 ounce regular process cheese. (Note, however, that one slice weighs only ¾ ounce.) Very high in fat.

PRODUCT	SERV	CAL	FAT (G)	% cal from fat	CHOL (mg)	SOD (mg)
Cheese, American (Formagg, Sliced American Flavor, yellow)	1 oz	67	5	67	0	307

◇

COMMENTS: 39 fewer calories, 4 grams less fat, 27 milligrams less cholesterol, 99 milligrams less sodium than 1 ounce regular process cheese. (Note, however, that one slice weighs only ¾ ounce.) Very high in fat.

PRODUCT	SERV	CAL	FAT (G)	% cal from fat	CHOL (mg)	SOD (mg)
Cheese, American (Kraft, Light n' Lively Cheese Slices, American)	1 oz	70	4	51	15	410

◇◇

COMMENTS: 40 fewer calories, 5 grams less fat, 10 milligrams less cholesterol, 50 milligrams less sodium than 1 ounce regular Kraft Deluxe process American cheese slices. Although lower in fat than most cheese, it's still very high in fat and sodium. (Note, however, that one slice weighs only ¾ ounce.)

PRODUCT	SERV	CAL	FAT (G)	% cal from fat	CHOL (mg)	SOD (mg)
Cheese, American (Lite-line, Low Cholesterol, American Flavor)	1 oz	90	7	70	5	430

◇◇

COMMENTS: Same calories and fat as, but 80 milligrams *more* sodium than 1 ounce regular Borden Processed American Cheese Singles. No direct cholesterol comparison, but 19 milligrams less than most regular process American cheese. (Note, however, that one slice weighs only ⅔ ounce.) Very high in fat.

PRODUCT	SERV	CAL	FAT (G)	% cal from fat	CHOL (mg)	SOD (mg)
Cheese, American (Lite-line, Reduced Sodium Slices, American Flavor)	1 oz	70	4	51	20	90

◇◇□□□

COMMENTS: 20 fewer calories, 3 grams less fat, 260 milligrams less sodium than 1 ounce regular Borden Processed American Cheese Singles. No direct cholesterol comparison, but only 4 milligrams less than most regular processed American cheese. Although lower in fat than most cheese, it's still very high in fat. (Note, however, that one slice weighs only ⅔ ounce.)

PRODUCT	SERV	CAL	FAT (G)	% cal from fat	CHOL (mg)	SOD (mg)
Cheese, American (Lite-line, Slices, American Flavor, yellow)	1 oz	50	2	36	10	410

◇◇

COMMENTS: 40 fewer calories, 5 grams less fat than 1 ounce regular Borden Processed American Cheese Singles, but 60 milligrams *more* sodium. No direct cholesterol comparison, but 14 milligrams less than most regular processed American cheese and much lower in fat. (Note, however, than one slice weighs only ⅔ ounce.)

PRODUCT	SERV	CAL	FAT (G)	% cal from fat	CHOL (mg)	SOD (mg)
Cheese, American (Lite-line, Cheese Slices, American, white)	1 oz	50	2	36	10	410

◇◇

COMMENTS: 40 fewer calories, 5 grams less fat, 60 milligrams less sodium than 1 ounce regular Borden Processed Cheese Singles. Although much lower in fat than most cheeses, it is high in sodium. (Note, however, that one slice weighs only ⅔ ounce.)

PRODUCT	SERV	CAL	FAT (G)	% cal from fat	CHOL (mg)	SOD (mg)
Cheese, cheddar (Armour, Lower Salt Cheddar)	1 oz	116	9	70	30	106

□□□

COMMENTS: 4 fewer calories, 46 milligrams less sodium than 1 ounce regular cheddar cheese, with the same amount of fat and cholesterol. Very high in fat.

PRODUCT	SERV	CAL	FAT (G)	% cal from fat	CHOL (mg)	SOD (mg)
Cheese, cheddar (Dorman's, Chedda-Delite, sliced, chunk or shredded)	1 oz	90	7	70	24	100

◇◇◇□□□

COMMENTS: 24 fewer calories, 2 grams less fat, 6 milligrams less cholesterol, and 76 milligrams less sodium than 1 ounce regular cheddar cheese. Slightly lower in fat than regular cheddar cheese, but still very high in fat.

PRODUCT	SERV	CAL	FAT (G)	% cal from fat	CHOL (mg)	SOD (mg)
Cheese, cheddar (Dorman's, Light Chedda-Delite)	1 oz	90	7	70	24	100

□□□

COMMENTS: 24 fewer calories, 2 grams less fat, 6 milligrams less cholesterol and 76 milligrams less sodium than regular cheddar cheese. Lower in fat than regular cheddar cheese, but still very high in fat.

PRODUCT	SERV	CAL	FAT (G)	% cal from fat	CHOL (mg)	SOD (mg)
Cheese, cheddar (Featherweight, Low Sodium)	1 oz	110	9	74	na	5

□□

COMMENTS: Light only in sodium. 4 fewer calories and 171 milligrams less sodium than 1 ounce regular cheddar cheese. Very high in fat.

PRODUCT	SERV	CAL	FAT (G)	% cal from fat	CHOL (mg)	SOD (mg)

Cheese, cheddar
(Formagg, Cheddar
Flavored, chunk)

	SERV	CAL	FAT (G)	% cal from fat	CHOL (mg)	SOD (mg)
	1 oz	75	5	60	0	195

◇

COMMENTS: 39 fewer calories, 4 grams less fat, 30 milligrams less cholesterol than 1 ounce regular cheddar, but 19 milligrams *more* sodium. Although lower in fat than the regular version, it's still very high in fat.

PRODUCT	SERV	CAL	FAT (G)	% cal from fat	CHOL (mg)	SOD (mg)

Cheese, cheddar
(Formagg, Cheddar
Flavored, shredded)

	SERV	CAL	FAT (G)	% cal from fat	CHOL (mg)	SOD (mg)
	1 oz	75	5	60	0	140

◇□□□

COMMENTS: 39 fewer calories, 4 grams less fat, 30 milligrams less cholesterol, 36 milligrams less sodium than 1 ounce regular cheddar. Although lower in fat than the regular version, it's still very high in fat.

PRODUCT	SERV	CAL	FAT (G)	% cal from fat	CHOL (mg)	SOD (mg)

Cheese, cheddar
(Kraft, Light n' Lively
Cheese Slices,
Cheddar, sharp)

	SERV	CAL	FAT (G)	% cal from fat	CHOL (mg)	SOD (mg)
	1 oz	70	4	51	15	380

◇◇

COMMENTS: 40 fewer calories, 5 grams less fat, 15 milligrams less cholesterol than 1 ounce regular Kraft natural cheddar cheese, but 200 milligrams *more* sodium. Although lower in fat than most cheese, it's still very high in fat. (Note, however, that one slice weighs only ¾ ounce.)

PRODUCT	SERV	CAL	FAT (G)	% cal from fat	CHOL (mg)	SOD (mg)
Cheese, cheddar (Lite-line, Slices, Cheddar, mild)	1 oz	50	2	36	10	380

◇◇

COMMENTS: 64 fewer calories, 7 grams less fat, 20 milligrams less cholesterol than 1 ounce regular cheddar cheese, but 204 milligrams *more* sodium. Much lower in fat than most cheese, but high in sodium. (Note, however, that one slice weighs only ⅔ ounce.)

PRODUCT	SERV	CAL	FAT (G)	% cal from fat	CHOL (mg)	SOD (mg)
Cheese, cheddar (Lite-line, Slices, Cheddar, sharp)	1 oz	50	2	36	10	440

◇◇

COMMENTS: 64 fewer calories, 7 grams less fat, 20 milligrams less cholesterol than 1 ounce regular cheddar cheese, but 264 milligrams *more* sodium. Much lower in fat than most cheese, but high in sodium. (Note, however, that one slice weighs only ⅔ ounce.)

PRODUCT	SERV	CAL	FAT (G)	% cal from fat	CHOL (mg)	SOD (mg)
Cheese, cheddar (Weight Watchers, Cheddar, shredded)	1 oz	80	5	56	na	150

COMMENTS: 34 fewer calories, 4 grams less fat, 26 milligrams less sodium than 1 ounce regular cheddar cheese. Although lower in fat than most cheese, it's still very high in fat.

PRODUCT	SERV	CAL	FAT (G)	% cal from fat	CHOL (mg)	SOD (mg)

Cheese, cheddar
(Weight Watchers,
Low Sodium,

Cheddar, shredded)	1 oz	80	5	56	na	70

☐☐☐

COMMENTS: 34 fewer calories, 4 grams less fat, 106 milligrams less sodium than 1 ounce regular cheddar cheese. Although lower in fat than most cheese, it's still very high in fat.

PRODUCT	SERV	CAL	FAT (G)	% cal from fat	CHOL (mg)	SOD (mg)

Cheese, cheddar
(Weight Watchers,
Slices, Cheddar,

sharp)	1 oz	50	2	36	na	400

COMMENTS: 64 fewer calories, 7 grams less fat, 20 milligrams less cholesterol than 1 ounce regular cheddar cheese, but 224 milligrams *more* sodium. Each slice weighs 1 ounce and, although much lower in fat than most cheese, is high in sodium.

PRODUCT	SERV	CAL	FAT (G)	% cal from fat	CHOL (mg)	SOD (mg)

Cheese, Colby
(Kraft, Light

Naturals, Colby)	1 oz	80	5	56	20	150

◇◇

COMMENTS: 30 fewer calories, 4 grams less fat, 10 milligrams less cholesterol, 30 milligrams less sodium than 1 ounce regular Kraft Natural Colby cheese. Although lower in fat than most cheese, it's still very high in fat.

PRODUCT	SERV	CAL	FAT (G)	% cal from fat	CHOL (mg)	SOD (mg)
Cheese, Colby (Lite-line, Slices, Colby Flavor)	1 oz	50	2	36	10	450

◇◇

COMMENTS: 62 fewer calories, 7 grams less fat, 17 milligrams less cholesterol and 279 milligrams less sodium than 1 ounce regular Colby cheese. Although much lower in fat than most cheese, it is high in sodium. (Note that one slice weighs only ⅔ ounce.)

PRODUCT	SERV	CAL	FAT (G)	% cal from fat	CHOL (mg)	SOD (mg)
Cheese, cottage (Formagg)	½ c	80	2	23	0	95

LITE PICK ○◇□□□

COMMENTS: 22 fewer calories, 10 milligrams less cholesterol, 364 milligrams less sodium than ½ cup 2% milkfat cottage cheese.

PRODUCT	SERV	CAL	FAT (G)	% cal from fat	CHOL (mg)	SOD (mg)
Cheese, cottage (Weight Watchers, Lowfat Cottage Cheese)	4 oz	90	1	10	na	420

○

COMMENTS: 12 fewer calories, 1 gram less fat, 39 milligrams less sodium than 4 ounces 2% milkfat lowfat cottage cheese, the same as any brand of lowfat 2% cottage cheese. Very low in fat.

PRODUCT	SERV	CAL	FAT (G)	% cal from fat	CHOL (mg)	SOD (mg)
Cheese, cream (Formagg, Soft Cream Cheese Style)	1 oz	80	7	79	0	70

◇☐☐☐

COMMENTS: 19 fewer calories, 13 grams less fat, 31 milligrams less cholesterol, 14 milligrams less sodium than 1 ounce regular cream cheese. Although lower in fat than the regular version, it's still very high in fat.

PRODUCT	SERV	CAL	FAT (G)	% cal from fat	CHOL (mg)	SOD (mg)
Cheese, cream (Kraft, Light Philadelphia Brand Cream Cheese Product)	1 oz	60	5	75	15	160

◇◇

COMMENTS: 40 fewer calories, 5 grams less fat, 15 milligrams less cholesterol, but 75 milligrams *more* sodium than 1 ounce regular Kraft Philadelphia Brand cream cheese. Although it provides only half the fat of the regular version, it's still very high in fat.

PRODUCT	SERV	CAL	FAT (G)	% cal from fat	CHOL (mg)	SOD (mg)
Cheese, cream (Weight Watchers, Reduced Calorie Cream Cheese)	1 oz	35	2	51	na	40

□□□

COMMENTS: 64 fewer calories, 8 grams less fat, 44 milligrams less sodium than 1 ounce regular cream cheese. In this case, the high percentage of calories from fat is deceiving; since it has only 2 grams fat, it's actually low in fat.

PRODUCT	SERV	CAL	FAT (G)	% cal from fat	CHOL (mg)	SOD (mg)
Cheese, cups (Weight Watchers, Cheese Cups, Cheddar-Onion Flavor)	1 oz	70	4	51	na	255

COMMENTS: 23 fewer calories, 3 grams less fat, and 15 milligrams less sodium than 1 ounce regular cheddar cheese product. Although lower in fat than most cheese, it's still very high in fat.

PRODUCT	SERV	CAL	FAT (G)	% cal from fat	CHOL (mg)	SOD (mg)
Cheese, cups (Weight Watchers, Cheese Cups, Port Wine Flavor)	1 oz	70	4	51	na	255

COMMENTS: 30 fewer calories, 5 grams less fat than 1 ounce regular port wine cheese product, but 5 milligrams *more* sodium. Although lower in fat than most cheese, it's still very high in fat.

PRODUCT	SERV	CAL	FAT (G)	% cal from fat	CHOL (mg)	SOD (mg)
Cheese, Jack (Armour, Lower Salt, Jack)	1 oz	116	9	74	30	111

□□□

COMMENTS: 4 fewer calories, 4 milligrams less cholesterol and 41 milligrams less sodium than 1 ounce regular Monterey Jack cheese. Very high in fat.

PRODUCT	SERV	CAL	FAT (G)	% cal from fat	CHOL (mg)	SOD (mg)
Cheese, Jack (Dorman's, Slim-Jack, slices or chunk)	1 oz	90	7	70	22	90

□□□

COMMENTS: 16 fewer calories, 2 grams less fat, 62 milligrams less sodium than 1 ounce regular Monterey Jack cheese. Slightly lower in fat than the regular version, but still very high in fat.

PRODUCT	SERV	CAL	FAT (G)	% cal from fat	CHOL (mg)	SOD (mg)
Cheese, Jack (Formagg, Jack Flavored, chunk)	1 oz	75	5	60	0	195

◇

COMMENTS: 31 fewer calories, 4 grams less fat, 26 milligrams less cholesterol than 1 ounce regular Monterey Jack, but 43 milligrams *more* sodium. Although lower in fat than the regular version, it's still very high in fat.

PRODUCT	SERV	CAL	FAT (G)	% cal from fat	CHOL (mg)	SOD (mg)
Cheese, Jack (Kraft, Light Naturals, Monterey Jack)	1 oz	80	6	68	20	160

◇◇

COMMENTS: 30 fewer calories, 3 grams less fat, 10 milligrams less cholesterol, 30 milligrams less sodium than 1 ounce regular Kraft Natural Monterey Jack cheese. Although lower in fat than the regular version, it's still very high in fat.

PRODUCT	SERV	CAL	FAT (G)	% cal from fat	CHOL (mg)	SOD (mg)
Cheese, Jack (Lite-line, Slices, Monterey Jack Flavor)	1 oz	50	2	36	10	450

◇◇

COMMENTS: 56 fewer calories, 7 grams less fat, 12 milligrams less cholesterol but 298 milligrams *more* sodium than 1 ounce regular Monterey Jack cheese. Much lower in fat than most cheese, but high in sodium. (Note, however, that one slice weighs only ⅔ ounce.)

PRODUCT	SERV	CAL	FAT (G)	% cal from fat	CHOL (mg)	SOD (mg)
Cheese, jalapeño (Formagg, Monterey Jack, jalapeño Flavored, chunk)	1 oz	75	5	60	0	195

 ◇

COMMENTS: 31 fewer calories, 4 grams less fat, 26 milligrams less cholesterol than 1 ounce regular Monterey Jack, but 43 milligrams *more* sodium. Although lower in fat than the regular version, it's still very high in fat.

PRODUCT	SERV	CAL	FAT (G)	% cal from fat	CHOL (mg)	SOD (mg)
Cheese, jalapeño (Lite-line, Slices, jalapeño Flavor, mild or hot)	1 oz	50	2	36	10	410

◇◇

COMMENTS: 56 fewer calories, 7 grams less fat, 17 milligrams less cholesterol than 1 ounce regular processed American cheese, but 4 milligrams *more* sodium. Much lower in fat than most cheese, but high in sodium. (Note, however, that one slice weighs only ⅔ ounce.)

PRODUCT	SERV	CAL	FAT (G)	% cal from fat	CHOL (mg)	SOD (mg)
Cheese, mozzarella (Dorman's, Light Low Moisture Part Skim Low Sodium Mozzarella, shredded or sliced)	1 oz	80	5	56	15	90

◇◇□□□

COMMENTS: Lighter only in sodium. 60 milligrams less sodium than 1 ounce regular part-skim low-moisture mozzarella cheese. Although lower in fat than most cheese, it's still very high in fat.

PRODUCT	SERV	CAL	FAT (G)	% cal from fat	CHOL (mg)	SOD (mg)
Cheese, mozzarella (Formagg, Mozzarella Flavored, shredded)	1 oz	75	5	60	0	195

COMMENTS: 10 fewer calories, 1 gram less fat, 22 milligrams less cholesterol than 1 ounce regular mozzarella, but 89 milligrams *more* sodium. Although lower in fat than most cheese, it's still very high in fat.

PRODUCT	SERV	CAL	FAT (G)	% cal from fat	CHOL (mg)	SOD (mg)
Cheese, mozzarella (Land O'Lakes, Low Moisture Part Skim Mozzarella)	1 oz	80	5	56	15	150

◇◇

COMMENTS: 1 gram less fat than 1 ounce regular mozzarella cheese. Although lower in fat than most cheese, it's still very high in fat.

PRODUCT	SERV	CAL	FAT (G)	% cal from fat	CHOL (mg)	SOD (mg)
Cheese, mozzarella (Lite-line, Slices, Mozzarella Flavored)	1 oz	50	2	36	10	340

◇◇

COMMENTS: 30 fewer calories, 4 grams less fat, 12 milligrams less cholesterol than 1 ounce regular mozzarella cheese, but 234 milligrams *more* sodium. Much lower in fat than most cheese, but high in sodium. (Note, however, that one slice weighs only ⅔ ounce.)

PRODUCT	SERV	CAL	FAT (G)	% cal from fat	CHOL (mg)	SOD (mg)
Cheese, mozzarella (Polly-O, All Natural Part Skim, shredded)	1 oz	80	6	68	na	280

COMMENTS: 10 fewer calories than, the same amount of fat as, and 60 milligrams *more* sodium than 1 ounce regular Polly-O Whole Milk Shredded Mozzarella. Very high in fat.

PRODUCT	SERV	CAL	FAT (G)	% cal from fat	CHOL (mg)	SOD (mg)
Cheese, mozzarella (Weight Watchers, Mozzarella, stick or shredded)	1 oz	70	4	51	na	150

COMMENTS: 10 fewer calories, 2 grams less fat, but 44 milligrams *more* sodium than 1 ounce regular mozzarella cheese. Although lower in fat than most cheese, it's still very high in fat.

PRODUCT	SERV	CAL	FAT (G)	% cal from fat	CHOL (mg)	SOD (mg)
Cheese, mozzarella (Formagg, Mozzarella Flavored, chunk)	1 oz	75	5	60	0	195

◇

COMMENTS: 5 fewer calories, 1 gram less fat, 22 milligrams less cholesterol than 1 ounce regular mozzarella, but 89 milligrams *more* sodium. Although lower in fat than most cheese, it's still very high in fat.

PRODUCT	SERV	CAL	FAT (G)	% cal from fat	CHOL (mg)	SOD (mg)
Cheese, Muenster (Dorman's, Light Low-Sodium Slices, Muenster)	1 oz	110	9	74	27	95

□□□

COMMENTS: Light only in sodium. 6 *more* calories but 83 milligrams sodium less than 1 ounce regular Muenster cheese. Very high in fat.

PRODUCT	SERV	CAL	FAT (G)	% cal from fat	CHOL (mg)	SOD (mg)
Cheese, Muenster (Lite-line, Slices, Muenster Flavored)	1 oz	50	2	36	10	450

◇◇

COMMENTS: 54 fewer calories, 7 grams less fat, 17 milligrams less cholesterol than 1 ounce regular Muenster cheese, but 272 milligrams *more* sodium. Although it's much lower in fat than most cheese, it's higher in sodium. (Note, however, that one slice weighs only ⅔ ounce.)

PRODUCT	SERV	CAL	FAT (G)	% cal from fat	CHOL (mg)	SOD (mg)
Cheese, Muenster (Lite-line, Cheese Slices, Muenster)	1 oz	50	2	36	10	450

◇◇

COMMENTS: 54 fewer calories, 7 grams less fat, 17 milligrams less cholesterol than 1 ounce regular Muenster cheese, but 272 milligrams *more* sodium. Much lower in fat than most cheese, but high in sodium. (Note, however, that one slice weighs only ⅔ ounce.)

PRODUCT	SERV	CAL	FAT (G)	% cal from fat	CHOL (mg)	SOD (mg)
Cheese, Parmesan (Formagg, Parmesan Flavored)	1 oz	70	5	64	0	400

◊

COMMENTS: 41 fewer calories, 3 grams less fat, 19 milligrams less cholesterol, 54 milligrams less sodium than 1 ounce regular Parmesan. Although lower in fat than the regular version, it's still very high in fat.

PRODUCT	SERV	CAL	FAT (G)	% cal from fat	CHOL (mg)	SOD (mg)
Cheese, Provolone (Dorman's, Light Low Sodium, Provolone)	1 oz	90	7	70	20	140

◊□□□

COMMENTS: 10 fewer calories, 1 gram less fat, 108 milligrams less sodium than 1 ounce regular Provolone. Very high in fat.

PRODUCT	SERV	CAL	FAT (G)	% cal from fat	CHOL (mg)	SOD (mg)
Cheese, Provolone (Formagg, Provolone Flavored, chunk)	1 oz	75	5	60	0	195

◊

COMMENTS: 25 fewer calories, 3 grams less fat, 202 milligrams less cholesterol, 53 milligrams less sodium than 1 ounce regular Provolone. Although lower in fat than the regular version, it's still very high in fat.

PRODUCT	SERV	CAL	FAT (G)	% cal from fat	CHOL (mg)	SOD (mg)
Cheese, Provolone (Formagg, Provolone Flavored, shredded)	1 oz	75	5	60	0	195

◇

COMMENTS: 25 fewer calories, 3 grams less fat, 20 milligrams less cholesterol, 53 milligrams less sodium than 1 ounce regular Provolone. Although lower in fat than the regular version, it's still very high in fat.

PRODUCT	SERV	CAL	FAT (G)	% cal from fat	CHOL (mg)	SOD (mg)
Cheese, Ricotta (Formagg)	½ c	130	5	35	0	40

◇□□□

COMMENTS: 41 fewer calories, 5 grams less fat, 38 milligrams less cholesterol, 115 milligrams less sodium than than ½ cup regular part-skim Ricotta cheese.

PRODUCT	SERV	CAL	FAT (G)	% cal from fat	CHOL (mg)	SOD (mg)
Cheese, Ricotta (Polly-O, Part Skim No Salt)	1 oz	45	3	60	10	10

◇◇□□

COMMENTS: The same number of calories, fat, and cholesterol as 1 ounce of regular Polly-O Part-Skim Ricotta, and 13 milligrams less sodium. Very high in fat.

PRODUCT	SERV	CAL	FAT (G)	% cal from fat	CHOL (mg)	SOD (mg)
Cheese, Ricotta (Polly-O, Whole Milk No Salt)	1 oz	50	3.5	63	18	10

◇◇□□

COMMENTS: The same number of calories, fat, and cholesterol as 1 ounce of regular Polly-O Whole Milk Ricotta, and 13 milligrams less sodium. Very high in fat.

PRODUCT	SERV	CAL	FAT (G)	% cal from fat	CHOL (mg)	SOD (mg)
Cheese, Ricotta (Polly-O, Lite)	1 oz	40	2	45	4	33

◇◇□□

COMMENTS: 10 fewer calories, 2 grams less fat, 8 milligrams less cholesterol than regular Polly-O Whole Milk Ricotta, but 10 milligrams *more* sodium. Lower in fat than most cheese. The high percentage of calories from fat is deceiving; with only 2 grams of fat this product is actually low in fat.

PRODUCT	SERV	CAL	FAT (G)	% cal from fat	CHOL (mg)	SOD (mg)
Cheese, Swiss (Dorman's, Light No-Salt-Added Swiss, slices, chunk, or shredded)	1 oz	100	8	72	26	8

□□

COMMENTS: 7 fewer calories, and 66 milligrams less sodium than 1 ounce regular Swiss cheese. Very high in fat.

PRODUCT	SERV	CAL	FAT (G)	% cal from fat	CHOL (mg)	SOD (mg)
Cheese, Swiss (Formagg, Swiss Flavored, chunk)	1 oz	75	5	60	0	195

◇

COMMENTS: 32 fewer calories, 3 grams less fat, 26 milligrams less cholesterol than 1 ounce regular Swiss, but 121 milligrams *more* sodium. Although lower in fat than the regular version, it's still very high in fat.

PRODUCT	SERV	CAL	FAT (G)	% cal from fat	CHOL (mg)	SOD (mg)
Cheese, Swiss (Formagg, Swiss Flavored, shredded)	1 oz	70	5	64	0	140

◇□□□

COMMENTS: 37 fewer calories, 3 grams less fat, 26 milligrams less cholesterol than 1 ounce regular Swiss, but 66 milligrams *more* sodium. Although lower in fat than the regular version, it's still very high in fat.

PRODUCT	SERV	CAL	FAT (G)	% cal from fat	CHOL (mg)	SOD (mg)
Cheese, Swiss (Formagg, Sliced Swiss Flavored)	1 oz	67	4	54	0	307

◇

COMMENTS: 40 fewer calories, 4 grams less fat, but 233 milligrams *more* sodium than 1 ounce regular Swiss cheese. Although lower in fat than the regular version, it's still very high in fat.

PRODUCT	SERV	CAL	FAT (G)	% cal from fat	CHOL (mg)	SOD (mg)
Cheese, Swiss (Kraft, Light Naturals 75% Less Sodium Swiss)	1 oz	110	8	65	30	10

□□

COMMENTS: Light only in sodium. 30 milligrams less sodium than 1 ounce regular Kraft Natural Swiss cheese, but 20 *more* calories and 5 milligrams more cholesterol. Very high in fat.

PRODUCT	SERV	CAL	FAT (G)	% cal from fat	CHOL (mg)	SOD (mg)
Cheese, Swiss (Kraft, Light Naturals Swiss)	1 oz	90	5	50	20	55

◇◇□□□

COMMENTS: 20 fewer calories, 3 grams less fat, 5 milligrams less cholesterol than 1 ounce regular Kraft Natural Swiss cheese, but 15 milligrams *more* sodium. Athough lower in fat than most cheese, it's still very high in fat.

PRODUCT	SERV	CAL	FAT (G)	% cal from fat	CHOL (mg)	SOD (mg)
Cheese, Swiss (Kraft, Light n' Lively Slices, Swiss)	1 oz	70	4	51	15	350

◇◇

COMMENTS: 40 fewer calories, 4 grams less fat, 10 milligrams less cholesterol than 1 ounce regular Kraft Natural Swiss cheese, but 310 milligrams *more* sodium. Although lower in fat than most cheese, it's still very high in fat and sodium. (Note that one slice weighs only ¾ ounce.)

PRODUCT	SERV	CAL	FAT (G)	% cal from fat	CHOL (mg)	SOD (mg)
Cheese, Swiss (Lite-line, Slices, Swiss Flavored)	1 oz	50	2	36	10	330

◇◇

COMMENTS: 57 fewer calories, 6 grams less fat, 16 milligrams less cholesterol than 1 ounce regular Swiss cheese, but 256 milligrams *more* sodium. Much lower in fat than most cheese, but high in sodium. (Note that one slice weighs only ⅔ ounce.)

PRODUCT	SERV	CAL	FAT (G)	% cal from fat	CHOL (mg)	SOD (mg)
Cheese, Swiss (Weight Watchers, Low Sodium Slices, Swiss)	1 oz	50	2	36	na	140

□□□

COMMENTS: 57 fewer calories, 6 grams less fat than 1 ounce regular Swiss cheese, but 66 milligrams *more* sodium. Much lower in fat than most cheese. (One slice weighs one ounce.)

PRODUCT	SERV	CAL	FAT (G)	% cal from fat	CHOL (mg)	SOD (mg)
Milk, evaporated (Pet 99, Light Evaporated Skimmed)	4 oz	100	0	0	1	150

○◇

COMMENTS: 70 fewer calories, 10 grams less fat, 36 milligrams less cholesterol than regular Pet evaporated milk, but 10 milligrams *more* sodium. There's a tremendous fat and calorie savings here, but it's slightly higher in sodium. Fat free.

PRODUCT	SERV	CAL	FAT (G)	% cal from fat	CHOL (mg)	SOD (mg)
Milk, instant (Land O'Lakes, Flash Instant Nonfat, reconstituted)	8 oz	80	<1	<11	5	120

LITE PICK ○◇◇□□□

COMMENTS: 6 fewer calories, 1 milligram less cholesterol, 6 milligrams less sodium than 8 ounces regular skim milk. Very low in fat.

PRODUCT	SERV	CAL	FAT (G)	% cal from fat	CHOL (mg)	SOD (mg)
Sour Cream (Formagg, Sour Cream Style)	2 T	40	3	68	0	10

◇□□

COMMENTS: 12 fewer calories, 2 grams less fat, 10 milligrams less cholesterol, 2 milligrams less sodium than 2 tablespoons regular sour cream.

PRODUCT	SERV	CAL	FAT (G)	% cal from fat	CHOL (mg)	SOD (mg)
Yogurt (Colombo, Lite Nonfat, fruit flavors)	8 oz	200	<1	<5	<1	110

LITE PICK ○◇□□□

COMMENTS: 25 fewer calories, 2 grams less fat, 9 milligrams less cholesterol, 11 milligrams less sodium than 8 ounces regular lowfat fruit-flavored yogurt. Very low in fat.

PRODUCT	SERV	CAL	FAT (G)	% cal from fat	CHOL (mg)	SOD (mg)
Yogurt (Colombo, Lite Nonfat, Vanilla)	8 oz	160	<1	<6	<1	130

LITE PICK ○◇□□□

COMMENTS: 34 fewer calories, 2 grams less fat, 10 milligrams less cholesterol, 19 milligrams less sodium than 8 ounces regular low-fat vanilla yogurt. Very low in fat.

PRODUCT	SERV	CAL	FAT (G)	% cal from fat	CHOL (mg)	SOD (mg)
Yogurt (Dannon, Lowfat Extra Smooth, all flavors)	4.4 oz	130	2	14	10	80

○◇◇□□□

COMMENTS: The same calories as, but 3 milligrams *more* sodium per ounce than low-fat fruit-on-the-bottom yogurt; 5 calories, 1 milligram cholesterol more than Dannon Fresh Flavors yogurt. Don't be fooled by the low calorie count: The carton is only half the size of most others. Very low in fat.

PRODUCT	SERV	CAL	FAT (G)	% cal from fat	CHOL (mg)	SOD (mg)
Yogurt (Dannon, Lowfat Fresh Flavors, Blueberry)	8 oz	200	4	18	10	160

○◇◇

COMMENTS: 40 fewer calories, 1 gram *more* fat, 40 milligrams *more* sodium than 8 ounces regular Dannon Lowfat Blueberry Fruit-on-the-Bottom yogurt. Very low in fat.

PRODUCT	SERV	CAL	FAT (G)	% cal from fat	CHOL (mg)	SOD (mg)
Yogurt (Dannon, Lowfat Fresh Flavors, Coffee)	8 oz	200	3	14	10	140

LITE PICK ○◇□□□

COMMENTS: 40 fewer calories than, same amount of fat and cholesterol as, but 20 milligrams *more* sodium than most Dannon Fruit-on-the-Bottom yogurts. Very low in fat.

PRODUCT	SERV	CAL	FAT (G)	% cal from fat	CHOL (mg)	SOD (mg)
Yogurt (Dannon, Lowfat Fresh Flavors, Lemon)	8 oz	200	3	14	10	140

LITE PICK ○◇□□□

COMMENTS: 40 fewer calories than, same amount of fat and cholesterol as, but 20 milligrams *more* sodium than Dannon Lowfat Fruit-on-the-Bottom yogurt. Very low in fat.

PRODUCT	SERV	CAL	FAT (G)	% cal from fat	CHOL (mg)	SOD (mg)
Yogurt (Dannon, Lowfat Fresh Flavors, Raspberry)	8 oz	200	4	18	10	160

○◇◇

COMMENTS: 40 fewer calories, 1 gram *more* fat, 40 milligrams *more* sodium than 8 ounces Dannon Lowfat Raspberry Fruit-on-the-Bottom yogurt. Very low in fat.

PRODUCT	SERV	CAL	FAT (G)	% cal from fat	CHOL (mg)	SOD (mg)
Yogurt (Dannon, Lowfat Fresh Flavors, Strawberry-Banana)	8 oz	200	4	18	10	160

○◇◇

COMMENTS: 40 fewer calories, 1 gram *more* fat, 40 milligrams *more* sodium than 8 ounces Dannon Lowfat Strawberry Banana Fruit-on-the-Bottom yogurt. Very low in fat.

PRODUCT	SERV	CAL	FAT (G)	% cal from fat	CHOL (mg)	SOD (mg)
Yogurt (Dannon, Lowfat Fresh Flavors, Strawberry)	8 oz	200	4	18	10	160

○◇◇

COMMENTS: 40 fewer calories, 1 gram *more* fat, 40 milligrams *more* sodium than 8 ounces Dannon Lowfat Strawberry Fruit-on-the-Bottom yogurt. Very low in fat.

PRODUCT	SERV	CAL	FAT (G)	% cal from fat	CHOL (mg)	SOD (mg)
Yogurt (Dannon, Lowfat Fresh Flavors, Vanilla)	8 oz	200	3	14	10	140

LITE PICK ○◇□□□

COMMENTS: 40 fewer calories than, same amount of fat and cholesterol as, but 20 milligrams *more* sodium than Dannon Fruit-on-the-Bottom yogurt; 60 fewer calories, 1 gram less fat, 5 milligrams less cholesterol, 20 milligrams less sodium than 8 ounces Dannon Lowfat Plain yogurt. Very low in fat.

PRODUCT	SERV	CAL	FAT (G)	% cal from fat	CHOL (mg)	SOD (mg)
Yogurt (Dannon, Lowfat Fruit-on-the-Bottom, all flavors)	8 oz	240	3	11	10	120

LITE PICK ○◇◇□□□

COMMENTS: 40 *more* calories, but 1 gram fat, 30 milligrams sodium less, than 8 ounces Dannon Lowfat Fresh Flavors Yogurt. Very low in fat.

PRODUCT	SERV	CAL	FAT (G)	% cal from fat	CHOL (mg)	SOD (mg)
Yogurt (Dannon, Lowfat Hearty Nuts and Raisins, Mixed Berries)	8 oz	260	3	10	10	120

LITE PICK ○◇◇□□□

COMMENTS: Same fat, cholesterol, and sodium as, but 20 *more* calories than, 8 ounces of most Dannon Fruit-on-the-Bottom yogurts. Very low in fat.

PRODUCT	SERV	CAL	FAT (G)	% cal from fat	CHOL (mg)	SOD (mg)
Yogurt (Dannon, Lowfat Hearty Nuts and Raisins, Orchard Fruit)	8 oz	260	3	10	10	120

LITE PICK ○◇◇□□□

COMMENTS: Same fat, cholesterol, and sodium as, but 20 *more* calories than 8 ounces of most Dannon Lowfat Fruit-on-the-Bottom yogurts. Very low in fat.

PRODUCT	SERV	CAL	FAT (G)	% cal from fat	CHOL (mg)	SOD (mg)
Yogurt (Dannon, Lowfat Hearty Nuts and Raisins, Vanilla)	8 oz	270	5	17	10	120

LITE PICK ○◇◇□□□

COMMENTS: Same cholesterol and sodium as, but 30 calories, 2 grams *more* fat than 8 ounces of most Dannon Lowfat Fruit-on-the-Bottom yogurt. Very low in fat.

PRODUCT	SERV	CAL	FAT (G)	% cal from fat	CHOL (mg)	SOD (mg)
Yogurt (Dannon, Lowfat, Plain)	8 oz	140	4	26	15	160

○◇◇

COMMENTS: 60 fewer calories, but 5 milligrams *more* cholesterol and 10 milligrams *more* sodium than 8 ounces of most Dannon Lowfat Fresh Flavors Yogurt. 30 calories, 10 milligrams *more* cholesterol than nonfat plain Dannon yogurt.

PRODUCT	SERV	CAL	FAT (G)	% cal from fat	CHOL (mg)	SOD (mg)
Yogurt (Dannon, Nonfat, Plain)	8 oz	110	0	0	5	160

○◇◇

COMMENTS: 30 fewer calories, 4 grams less fat, 10 milligrams less cholesterol than 8 ounces Dannon Lowfat Plain yogurt. Fat free.

PRODUCT	SERV	CAL	FAT (G)	% cal from fat	CHOL (mg)	SOD (mg)
Yogurt (La Yogurt 25 Nonfat, all flavors)	8 oz	200	0	0	na	140

LITE PICK ○□□

COMMENTS: 25 fewer calories, 3 grams less fat than 8 ounces regular low-fat fruit-flavored yogurt, but 19 milligrams *more* sodium. Fat free. Regular low-fat La Yogurt comes in 6 ounce containers which provide 190 calories.

PRODUCT	SERV	CAL	FAT (G)	% cal from fat	CHOL (mg)	SOD (mg)
Yogurt (Lite-Line, Lowfat Swiss Style, 1½% Milk Fat, Plain)	8 oz	140	2	13	na	150

○

COMMENTS: Same fat and sodium as, but an average of 97 calories fewer than 8 ounces Lite-Line fruit-flavored yogurts. Very low in fat.

PRODUCT	SERV	CAL	FAT (G)	% cal from fat	CHOL (mg)	SOD (mg)
Yogurt (Lite-Line, Low Fat Swiss Style 1% Milk Fat, Natural Peach)	8 oz	230	2	8	na	150

○

COMMENTS: Same fat and sodium as, but 90 *more* calories than 8 ounces Lite-Line fruit-flavored yogurts. Very low in fat.

PRODUCT	SERV	CAL	FAT (G)	% cal from fat	CHOL (mg)	SOD (mg)

Yogurt
(Lite-Line, Lowfat
Swiss Style 1% Milk
Fat, Natural Cherry-
Vanilla)

| | 8 oz | 240 | 2 | 8 | na | 150 |

○

COMMENTS: Same fat and sodium as, but 100 calories *more* than 8 ounces Lite-Line lowfat plain yogurt. Very low in fat.

PRODUCT	SERV	CAL	FAT (G)	% cal from fat	CHOL (mg)	SOD (mg)

Yogurt
(Lite-Line, Lowfat
Swiss Style 1% Milk
Fat, Natural
Strawberry)

| | 8 oz | 240 | 2 | 8 | na | 150 |

○

COMMENTS: Same fat and sodium as, but 100 calories *more* than 8 ounces Lite-Line fruit-flavored yogurts. Very low in fat.

PRODUCT	SERV	CAL	FAT (G)	% cal from fat	CHOL (mg)	SOD (mg)

Yogurt
(Meadow Gold, 1.5%
Milk Fat Sundae
Style, Natural
Raspberry)

| | 8 oz | 250 | 4 | 14 | na | 160 |

○

COMMENTS: 10 calories, 2 grams fat, 10 milligrams *more* sodium than 8 ounces Lite-Line low-fat fruit-flavored yogurts (both are Borden products). Very low in fat.

PRODUCT	SERV	CAL	FAT (G)	% cal from fat	CHOL (mg)	SOD (mg)

Yogurt
(Meadow Gold, 2%
Milk Fat, Plain)

| | 8 oz | 160 | 5 | 28 | na | 160 |

○

COMMENTS: 20 calories, 3 grams fat, 10 milligrams sodium *more* than 8 ounces Lite-Line low-fat plain yogurt (both are Borden products).

PRODUCT	SERV	CAL	FAT (G)	% cal from fat	CHOL (mg)	SOD (mg)

Yogurt
(Weight Watchers,
Nonfat, all flavors)

| | 8 oz | 150 | <1 | <6 | na | 120 |

LITE PICK ○□□□

COMMENTS: No direct comparison, but generally lower in fat than most fruit-flavored yogurts. Very low in fat.

PRODUCT	SERV	CAL	FAT (G)	% cal from fat	CHOL (mg)	SOD (mg)

Yogurt
(Weight Watchers,
Nonfat, Plain)

| | 8 oz | 90 | <1 | <10 | na | 130 |

LITE PICK ○□□□

COMMENTS: 50 less calories, 4 grams less fat, 30 milligrams less sodium than 8 ounces Dannon Low-Fat, plain yogurt. Very low in fat.

PRODUCT	SERV	CAL	FAT (G)	% cal from fat	CHOL (mg)	SOD (mg)
Yogurt (Yoplait Light, Lowfat, all flavors)	6 oz	90	<1	<10	5	110

LITE PICK ○◇◇□□□

COMMENTS: 100 less calories, 3 grams less fat, 5 milligrams less cholesterol, 5 milligrams *more* sodium than 6 ounces original fruit flavor Yoplait. Very low in fat. Because it is sweetened with aspartame it is lower in calories than most other yogurts. However, when compared to other brands, note Yoplait's small serving size. Yogurts in 8 ounce containers might have *more* calories per serving, but the same or fewer calories per ounce than Yoplait.

PRODUCT	SERV	CAL	FAT (G)	% cal from fat	CHOL (mg)	SOD (mg)
Yogurt (Yoplait 150, all flavors)	6 oz	150	<1	<6	5	95

LITE PICK ○◇◇□□□

COMMENTS: 40 fewer calories, 2 grams less fat, 5 milligrams less cholesterol and 10 milligrams less sodium than 6 ounces regular Yoplait fruit flavors. Very low in fat. (When compared to other brands, note Yoplait's small serving size.)

PRODUCT	SERV	CAL	FAT (G)	% cal from fat	CHOL (mg)	SOD (mg)
Yogurt (Yoplait, Breakfast Yogurt, Apple-Cinnamon)	6 oz	220	4	16	10	90

LITE PICK ○◇◇□□□

COMMENTS: Same amount of fat as, but 37 calories, 5 milligrams cholesterol, and 10 milligrams sodium on average less than Yoplait's regular 6 ounce fruit-flavored yogurts. Very low in fat. (When compared to other brands, note Yoplait's small serving size.)

PRODUCT	SERV	CAL	FAT (G)	% cal from fat	CHOL (mg)	SOD (mg)
Yogurt (Yoplait, Breakfast Yogurt, Berries)	6 oz	230	4	16	10	95

LITE PICK ○◇◇□□□

COMMENTS: Same amount of fat as, but 47 *more* calories, and 5 milligrams cholesterol, 5 milligrams sodium on average less, than Yoplait's regular 6 ounce fruit-flavored yogurts. Very low in fat. (When compared to other brands, note Yoplait's small serving size.)

PRODUCT	SERV	CAL	FAT (G)	% cal from fat	CHOL (mg)	SOD (mg)
Yogurt (Yoplait, Breakfast Yogurt, Cherry with Almonds)	6 oz	210	3	13	10	90

LITE PICK ○◇◇□□□

COMMENTS: 27 *more* calories, but 1 gram fat, 5 milligrams cholesterol, and 10 milligrams sodium on average less than Yoplait's regular 6 ounce fruit-flavored yogurts. Very low in fat. (When compared to other brands, note Yoplait's small serving size.)

PRODUCT	SERV	CAL	FAT (G)	% cal from fat	CHOL (mg)	SOD (mg)
Yogurt (Yoplait, Breakfast Yogurt, Strawberry with Almonds)	6 oz	210	3	13	10	90

LITE PICK ○◇◇□□□

COMMENTS: 27 *more* calories, but 1 gram fat, 5 milligrams cholesterol, and 10 milligrams sodium on average less than Yoplait's regular 6 ounce fruit-flavored yogurts. Very low in fat. (When compared to other brands, note Yoplait's small serving size.)

PRODUCT	SERV	CAL	FAT (G)	% cal from fat	CHOL (mg)	SOD (mg)
Yogurt (Yoplait, Breakfast Yogurt, Strawberry-Banana)	6 oz	240	4	15	10	90

LITE PICK ○◇◇□□□

COMMENTS: Same amount of fat as, but 57 *more* calories, and 5 milligrams cholesterol, 10 milligrams sodium on average less, than Yoplait's regular 6 ounce fruit-flavored yogurts. Very low in fat. (When compared to other brands, note Yoplait's small serving size.)

PRODUCT	SERV	CAL	FAT (G)	% cal from fat	CHOL (mg)	SOD (mg)
Yogurt (Yoplait, Breakfast Yogurt, Tropical Fruits)	6 oz	230	4	16	10	90

LITE PICK ○◇◇□□□

COMMENTS: Same amount of fat as, but 47 *more* calories, and 5 milligrams cholesterol, 10 milligrams sodium on average less, than Yoplait's regular 6 ounce fruit-flavored yogurts. Very low in fat. (When compared to other brands, note Yoplait's small serving size.)

DRESSINGS AND SAUCES

PRODUCT	SERV	CAL	FAT (G)	% cal from fat	CHOL (mg)	SOD (mg)
Gravy mix (Weight Watchers, Brown Gravy)	¼ c	10	0	0	na	360

○

COMMENTS: 10 fewer calories, 1 gram less fat than ¼ cup regular brown gravy mix, but 74 milligrams *more* sodium. Fat free.

PRODUCT	SERV	CAL	FAT (G)	% cal from fat	CHOL (mg)	SOD (mg)
Gravy mix (Weight Watchers, Brown Gravy with Mushrooms)	¼ c	10	0	0	na	270

○

COMMENTS: 8 fewer calories, 81 milligrams less sodium than ¼ cup regular mushroom gravy mix. Fat free.

PRODUCT	SERV	CAL	FAT (G)	% cal from fat	CHOL (mg)	SOD (mg)
Gravy mix (Weight Watchers, Brown Gravy with Onions)	¼ c	10	0	0	na	310

○

COMMENTS: 10 fewer calories, 1 gram less fat, 327 milligrams less sodium than ¼ cup regular brown gravy mix. Fat free.

PRODUCT	SERV	CAL	FAT (G)	% cal from fat	CHOL (mg)	SOD (mg)
Gravy mix (Weight Watchers, Chicken)	¼ c	10	0	0	na	410

○

COMMENTS: 11 fewer calories, 1 gram less fat than ¼ cup regular chicken gravy mix, but 127 milligrams *more* sodium. Fat free.

PRODUCT	SERV	CAL	FAT (G)	% cal from fat	CHOL (mg)	SOD (mg)
Mayonnaise (Estee)	1 T	100	10	90	0	35

◇□□

COMMENTS: Light only in sodium. The same number of calories as but 43 milligrams less sodium than 1 tablespoon regular mayonnaise. Like all mayonnaise, it is very high in fat.

PRODUCT	SERV	CAL	FAT (G)	% cal from fat	CHOL (mg)	SOD (mg)
Mayonnaise (Hellman's/Best Foods, Light Reduced Calorie)	1 T	50	5	90	5	115

◇□□□

COMMENTS: Same cholesterol as, but 50 fewer calories and 6 grams less fat than 1 tablespoon regular Hellman's/Best Foods mayonnaise, and 35 milligrams *more* sodium. Although fat is reduced, like all mayonnaise, it is very high in fat.

PRODUCT	SERV	CAL	FAT (G)	% cal from fat	CHOL (mg)	SOD (mg)
Mayonnaise (Kraft, Light Reduced Calorie)	1 T	45	5	100	5	90

◇◇□□□

COMMENTS: Fat and calories are cut by more than one half. 55 fewer calories, 7 grams less fat, 25 milligrams less sodium than 1 tablespoon regular Kraft Real Mayonnaise. Although fat is reduced, like all mayonnaise, it is very high in fat.

PRODUCT	SERV	CAL	FAT (G)	% cal from fat	CHOL (mg)	SOD (mg)
Mayonnaise (Weight Watchers, Reduced Calorie Cholesterol Free)	1 T	40	4	90	na	80

□□□

COMMENTS: 59 fewer calories, 7 grams less fat, 2 milligrams less sodium than than 1 tablespoon regular mayonnaise. Although fat is reduced by more than 70 percent, it is still very high in fat.

PRODUCT	SERV	CAL	FAT (G)	% cal from fat	CHOL (mg)	SOD (mg)
Mayonnaise (Weight Watchers, Reduced Calorie)	1 T	40	4	90	na	80

□□□

COMMENTS: 59 fewer calories, 7 grams less fat than 1 tablespoon regular mayonnaise, but 2 milligrams *more* sodium. Although fat is reduced by more than 70 percent, it is still very high in fat.

PRODUCT	SERV	CAL	FAT (G)	% cal from fat	CHOL (mg)	SOD (mg)
Mayonnaise (Weight Watchers, Reduced Calorie Low Sodium)	1 T	40	4	90	na	35

□□

COMMENTS: 59 fewer calories, 7 grams less fat, 43 milligrams less sodium than 1 tablespoon mayonnaise. Although fat is reduced by more than 70 percent, it is still very high in fat.

PRODUCT	SERV	CAL	FAT (G)	% cal from fat	CHOL (mg)	SOD (mg)
Mayonnaise substitute (Featherweight, Soyamaise)	1 T	100	11	99	5	3

◇◇□

COMMENTS: Same calories as, but 75 milligrams sodium less than 1 tablespoon regular mayonnaise. Like all mayonnaise, it is very high in fat.

PRODUCT	SERV	CAL	FAT (G)	% cal from fat	CHOL (mg)	SOD (mg)
Salad dressing (Kraft, Reduced Calorie Thousand Island)	1 T	30	2	60	5	150

COMMENTS: Same cholesterol and sodium as, but 30 fewer calories and 3 grams less fat than 1 tablespoon regular Kraft Thousand Island Dressing. The high percentage of calories from fat is deceiving; since it contains only 2 grams of fat per tablespoon, this product is actually low in fat.

PRODUCT	SERV	CAL	FAT (G)	% cal from fat	CHOL (mg)	SOD (mg)
Salad dressing (Miracle Whip, Light Reduced Calorie)	1 T	45	4	80	5	95

◇◇□□□

COMMENTS: 25 fewer calories and 3 grams less fat than 1 tablespoon regular Miracle Whip, but 10 milligrams *more* sodium. Although fat is reduced by 43 percent, it is still very high in fat.

PRODUCT	SERV	CAL	FAT (G)	% cal from fat	CHOL (mg)	SOD (mg)
Salad dressing (Weight Watchers, Reduced Calorie Whipped)	1 T	35	3	77	na	80

□□□

COMMENTS: 22 fewer calories, 2 grams less fat, 25 milligrams less sodium than 1 tablespoon regular whipped salad dressing. Very high in fat.

PRODUCT	SERV	CAL	FAT (G)	% cal from fat	CHOL (mg)	SOD (mg)
Salad dressing, bacon and tomato (Kraft, Reduced Calorie Bacon and Tomato)	1 T	30	2	60	0	150

◇

COMMENTS: 40 fewer calories and 5 grams less fat than 1 tablespoon regular Kraft Bacon and Tomato Dressing, but 20 milligrams *more* sodium. The high percentage of calories from fat is deceiving; since it contains only 2 grams of fat per tablespoon, this product is actually low in fat.

PRODUCT	SERV	CAL	FAT (G)	% cal from fat	CHOL (mg)	SOD (mg)
Salad dressing, bacon (Kraft, Reduced Calorie Creamy Bacon)	1 T	30	2	60	0	150

◇

COMMENTS: 50 fewer calories and 6 grams less fat than 1 tablespoon regular Kraft Bacon and Buttermilk Dressing, but 25 milligrams *more* sodium. The high percentage of calories from fat is deceiving; since it contains only 2 grams of fat per tablespoon, this product is actually low in fat.

PRODUCT	SERV	CAL	FAT (G)	% cal from fat	CHOL (mg)	SOD (mg)
Salad dressing, bacon (Estee, Bacon and Tomato)	1 T	8	<1	na	3	35

LITE PICK ◇◇□□

COMMENTS: 63 fewer calories, 6 grams less fat, 95 milligrams less sodium than 1 tablespoon regular bacon-and-tomato dressing, but 3 milligrams *more* cholesterol. Very low in fat.

PRODUCT	SERV	CAL	FAT (G)	% cal from fat	CHOL (mg)	SOD (mg)
Salad dressing, blue cheese (Estee)	1 T	8	<1	na	10	50

LITE PICK ◇◇□□□

COMMENTS: 68 fewer calories, 7 grams less fat, 114 milligrams less sodium than 1 tablespoon regular blue cheese dressing. Very low in fat.

PRODUCT	SERV	CAL	FAT (G)	% cal from fat	CHOL (mg)	SOD (mg)
Salad dressing, blue cheese (Featherweight, Neu Bleu)	1 T	4	0	0	0	110

LITE PICK ◇◇□□□

COMMENTS: 71 fewer calories, 8 grams less fat and 54 milligrams less sodium than 1 tablespoon regular blue cheese dressing. Fat free.

PRODUCT	SERV	CAL	FAT (G)	% cal from fat	CHOL (mg)	SOD (mg)
Salad dressing, blue cheese (Kraft, Reduced Calorie Chunky Blue Cheese)	1 T	30	2	60	0	240

◇

COMMENTS: 40 fewer calories and 4 grams less fat than 1 tablespoon regular Kraft Chunky Blue Cheese dressing, but 10 milligrams *more* sodium. The high percentage of calories from fat is deceiving; since it contains only 2 grams of fat per tablespoon, this product is actually low in fat.

PRODUCT	SERV	CAL	FAT (G)	% cal from fat	CHOL (mg)	SOD (mg)
Salad dressing, blue cheese (Kraft, Reduced Calorie Roka Brand Blue Cheese)	1 T	14	1	64	5	280

◇◇

COMMENTS: 46 fewer calories, 5 grams less fat, 5 milligrams less cholesterol than 1 tablespoon regular Kraft Roka Brand Blue Cheese Dressing, but 110 milligrams *more* sodium. The high percentage of calories from fat is deceiving; since it contains only 1 gram of fat per tablespoon, this product is actually low in fat.

PRODUCT	SERV	CAL	FAT (G)	% cal from fat	CHOL (mg)	SOD (mg)
Salad dressing, blue cheese (Marie's, Lite Blue Cheese)	1 T	40	4	90	3.3	190

◇◇

COMMENTS: 54 fewer calories, 6 grams less fat, 8 milligrams less cholesterol than 1 tablespoon regular Marie's Blue Cheese dressing, but 106 milligrams *more* sodium. Although fat is reduced by 60 percent, it is still very high in fat.

PRODUCT	SERV	CAL	FAT (G)	% cal from fat	CHOL (mg)	SOD (mg)
Salad dressing, blue cheese (Walden Farms, Reduced Calorie)	1 T	27	2	67	5	270

◇◇

COMMENTS: 49 fewer calories and 6 grams less fat than 1 tablespoon regular blue cheese dressing, but 106 milligrams *more* sodium. The high percentage of calories from fat is deceiving; since it contains only 2 grams of fat per tablespoon, this product is actually low in fat.

PRODUCT	SERV	CAL	FAT (G)	% cal from fat	CHOL (mg)	SOD (mg)
Salad dressing, blue cheese (Wishbone, Lite Chunky)	1 T	40	4	90	0	200

◇

COMMENTS: 30 fewer calories and 4 grams less fat than 1 tablespoon regular Wishbone Chunky Blue Cheese Dressing, but 50 milligrams *more* sodium. Although fat is reduced by 50 percent, it is still very high in fat.

PRODUCT	SERV	CAL	FAT (G)	% cal from fat	CHOL (mg)	SOD (mg)
Salad dressing, buttermilk (Estee, Creamy)	1 T	6	0	0	5	30

○◇◇□□

COMMENTS: 74 fewer calories, 8 grams less fat, 90 milligrams less sodium than 1 tablespoon regular creamy buttermilk dressing. Fat free.

PRODUCT	SERV	CAL	FAT (G)	% cal from fat	CHOL (mg)	SOD (mg)
Salad dressing, buttermilk (Kraft, Reduced Calorie Buttermilk Creamy)	1 T	30	3	90	0	125

◇□□□

COMMENTS: 50 fewer calories, 5 grams less fat, and 5 milligrams less cholesterol than 1 tablespoon regular Kraft Creamy Buttermilk Dressing, but 5 milligrams *more* sodium.

PRODUCT	SERV	CAL	FAT (G)	% cal from fat	CHOL (mg)	SOD (mg)
Salad dressing, Caesar (Featherweight, Caesar)	1 T	14	1	64	0	3

◇○□

COMMENTS: 56 fewer calories, 6 grams less fat, 177 milligrams less sodium than 1 tablespoon regular Caesar salad dressing. The high percentage of calories from fat is deceiving; since it contains only 1 gram of fat per tablespoon, this product is actually low in fat.

PRODUCT	SERV	CAL	FAT (G)	% cal from fat	CHOL (mg)	SOD (mg)
Salad dressing, Caesar (Weight Watchers, Caesar)	1 T	4	0	0	na	195

○

COMMENTS: 66 fewer calories and 7 grams less fat than 1 tablespoon regular Caesar dressing, but 15 milligrams more sodium. Fat free.

PRODUCT	SERV	CAL	FAT (G)	% cal from fat	CHOL (mg)	SOD (mg)
Salad dressing, cucumber (Featherweight, Creamy Cucumber)	1 T	4	0	0	0	80

LITE PICK ◇○□□□

COMMENTS: 76 fewer calories, 8 grams less fat, 40 milligrams less sodium than 1 tablespoon creamy cucumber dressing. Fat free.

PRODUCT	SERV	CAL	FAT (G)	% cal from fat	CHOL (mg)	SOD (mg)
Salad dressing, cucumber (Kraft, Reduced Calorie Creamy Cucumber)	1 T	30	3	90	0	210

◇

COMMENTS: 40 fewer calories and 5 grams less fat than 1 tablespoon regular Kraft Creamy Cucumber Dressing, but 10 milligrams *more* sodium.

PRODUCT	SERV	CAL	FAT (G)	% cal from fat	CHOL (mg)	SOD (mg)
Salad dressing, Dijon (Estee, Creamy)	1 T	8	<1	na	30	100

□□□

COMMENTS: No direct comparison, but this dressing is very low in fat.

PRODUCT	SERV	CAL	FAT (G)	% cal from fat	CHOL (mg)	SOD (mg)
Salad dressing, Dijon (Wishbone, Lite Classic Dijon Vinaigrette)	1 T	25	2	72	0	190

◇

COMMENTS: No direct comparison. The high percentage of calories from fat is deceiving; since it contains only 2 grams of fat per tablespoon, this product is actually low in fat.

PRODUCT	SERV	CAL	FAT (G)	% cal from fat	CHOL (mg)	SOD (mg)
Salad dressing, Dijon (Wishbone, Lite Creamy)	1 T	25	2	72	5	140

◇◇□□□

COMMENTS: Same cholesterol and sodium as, but 35 calories and 4 grams fat less than 1 tablespoon regular Wishbone Creamy Dijon Dressing. The high percentage of calories from fat is deceiving; since it contains only 2 grams of fat per tablespoon, this product is actually low in fat.

PRODUCT	SERV	CAL	FAT (G)	% cal from fat	CHOL (mg)	SOD (mg)
Salad dressing, French (Featherweight, French)	1 T	14	0	0	0	15

LITE PICK ◇○□□

COMMENTS: 53 fewer calories, 6 grams less fat, 199 milligrams less sodium than 1 tablespoon regular French dressing. Fat free.

PRODUCT	SERV	CAL	FAT (G)	% cal from fat	CHOL (mg)	SOD (mg)
Salad dressing, French (Kraft, Reduced Calorie Catalina Brand French)	1 T	16	0	0	0	125

LITE PICK ○◇□□□

COMMENTS: 54 fewer calories, 6 grams less fat, 55 milligrams less sodium than 1 tablespoon regular Kraft Catalina dressing. Fat free.

PRODUCT	SERV	CAL	FAT (G)	% cal from fat	CHOL (mg)	SOD (mg)
Salad dressing, French (Kraft, Reduced Calorie French)	1 T	25	2	72	0	150

◇

COMMENTS: 35 fewer calories and 4 grams less fat, but 25 milligrams *more* sodium than 1 tablespoon regular Kraft French Dressing. The high percentage of calories as fat is deceiving; since it contains only 2 grams of fat per tablespoon, this product is actually low in fat.

PRODUCT	SERV	CAL	FAT (G)	% cal from fat	CHOL (mg)	SOD (mg)
Salad dressing, French (Pritikin)	1 T	10	0	0	0	0

○◇□

COMMENTS: 57 fewer calories, 6 grams less fat, and 214 milligrams less sodium than 1 tablespoon regular French dressing. Fat free.

PRODUCT	SERV	CAL	FAT (G)	% cal from fat	CHOL (mg)	SOD (mg)
Salad dressing, French (Walden Farms)	1 T	33	2.4	65	2	132

◇◇□□□

COMMENTS: 34 fewer calories, 4 grams less fat, 82 milligrams less sodium than 1 tablespoon regular French dressing. The high percentage of calories from fat is deceiving; since it contains only 2.4 grams of fat per tablespoon, this product is actually low in fat.

PRODUCT	SERV	CAL	FAT (G)	% cal from fat	CHOL (mg)	SOD (mg)
Salad dressing, French (Weight Watchers, French)	1 T	10	0	0	na	170

○

COMMENTS: 57 fewer calories, 6 grams less fat, 44 milligrams less sodium than 1 tablespoon regular French dressing. Fat free.

PRODUCT	SERV	CAL	FAT (G)	% cal from fat	CHOL (mg)	SOD (mg)
Salad dressing, French (Wishbone, Lite French Style)	1 T	30	2	6	0	70

◇□□□

COMMENTS: 30 fewer calories, 4 grams less fat, 10 milligrams less sodium than 1 tablespoon Wishbone Deluxe French Dressing. The high percentage of calories from fat is deceiving; since it contains only 2 grams of fat per tablespoon, this product is actually low in fat.

PRODUCT	SERV	CAL	FAT (G)	% cal from fat	CHOL (mg)	SOD (mg)
Salad dressing, French (Wishbone, Lite Sweet n' Spicy (R) French Style)	1 T	18	<1	na	0	130

◇□□□

COMMENTS: 52 fewer calories, 5 grams less fat, 20 milligrams less sodium than 1 tablespoon regular Wishbone Sweet n' Spicy French Style Dressing. Very low in fat.

PRODUCT	SERV	CAL	FAT (G)	% cal from fat	CHOL (mg)	SOD (mg)
Salad dressing, garlic (Estee, Creamy)	1 T	2	0	0	0	10

LITE PICK ◇◇□□

COMMENTS: 81 fewer calories, 9 grams less fat, 212 milligrams less sodium than regular creamy garlic dressing. Fat free.

PRODUCT	SERV	CAL	FAT (G)	% cal from fat	CHOL (mg)	SOD (mg)

Salad dressing, herb

| (Featherweight, Herb) | 1 T | 6 | 0 | 0 | 0 | 5 |

LITE PICK ◇○□

COMMENTS: No direct comparison, but this dressing is fat free.

PRODUCT	SERV	CAL	FAT (G)	% cal from fat	CHOL (mg)	SOD (mg)

Salad dressing, Italian

| | | | | | | 10/ |
| (Estee, Creamy) | 1 T | 4 | 0 | 0 | 5 | 15 |

LITE PICK ○◇□□

COMMENTS: 48 fewer calories, 5 grams less fat, 90 milligrams less sodium than 1 tablespoon regular creamy Italian dressing. Fat free.

PRODUCT	SERV	CAL	FAT (G)	% cal from fat	CHOL (mg)	SOD (mg)

Salad dressing, Italian

| (Featherweight, Italian) | 1 T | 4 | 0 | 0 | 0 | 120 |

LITE PICK ◇○□□□

COMMENTS: 65 fewer calories, 7 grams less fat, 4 milligrams *more* sodium than 1 tablespoon regular Italian dressing. Fat free.

PRODUCT	SERV	CAL	FAT (G)	% cal from fat	CHOL (mg)	SOD (mg)
Salad dressing, Italian						
(Good Seasons, Lite)	1 T	25	3	100	0	180

◇

COMMENTS: 35 fewer calories, 6 grams less fat than regular Good Seasons Italian, with the same cholesterol, but 30 milligrams *more* sodium.

PRODUCT	SERV	CAL	FAT (G)	% cal from fat	CHOL (mg)	SOD (mg)
Salad dressing, Italian						
(Good Seasons, Lite Zesty Italian)	1 T	25	3	100	0	130

◇□□□

COMMENTS: 55 fewer calories, 6 grams less fat than regular Good Seasons Zesty Italian, but 10 milligrams *more* sodium.

PRODUCT	SERV	CAL	FAT (G)	% cal from fat	CHOL (mg)	SOD (mg)
Salad dressing, Italian (Kraft, Reduced Calorie Creamy Italian)	1 T	25	2	72	0	125

◇☐☐☐

COMMENTS: 35 fewer calories, 4 grams less fat, but 5 milligrams *more* sodium than 1 tablespoon regular Kraft Creamy Italian dressing. The high percentage of calories from fat is deceiving; since it contains only 2 grams of fat per tablespoon, this product is actually low in fat.

PRODUCT	SERV	CAL	FAT (G)	% cal from fat	CHOL (mg)	SOD (mg)
Salad dressing, Italian (Kraft, Reduced Calorie Italian)	1 T	6	0	0	0	210

◇◇

COMMENTS: 64 fewer calories, 8 grams less fat, 70 milligrams less sodium than 1 tablespoon regular Kraft Zesty Italian Dressing. Fat free.

PRODUCT	SERV	CAL	FAT (G)	% cal from fat	CHOL (mg)	SOD (mg)
Salad dressing, Italian (Marie's, Lite Italian Garlic)	1 T	36	3	75	2.3	165

◇◇

COMMENTS: 64 fewer calories, 8 grams less fat, 10 milligrams less cholesterol and 57 milligrams *more* sodium than 1 tablespoon regular Marie's Italian garlic dressing.

PRODUCT	SERV	CAL	FAT (G)	% cal from fat	CHOL (mg)	SOD (mg)
Salad dressing, Italian (Pritikin, Creamy)	1 T	12	0	0	0	0

LITE PICK ○◇□

COMMENTS: 40 fewer calories, 5 grams less fat, 105 milligrams less sodium than 1 tablespoon regular creamy Italian dressing. Fat free.

PRODUCT	SERV	CAL	FAT (G)	% cal from fat	CHOL (mg)	SOD (mg)
Salad dressing, Italian (Pritikin)	1 T	6	0	0	0	0

LITE PICK ○◇□

COMMENTS: 57 fewer calories, 7 grams less fat, 116 milligrams less sodium than regular Italian dressing. Fat free.

PRODUCT	SERV	CAL	FAT (G)	% cal from fat	CHOL (mg)	SOD (mg)
Salad dressing, Italian (Walden Farms, Creamy Italian with Parmesan)	1 T	35	2.5	64	4	21

◇◇

COMMENTS: 17 fewer calories, 2 grams less fat, 84 milligrams less sodium than 1 tablespoon regular creamy Italian dressing. The high percentage of calories from fat is deceiving; since it contains only 2.5 grams of fat per tablespoon, this product is actually low in fat.

PRODUCT	SERV	CAL	FAT (G)	% cal from fat	CHOL (mg)	SOD (mg)
Salad dressing, Italian (Walden Farms, No Sugar Added)	1 T	6	<1	na	0	180

◇

COMMENTS: 63 fewer calories, 6 grams less fat, 64 milligrams less sodium than regular Italian dressing. Very low in fat.

PRODUCT	SERV	CAL	FAT (G)	% cal from fat	CHOL (mg)	SOD (mg)
Salad dressing, Italian (Walden Farms, Reduced Calorie)	1 T	9	<1	na	0	300

◇

COMMENTS: 60 fewer calories, 6 grams less fat than regular Italian dressing, but 184 milligrams *more* sodium. Very low in fat.

PRODUCT	SERV	CAL	FAT (G)	% cal from fat	CHOL (mg)	SOD (mg)
Salad dressing, Italian (Walden Farms, Sodium Free)	1 T	9	<1	na	0	5

◇□□

COMMENTS: 60 fewer calories, 6 grams less fat, 111 milligrams less sodium than 1 tablespoon regular Italian dressing. Very low in fat.

PRODUCT	SERV	CAL	FAT (G)	% cal from fat	CHOL (mg)	SOD (mg)
Salad dressing, Italian (Weight Watchers, Creamy Italian)	1 T	50	5	90	na	80

NO LITE BARGAIN □□□

COMMENTS: 2 fewer calories, 25 milligrams less sodium than 1 tablespoon regular creamy Italian dressing. Very high in fat.

PRODUCT	SERV	CAL	FAT (G)	% cal from fat	CHOL (mg)	SOD (mg)
Salad dressing, Italian (Weight Watchers, Italian)	1 T	6	0	0	na	310

○

COMMENTS: 63 fewer calories, 7 grams less fat than 1 tablespoon regular Italian dressing, but 194 milligrams *more* sodium. Fat free.

PRODUCT	SERV	CAL	FAT (G)	% cal from fat	CHOL (mg)	SOD (mg)
Salad dressing, Italian (Wishbone, Lite Creamy)	1 T	25	2	72	0	160

○

COMMENTS: 35 fewer calories, 3 grams less fat than 1 tablespoon regular Wishbone Creamy Italian Dressing, but 10 milligrams *more* sodium. The high percentage of calories from fat is deceiving; since it contains only 2 grams of fat per tablespoon, this product is actually low in fat.

PRODUCT	SERV	CAL	FAT (G)	% cal from fat	CHOL (mg)	SOD (mg)
Salad dressing, Italian (Wishbone, Lite)	1 T	6	<1	na	0	210

◇

COMMENTS: 39 fewer calories, 3 grams less fat, 70 milligrams less sodium than 1 tablespoon Wishbone Italian Dressing. Very low in fat.

PRODUCT	SERV	CAL	FAT (G)	% cal from fat	CHOL (mg)	SOD (mg)
Salad dressing, onion (Wishbone, Lite Onion and Chive)	1 T	35	3	77	0	160

◇

COMMENTS: 35 fewer calories, 4 grams less fat, but 20 milligrams *more* sodium than 1 tablespoon regular onion-and-chive dressing.

PRODUCT	SERV	CAL	FAT (G)	% cal from fat	CHOL (mg)	SOD (mg)
Salad dressing, ranch (Kraft, Reduced Calorie Rancher's Choice Creamy)	1 T	30	3	90	5	130

◇◇□□□

COMMENTS: 50 fewer calories, 5 grams less fat than 1 tablespoon regular Kraft Rancher's Choice Creamy Dressing, but 10 milligrams *more* sodium.

PRODUCT	SERV	CAL	FAT (G)	% cal from fat	CHOL (mg)	SOD (mg)
Salad dressing, ranch (Marie's, Lite Ranch)	1 T	40	3	68	2.2	200

◇◇

COMMENTS: 65 fewer calories, 8 grams less fat, 10 milligrams less cholesterol and 121 milligrams *more* sodium than 1 tablespoon regular Marie's ranch dressing.

PRODUCT	SERV	CAL	FAT (G)	% cal from fat	CHOL (mg)	SOD (mg)
Salad dressing, ranch (Pritikin)	1 T	18	0	0	0	0

LITE PICK ○◇□

COMMENTS: 36 fewer calories, 6 grams less fat and 97 milligrams less sodium than 1 tablespoon regular ranch dressing. Fat free.

PRODUCT	SERV	CAL	FAT (G)	% cal from fat	CHOL (mg)	SOD (mg)
Salad dressing, ranch						
(Walden Farms)	1 T	35	2	51	8	165

◇◇

COMMENTS: 19 fewer calories, 4 grams less fat than 1 tablespoon regular ranch dressing, but 68 milligrams *more* sodium. The high percentage of calories from fat is deceiving; since it contains only 2 grams of fat per tablespoon, this product is actually low in fat.

PRODUCT	SERV	CAL	FAT (G)	% cal from fat	CHOL (mg)	SOD (mg)
Salad dressing, ranch						
(Wishbone, Lite)	1 T	40	3	68	<1	150

◇

COMMENTS: 40 fewer calories, 5 grams less fat than 1 tablespoon regular ranch dressing.

PRODUCT	SERV	CAL	FAT (G)	% cal from fat	CHOL (mg)	SOD (mg)
Salad dressing, Russian						
(Featherweight, Russian)	1 T	6	0	0	0	125

LITE PICK ◇○□□□

COMMENTS: 70 fewer calories, 8 grams less fat, 8 milligrams less sodium than 1 tablespoon regular Russian dressing. Fat free.

PRODUCT	SERV	CAL	FAT (G)	% cal from fat	CHOL (mg)	SOD (mg)
Salad dressing, Russian (Kraft, Reduced Calorie Russian)	1 T	30	1	30	0	120

LITE PICK ○◇□□□

COMMENTS: 30 fewer calories, 4 grams less fat, 5 milligrams less sodium than 1 tablespoon regular Kraft Russian dressing.

PRODUCT	SERV	CAL	FAT (G)	% cal from fat	CHOL (mg)	SOD (mg)
Salad dressing, Russian (Pritikin)	1 T	6	0	0	0	20

LITE PICK ○◇□□

COMMENTS: 70 fewer calories, 8 grams less fat, 113 milligrams less sodium than regular Russian dressing. Fat free.

PRODUCT	SERV	CAL	FAT (G)	% cal from fat	CHOL (mg)	SOD (mg)
Salad dressing, Russian (Weight Watchers, Russian)	1 T	50	5	90	na	80

□□□

COMMENTS: 26 fewer calories, 3 grams less fat, 33 milligrams less sodium than 1 tablespoon regular Russian dressing. Very high in fat.

PRODUCT	SERV	CAL	FAT (G)	% cal from fat	CHOL (mg)	SOD (mg)
Salad dressing, Russian						
(Wishbone, Lite)	1 T	25	<1	na	0	140

◇☐☐☐

COMMENTS: Same cholesterol as, but 20 fewer calories, 2 grams less fat, and 10 milligrams *more* sodium than 1 tablespoon regular Wishbone Russian Dressing. Very low in fat.

PRODUCT	SERV	CAL	FAT (G)	% cal from fat	CHOL (mg)	SOD (mg)
Salad dressing, Thousand Island						
(Estee)	1 T	6	0	0	5	30

◇◇◇☐☐

COMMENTS: 53 fewer calories, 6 grams less fat, 79 milligrams less sodium than 1 tablespoon regular Thousand Island dressing. Fat free.

PRODUCT	SERV	CAL	FAT (G)	% cal from fat	CHOL (mg)	SOD (mg)
Salad dressing, Thousand Island						
(Featherweight, Thousand Island)	1 T	18	0	0	0	70

LITE PICK ◇◇☐☐☐

COMMENTS: 41 fewer calories, 6 grams less fat, 39 milligrams less sodium than 1 tablespoon regular Thousand Island dressing. Fat free.

PRODUCT	SERV	CAL	FAT (G)	% cal from fat	CHOL (mg)	SOD (mg)
Salad dressing, Thousand Island (Marie's, Lite Thousand Island)	1 T	40	3	68	2.3	160

◇◇

COMMENTS: 48 fewer calories, 6 grams less fat, 5 milligrams less cholesterol but 57 milligrams *more* sodium than 1 tablespoon regular Marie's Thousand Island dressing.

PRODUCT	SERV	CAL	FAT (G)	% cal from fat	CHOL (mg)	SOD (mg)
Salad dressing, Thousand Island (Walden Farms)	1 T	24	1.7	64	8	132

◇◇□□□

COMMENTS: 56 fewer calories, 6 grams less fat than 1 tablespoon regular Thousand Island dressing, but 20 milligrams *more* sodium. The high percentage of calories from fat is deceiving; since it contains only 1.7 grams of fat per tablespoon, this product is actually low in fat.

PRODUCT	SERV	CAL	FAT (G)	% cal from fat	CHOL (mg)	SOD (mg)
Salad dressing, Thousand Island (Weight Watchers, Thousand Island)	1 T	50	5	90	na	80

NO LITE BARGAIN □□□

COMMENTS: 9 fewer calories, 1 gram less fat, 29 milligrams less sodium than 1 tablespoon regular Thousand Island dressing. Very high in fat.

PRODUCT	SERV	CAL	FAT (G)	% cal from fat	CHOL (mg)	SOD (mg)
Salad dressing, Thousand Island (Wishbone, Lite)	1 T	40	3	68	10	105

◇◇□□□

COMMENTS: 20 fewer calories, 2 grams less fat, 55 milligrams less sodium than 1 tablespoon regular Wishbone Thousand Island Dressing, but 5 milligrams *more* cholesterol.

PRODUCT	SERV	CAL	FAT (G)	% cal from fat	CHOL (mg)	SOD (mg)
Salad dressing, tomato (Featherweight, Zesty Tomato)	1 T	2	0	0	0	5

LITE PICK ◇○□

COMMENTS: No direct comparison, but this dressing is fat free.

PRODUCT	SERV	CAL	FAT (G)	% cal from fat	CHOL (mg)	SOD (mg)
Salad dressing, tomato (Pritikin, Zesty Tomato)	1 T	18	0	0	0	0

LITE PICK ○◇□

COMMENTS: No direct comparison, but this dressing is fat free.

PRODUCT	SERV	CAL	FAT (G)	% cal from fat	CHOL (mg)	SOD (mg)
Salad dressing, tomato (Weight Watchers, Tomato Vinaigrette)	1 T	8	0	0	na	150

○

COMMENTS: No direct comparison, but this dressing is fat free.

PRODUCT	SERV	CAL	FAT (G)	% cal from fat	CHOL (mg)	SOD (mg)
Salad dressing, vinaigrette (Pritikin)	1 T	10	0	0	0	0

LITE PICK ○◇□

COMMENTS: 62 calories and 8 grams less fat than 1 tablespoon home-made vinegar-and-oil dressing. Fat free.

PRODUCT	SERV	CAL	FAT (G)	% cal from fat	CHOL (mg)	SOD (mg)
Salad dressing, wine vinegar (Estee, Red Wine Vinegar)	1 T	2	0	0	0	10

LITE PICK ○◇□□

COMMENTS: 101 fewer calories, 9 grams less fat, 413 milligrams less sodium than 1 tablespoon regular red wine vinegar-and-oil dressing. Fat free.

PRODUCT	SERV	CAL	FAT (G)	% cal from fat	CHOL (mg)	SOD (mg)
Salad dressing, wine vinegar (Featherweight, Red Wine Vinegar)	1 T	6	0	0	0	100

LITE PICK ◇○□□□

COMMENTS: 97 fewer calories, 9 grams less fat, 323 milligrams less sodium than 1 tablespoon regular red wine vinegar-and-oil dressing. Fat free.

PRODUCT	SERV	CAL	FAT (G)	% cal from fat	CHOL (mg)	SOD (mg)
Salad dressing mix, blue cheese (Weight Watchers)	1 T	8	0	0	na	110

○□□□

COMMENTS: 76 fewer calories, 9 grams less fat, 104 milligrams less sodium than 1 tablespoon regular blue cheese dressing mix. Fat free.

PRODUCT	SERV	CAL	FAT (G)	% cal from fat	CHOL (mg)	SOD (mg)
Salad dressing mix, French (Weight Watchers)	1 T	4	0	0	na	150

○

COMMENTS: 93 fewer calories, 9 grams less fat, 56 milligrams less sodium than 1 tablespoon regular French dressing from a mix. Fat free.

PRODUCT	SERV	CAL	FAT (G)	% cal from fat	CHOL (mg)	SOD (mg)
Salad dressing mix, Italian (Good Seasons, No Oil)	1 T	6	0	0	0	30

LITE PICK ○◇□□

COMMENTS: 74 fewer calories, 9 grams less fat, and 120 milligrams less sodium than 1 tablespoon Good Seasons regular Italian dressing mix. Fat free.

PRODUCT	SERV	CAL	FAT (G)	% cal from fat	CHOL (mg)	SOD (mg)
Salad dressing mix, Italian (Weight Watchers, Creamy)	1 T	4	0	0	na	180

○

COMMENTS: 48 fewer calories, 5 grams less fat, 75 milligrams less sodium than 1 tablespoon regular creamy Italian dressing. Fat free.

PRODUCT	SERV	CAL	FAT (G)	% cal from fat	CHOL (mg)	SOD (mg)
Salad dressing mix, Italian (Weight Watchers)	1 T	8	0	0	na	140

LITE PICK

COMMENTS: 76 fewer calories, 9 grams less fat, 32 milligrams less sodium than 1 tablespoon regular Italian dressing from a mix. Fat free.

PRODUCT	SERV	CAL	FAT (G)	% cal from fat	CHOL (mg)	SOD (mg)
Salad dressing mix, Russian (Weight Watchers)	1 T	4	0	0	na	120

○□□□

COMMENTS: 72 fewer calories, 8 grams less fat, 13 milligrams less sodium than 1 tablespoon regular bottled Russian dressing, and is fat free.

PRODUCT	SERV	CAL	FAT (G)	% cal from fat	CHOL (mg)	SOD (mg)
Salad dressing mix, Thousand Island (Weight Watchers)	1 T	4	0	0	na	140

○□□□

COMMENTS: 55 fewer calories, 6 grams less fat than 1 tablespoon regular bottled Thousand Island dressing, and is fat free.

PRODUCT	SERV	CAL	FAT (G)	% cal from fat	CHOL (mg)	SOD (mg)
Sauce, barbecue (Estee)	1 T	18	<1	na	0	0

◇□

COMMENTS: 127 milligrams less sodium than 1 tablespoon regular barbecue sauce, but 6 *more* calories. Very low in fat.

PRODUCT	SERV	CAL	FAT (G)	% cal from fat	CHOL (mg)	SOD (mg)
Sauce, barbecue (Featherweight, Low Sodium)	2 T	14	0	0	na	38

○□□□

COMMENTS: 5 fewer calories, 108 milligrams less sodium than 1 tablespoon regular barbecue sauce. Fat free.

PRODUCT	SERV	CAL	FAT (G)	% cal from fat	CHOL (mg)	SOD (mg)
Sauce, chili (Featherweight, Low Sodium)	1 T	8	0	0	0	10

○□□

COMMENTS: 8 fewer calories and 191 milligrams less sodium than 1 tablespoon regular chili sauce. Fat free.

PRODUCT	SERV	CAL	FAT (G)	% cal from fat	CHOL (mg)	SOD (mg)
Sauce, cocktail (Estee)	1 T	10	<1	na	0	35

◇□□

COMMENTS: 10 fewer calories and 125 milligrams less sodium than 1 tablespoon regular seafood cocktail sauce. Very low in fat.

PRODUCT	SERV	CAL	FAT (G)	% cal from fat	CHOL (mg)	SOD (mg)
Sauce, Mexican (Pritikin)	4 oz	50	1	18	0	356

LITE PICK ○◇□□

COMMENTS: 3 fewer calories and 605 milligrams less sodium than 4 ounces regular picante sauce. Very low in fat.

PRODUCT	SERV	CAL	FAT (G)	% cal from fat	CHOL (mg)	SOD (mg)
Sauce, picante (Estee)	2 T	8	0	0	0	60

LITE PICK ○◇□□□

COMMENTS: 5 fewer calories and 100 milligrams less sodium than 2 tablespoons regular picante sauce. Fat free.

PRODUCT	SERV	CAL	FAT (G)	% cal from fat	CHOL (mg)	SOD (mg)
Sauce, soy (Angostura, Low Sodium)	1 tsp	2	0	0	0	130

LITE PICK ○◇□□□

COMMENTS: 2 fewer calories and 213 milligrams less sodium than 1 teaspoon regular soy sauce. Fat free.

PRODUCT	SERV	CAL	FAT (G)	% cal from fat	CHOL (mg)	SOD (mg)
Sauce, spaghetti (Estee)	4 oz	70	2	26	0	30

LITE PICK ○◇□□

COMMENTS: 1 gram fat, 800 milligrams less sodium than 4 ounces regular canned spaghetti sauce.

PRODUCT	SERV	CAL	FAT (G)	% cal from fat	CHOL (mg)	SOD (mg)
Sauce, spaghetti (Featherweight, Low Sodium)	⅓ c	50	1	18	0	44

○□□□

COMMENTS: 41 fewer calories, 3 grams less fat, 368 milligrams less sodium than ⅓ cup regular canned spaghetti sauce. Very low in fat.

PRODUCT	SERV	CAL	FAT (G)	% cal from fat	CHOL (mg)	SOD (mg)
Sauce, spaghetti (Prego, No Salt Added)	4 oz	100	6	54	na	30

□□

COMMENTS: 40 fewer calories, 640 milligrams less sodium than 4 ounces regular Prego Spaghetti Sauce. Very high in fat.

PRODUCT	SERV	CAL	FAT (G)	% cal from fat	CHOL (mg)	SOD (mg)
Sauce, spaghetti (Pritikin, Spaghetti Sauce with Mushrooms)	4 oz	60	0	0	0	35

LITE PICK ○◇□□

COMMENTS: 11 fewer calories, 3 grams less fat, 380 milligrams less sodium than regular canned spaghetti sauce. Fat free.

PRODUCT	SERV	CAL	FAT (G)	% cal from fat	CHOL (mg)	SOD (mg)
Sauce, spaghetti (Pritikin)	4 oz	60	0	0	0	35

LITE PICK ○◇□□

COMMENTS: 11 fewer calories, 3 grams less fat, 795 milligrams less sodium than regular canned spaghetti sauce. Fat free.

PRODUCT	SERV	CAL	FAT (G)	% cal from fat	CHOL (mg)	SOD (mg)
Sauce, spaghetti (Weight Watchers, Spaghetti Sauce Flavored with Meat)	⅓ c	50	1	18	na	440

○

COMMENTS: 22 fewer calories, 1 gram less fat than ⅓ cup regular canned spaghetti sauce with meat, but 5 milligrams *more* sodium. Very low in fat, but high in sodium.

PRODUCT	SERV	CAL	FAT (G)	% cal from fat	CHOL (mg)	SOD (mg)
Sauce, spaghetti (Weight Watchers, Spaghetti Sauce with Mushrooms)	⅓ c	40	0	0	na	430

○

COMMENTS: 32 fewer calories, 2 grams less fat than ⅓ cup regular canned spaghetti sauce with mushrooms, but 98 milligrams *more* sodium. Fat free, but high in sodium.

PRODUCT	SERV	CAL	FAT (G)	% cal from fat	CHOL (mg)	SOD (mg)
Sauce, steak (Estee)	½ oz	15	<1	na	0	10

◇□□

COMMENTS: 3 fewer calories and 139 milligrams less sodium per tablespoon than regular steak sauce. Very low in fat.

PRODUCT	SERV	CAL	FAT (G)	% cal from fat	CHOL (mg)	SOD (mg)
Sauce, taco (Estee)	2 T	14	0	0	0	25

○◇□□

COMMENTS: 135 milligrams less sodium than 2 tablespoons regular picante sauce. Fat free.

PRODUCT	SERV	CAL	FAT (G)	% cal from fat	CHOL (mg)	SOD (mg)
Sauce, tartar (Weight Watchers)	1 T	35	3	77	na	80

□□□

COMMENTS: 35 fewer calories, 5 grams less fat, 105 milligrams less sodium than 1 tablespoon regular tartar sauce. Fat is reduced by more than one-half compared to regular version.

PRODUCT	SERV	CAL	FAT (G)	% cal from fat	CHOL (mg)	SOD (mg)
Sauce, teriyaki (Angostura, Low Sodium)	1 tsp	4	0	0	0	85

LITE PICK ○◇□□□

COMMENTS: 145 milligrams less sodium than 1 teaspoon regular teriyaki sauce. Fat free.

PRODUCT	SERV	CAL	FAT (G)	% cal from fat	CHOL (mg)	SOD (mg)
Sauce, tomato (Del Monte, No Salt Added)	1 c	70	1	13	0	50

LITE PICK ○◇□□□

COMMENTS: The same number of calories as 1 cup of Del Monte's regular tomato sauce, but 1,280 milligrams less sodium.

PRODUCT	SERV	CAL	FAT (G)	% cal from fat	CHOL (mg)	SOD (mg)
Sauce, tomato (Health Valley, No Salt)	4 oz	31	<1	<29	0	23

LITE PICK ○◇□□

COMMENTS: Same fat and cholesterol as but 6 fewer calories and 717 milligrams less sodium than 4 ounces regular tomato sauce.

PRODUCT	SERV	CAL	FAT (G)	% cal from fat	CHOL (mg)	SOD (mg)
Sauce, Worcestershire (Angostura, Low Sodium)	1 tsp	4	0	0	na	19

LITE PICK ○◇□□

COMMENTS: Same calories as, and 128 milligrams less sodium than, regular Worcestershire sauce. Fat free.

PRODUCT	SERV	CAL	FAT (G)	% cal from fat	CHOL (mg)	SOD (mg)
Sauce mix, butter (Weight Watchers, Lemon butter)	1 T	6	0	0	na	90

○□□□

COMMENTS: 102 fewer calories, 12 grams less fat, 33 milligrams less sodium than 1 tablespoon butter. Fat free.

PRODUCT	SERV	CAL	FAT (G)	% cal from fat	CHOL (mg)	SOD (mg)
Tomato paste (Del Monte, No Salt Added)	6 oz	150	1	6	0	110

LITE PICK ○◇□□□

COMMENTS: No lighter in sodium than regular tomato paste. The same number of calories, and the same amount of fat and sodium as 6 ounces of Del Monte's regular tomato paste.

EGGS

PRODUCT	SERV	CAL	FAT (G)	% cal from fat	CHOL (mg)	SOD (mg)
Egg substitute (Egg Magic Featherweight)	1 packet equivalent of 2 eggs	120	8	60	15	250

COMMENTS: 30 fewer calories, 2 grams less fat, 124 milligrams *more* sodium and 411 milligrams less cholesterol than two large eggs. Very high in fat.

PRODUCT	SERV	CAL	FAT (G)	% cal from fat	CHOL (mg)	SOD (mg)
Egg substitute (Fleischmann's, Egg Beaters)	¼ c equivalent of 1 egg	25	0	0	0	80

LITE PICK ○◇□□□

COMMENTS: 50 fewer calories, 5 grams less fat, 213 milligrams less cholesterol than the equivalent of one large egg, but 17 milligrams *more* sodium. Fat free.

PRODUCT	SERV	CAL	FAT (G)	% cal from fat	CHOL (mg)	SOD (mg)
Egg substitute (Fleischmann's, Egg Beaters with Cheez)	¼ c equivalent of 1 egg	65	3	42	3	220

COMMENTS: 10 fewer calories, 2 grams less fat, and 157 milligrams *more* sodium than one large egg. 210 milligrams less cholesterol, but high in fat.

PRODUCT	SERV	CAL	FAT (G)	% cal from fat	CHOL (mg)	SOD (mg)
Egg substitute (Tofutti, Egg Watchers)	2 oz equivalent of 1 egg	50	2	36	0	100

◇□□□

COMMENTS: 25 fewer calories, 3 grams less fat, 113 milligrams less cholesterol than one large egg, but 37 milligrams *more* sodium.

ENTREES
and
DINNERS

Frozen entrees and dinners have their own set of standards to determine if they are truly light. To be designated a ''LITE PICK,'' a frozen entree or dinner was required to meet the following guidelines:

• provides 300 calories or fewer per serving, so that it can easily be part of a weight loss program

• contains 30% or less calories from fat in order to fall within heart-healthy guidelines

• contains no more than 1,000 milligrams of sodium

• provides no more than 100 milligrams of cholesterol

PRODUCT	SERV	CAL	FAT (G)	% cal from fat	CHOL (mg)	SOD (mg)
Beef, frozen (Armour Dinner Classics, Lite Beef Pepper Steak)	10½ oz	290	8	25	na	1010

○

COMMENTS: Too high in sodium.

PRODUCT	SERV	CAL	FAT (G)	% cal from fat	CHOL (mg)	SOD (mg)
Beef, frozen (Armour Dinner Classics, Lite Salisbury Steak)	10 oz	270	13	43	na	1000

COMMENTS: Very high in fat.

PRODUCT	SERV	CAL	FAT (G)	% cal from fat	CHOL (mg)	SOD (mg)
Beef, frozen (Armour Dinner Classics, Lite Steak Diane)	10 oz	290	9	28	na	770

LITE PICK ○

COMMENTS: Meets the healthful guidelines described on page 168. Cholesterol information not available.

PRODUCT	SERV	CAL	FAT (G)	% cal from fat	CHOL (mg)	SOD (mg)
Beef, frozen (Budget Gourmet Slim Selects, Beef Stroganoff)	8¾ oz	280	10	32	60	560

COMMENTS: Too high in fat. Note small serving size. Most entrees are 9–11 ounces.

PRODUCT	SERV	CAL	FAT (G)	% cal from fat	CHOL (mg)	SOD (mg)
Beef, frozen (Budget Gourmet Slim Selects, Sirloin of Beef in Herb Sauce)	10 oz	290	12	37	25	770

COMMENTS: Too high in fat.

PRODUCT	SERV	CAL	FAT (G)	% cal from fat	CHOL (mg)	SOD (mg)
Beef, frozen (Budget Gourmet Slim Selects, Sirloin Salisbury Steak)	9 oz	280	8	26	75	870

LITE PICK ○

COMMENTS: Meets the healthful guidelines described on page 168.

PRODUCT	SERV	CAL	FAT (G)	% cal from fat	CHOL (mg)	SOD (mg)
Beef, frozen (Dining Lite, Salisbury Steak with Zesty Italian Sauce)	9 oz	230	12	47	70	930

COMMENTS: Very high in fat.

PRODUCT	SERV	CAL	FAT (G)	% cal from fat	CHOL (mg)	SOD (mg)
Beef, frozen (Dining Lite, Sauce and Swedish Meatballs)	9 oz	280	10	32	55	660

COMMENTS: Too high in fat.

PRODUCT	SERV	CAL	FAT (G)	% cal from fat	CHOL (mg)	SOD (mg)
Beef, frozen (Healthy Choice, Salisbury Steak Dinner)	11¼ oz	300	7	21	50	560

LITE PICK ○

COMMENTS: Meets the healthful guidelines described on page 168.

PRODUCT	SERV	CAL	FAT (G)	% cal from fat	CHOL (mg)	SOD (mg)
Beef, frozen (Healthy Choice, Sirloin Tips Dinner)	11½ oz	280	6	19	55	320

LITE PICK ○

COMMENTS: Very low in fat and lower in sodium than most frozen entrees.

PRODUCT	SERV	CAL	FAT (G)	% cal from fat	CHOL (mg)	SOD (mg)
Beef, frozen (Le Menu LightStyle, Salisbury Steak)	10 oz	220	7	29	45	930

○

COMMENTS: Meets the healthful guidelines described on page 168.

PRODUCT	SERV	CAL	FAT (G)	% cal from fat	CHOL (mg)	SOD (mg)
Beef, frozen (Right Course, Homestyle Pot Roast)	9¼ oz	220	7	29	35	550

LITE PICK ○

COMMENTS: Meets the healthful guidelines described on page 168.

PRODUCT	SERV	CAL	FAT (G)	% cal from fat	CHOL (mg)	SOD (mg)
Beef, frozen (Sensible Chef, Beef Stroganoff with Gravy)	9 oz	240	8	30	27	1060

○

COMMENTS: Too high in sodium.

PRODUCT	SERV	CAL	FAT (G)	% cal from fat	CHOL (mg)	SOD (mg)
Beef, frozen (Sensible Chef, Swedish Meatballs with Gravy)	9 oz	360	20	50	22	1570

COMMENTS: Too high in calories and sodium. Very high in fat.

PRODUCT	SERV	CAL	FAT (G)	% cal from fat	CHOL (mg)	SOD (mg)
Beef, frozen, w/vegetables (Sensible Chef, Beef Tips with Vegetables and Noodles)	9 oz	250	9	32	20	960

◇◇

COMMENTS: Too high in fat.

PRODUCT	SERV	CAL	FAT (G)	% cal from fat	CHOL (mg)	SOD (mg)
Beef, frozen, w/pasta (Right Course, Beef Dijon with Pasta and Vegetables)	9½ oz	290	9	28	40	580

LITE PICK ○

COMMENTS: Meets the healthful guidelines described on page 168.

PRODUCT	SERV	CAL	FAT (G)	% cal from fat	CHOL (mg)	SOD (mg)
Beef, frozen (Right Course, Fiesta Beef with Corn Pasta)	8⅞ oz	270	7	23	30	590

LITE PICK ○

COMMENTS: Meets the healthful guidelines described on page 168. Note small serving size. Most entrees are 9–11 oz.

PRODUCT	SERV	CAL	FAT (G)	% cal from fat	CHOL (mg)	SOD (mg)
Beef, frozen, w/pasta (Weight Watchers, Beef Stroganoff with Parsley Noodles)	9 oz	340	15	40	95	930

COMMENTS: Too high in calories and very high in fat.

PRODUCT	SERV	CAL	FAT (G)	% cal from fat	CHOL (mg)	SOD (mg)
Beef, frozen, w/pasta (Weight Watchers, Beef Salisbury Steak Romana with Rotini Noodles)	8¾ oz	320	12	34	80	910

COMMENTS: Too high in calories and fat. Note small serving size. Most entrees are 9–11 ounces.

PRODUCT	SERV	CAL	FAT (G)	% cal from fat	CHOL (mg)	SOD (mg)
Beef, frozen, w/rice (Right Course, Beef Ragout with Rice Pilaf)	10 oz	300	8	24	50	550

LITE PICK ○

COMMENTS: Meets the healthful guidelines described on page 168.

PRODUCT	SERV	CAL	FAT (G)	% cal from fat	CHOL (mg)	SOD (mg)
Beef, frozen, w/rice (Sensible Chef, Beef Pepper Steak with Rice)	9 oz	250	10	36	21	1150

COMMENTS: Too high in fat and sodium.

PRODUCT	SERV	CAL	FAT (G)	% cal from fat	CHOL (mg)	SOD (mg)
Beef, frozen, w/vegetables (Lean Cuisine, Salisbury Steak with Italian Style Sauce and Vegetables)	9½ oz	270	13	43	95	700

COMMENTS: Very high in fat.

PRODUCT	SERV	CAL	FAT (G)	% cal from fat	CHOL (mg)	SOD (mg)
Beef, frozen, w/vegetables (Weight Watchers, Chopped Beef Steak in Green Pepper and Mushroom Sauce with Carrots and Green Beans)	9 oz	280	17	55	100	800

COMMENTS: Very high in fat.

PRODUCT	SERV	CAL	FAT (G)	% cal from fat	CHOL (mg)	SOD (mg)
Cabbage, frozen, w/meat (Lean Cuisine, Stuffed Cabbage with Meat in Tomato Sauce)	10¾ oz	220	9	37	40	930

COMMENTS: Too high in fat.

PRODUCT	SERV	CAL	FAT (G)	% cal from fat	CHOL (mg)	SOD (mg)
Chicken, frozen (Armour Dinner Classics, Lite Chicken Burgundy)	10½ oz	210	2	9	na	1360

○

COMMENTS: Too high in sodium. Very low in fat.

PRODUCT	SERV	CAL	FAT (G)	% cal from fat	CHOL (mg)	SOD (mg)
Chicken, frozen (Armour Dinner Classics, Lite Chicken Cacciatore)	11 oz	240	4	15	na	840

LITE PICK ○

COMMENTS: Very low in fat. Meets the healthful guidelines described on page 168. Cholesterol information not available.

PRODUCT	SERV	CAL	FAT (G)	% cal from fat	CHOL (mg)	SOD (mg)
Chicken, frozen (Armour Dinner Classics, Lite Chicken Breast Marsala)	11 oz	270	7	23	na	970

LITE PICK ○

COMMENTS: Meets the healthful guidelines described on page 168. Cholesterol information not available.

PRODUCT	SERV	CAL	FAT (G)	% cal from fat	CHOL (mg)	SOD (mg)
Chicken, frozen (Armour Dinner Classics, Lite Chicken Breast with Tomato and Mushroom Sauce)	10 oz	250	5	18	na	890

LITE PICK ○

COMMENTS: Very low in fat. Meets the healthful guidelines described on page 168. Cholesterol information not available.

PRODUCT	SERV	CAL	FAT (G)	% cal from fat	CHOL (mg)	SOD (mg)
Chicken, frozen (Budget Gourmet, Slim Selects, Chicken-au-Gratin)	9.1 ounces	260	11	38	70	820

COMMENTS: Too high in fat.

PRODUCT	SERV	CAL	FAT (G)	% cal from fat	CHOL (mg)	SOD (mg)
Chicken, frozen (Budget Gourmet, Slim Selects, French Recipe Chicken)	10 oz	260	10	35	60	790

COMMENTS: Too high in fat.

PRODUCT	SERV	CAL	FAT (G)	% cal from fat	CHOL (mg)	SOD (mg)
Chicken, frozen (Healthy Choice, Chicken Parmigiana Dinner)	11½ oz	290	5	16	65	320

LITE PICK ○

COMMENTS: Very low in fat and lower in sodium than most frozen entrees. Meets the healthful guidelines described on page 168.

PRODUCT	SERV	CAL	FAT (G)	% cal from fat	CHOL (mg)	SOD (mg)
Chicken, frozen (Le Menu LightStyle, Chicken Cacciatore)	10 oz	270	8	27	85	640

LITE PICK ○

COMMENTS: Meets the healthful guidelines described on page 168.

PRODUCT	SERV	CAL	FAT (G)	% cal from fat	CHOL (mg)	SOD (mg)
Chicken, frozen (Le Menu LightStyle, Glazed Chicken)	10 oz	270	6	20	70	740

LITE PICK ○

COMMENTS: Very low in fat. Meets the healthful guidelines described on page 168.

PRODUCT	SERV	CAL	FAT (G)	% cal from fat	CHOL (mg)	SOD (mg)
Chicken, frozen (Le Menu LightStyle, Herb Roasted Chicken)	10 oz	220	6	25	55	610

LITE PICK ○

COMMENTS: Meets the healthful guidelines described on page 168.

PRODUCT	SERV	CAL	FAT (G)	% cal from fat	CHOL (mg)	SOD (mg)
Chicken, frozen (Right Course, Sesame Chicken)	10 oz	320	9	25	50	590

LITE PICK ○

COMMENTS: Too high in calories.

PRODUCT	SERV	CAL	FAT (G)	% cal from fat	CHOL (mg)	SOD (mg)
Chicken, frozen (Tyson, Lightly Breaded Cooked Chicken)	3½ oz	255	4.5	16	94	724

COMMENTS: Very low in fat, but high in sodium and cholesterol for such a small portion.

PRODUCT	SERV	CAL	FAT (G)	% cal from fat	CHOL (mg)	SOD (mg)
Chicken, frozen (Weaver's Crispy Light Fried Chicken)	2.9 oz	160	8.5	48	na	300

COMMENTS: Very high in fat. Note small serving size.

PRODUCT	SERV	CAL	FAT (G)	% cal from fat	CHOL (mg)	SOD (mg)
Chicken, frozen (Weight Watchers, Chicken Nuggets Breaded Chicken Patties)	3 oz	180	11	55	55	360

COMMENTS: 29 fewer calories, 2 grams less fat than four regular chicken nuggets, but 10 milligrams *more* sodium and 4 milligrams *more* cholesterol. Very high in fat. Note small serving size.

PRODUCT	SERV	CAL	FAT (G)	% cal from fat	CHOL (mg)	SOD (mg)
Chicken, frozen (Weight Watchers, Chicken à la King)	9 oz	230	8	31	60	900

COMMENTS: Too high in fat.

PRODUCT	SERV	CAL	FAT (G)	% cal from fat	CHOL (mg)	SOD (mg)
Chicken, frozen, w/dumplings (Sensible Chef, Chicken and Dumplings)	9 oz	330	16	44	23	1410

COMMENTS: Too high in calories and sodium. Very high in fat.

PRODUCT	SERV	CAL	FAT (G)	% cal from fat	CHOL (mg)	SOD (mg)
Chicken, frozen, w/vegetables (Weight Watchers, Breaded Chicken Patty Parmigiana with Vegetable Medley)	8 1/16 oz	280	16	51	85	840

COMMENTS: Note small serving size. Most entrees are 9–11 ounces. Very high in fat.

PRODUCT	SERV	CAL	FAT (G)	% cal from fat	CHOL (mg)	SOD (mg)
Chicken, frozen, w/pasta (Healthy Choice, Chicken and Pasta Divan Dinner)	11 1/4 oz	310	4	12	60	560

○

COMMENTS: Very low in fat.

PRODUCT	SERV	CAL	FAT (G)	% cal from fat	CHOL (mg)	SOD (mg)
Chicken, frozen, w/pasta (Lean Cuisine, Chicken Cacciatore with Vermicelli)	10 7/8 oz	280	10	32	45	950

COMMENTS: Too high in fat.

PRODUCT	SERV	CAL	FAT (G)	% cal from fat	CHOL (mg)	SOD (mg)
Chicken, frozen, w/pasta (Lean Cuisine, Chicken and Vegetables with Vermicelli)	12¾ oz	270	7	23	45	1120

○

COMMENTS: Too high in sodium.

PRODUCT	SERV	CAL	FAT (G)	% cal from fat	CHOL (mg)	SOD (mg)
Chicken, frozen (Right Course, Chicken Italiano with Fettucini and Vegetables)	9⅝ oz	280	8	26	45	560

LITE PICK ○

COMMENTS: Meets the healthful guidelines described on page 168.

PRODUCT	SERV	CAL	FAT (G)	% cal from fat	CHOL (mg)	SOD (mg)
Chicken, frozen (Right Course, Chicken Tenderloins in Peanut Sauce with Linguini and Vegetables)	9¼ oz	330	10	27	50	570

○

COMMENTS: Too high in calories.

PRODUCT	SERV	CAL	FAT (G)	% cal from fat	CHOL (mg)	SOD (mg)
Chicken, frozen, w/pasta (Weight Watchers, Chicken Fettucini)	8¼ oz	300	10	30	85	630

LITE PICK ○

COMMENTS: Note small serving size. Most entrees are 9–11 ounces. Meets the healthful guidelines described on page 168.

PRODUCT	SERV	CAL	FAT (G)	% cal from fat	CHOL (mg)	SOD (mg)
Chicken, frozen, w/rice (Dining Lite, Chicken à la King with Rice)	9½ oz	290	10	31	40	900

LITE PICK ○

COMMENTS: Too high in fat.

PRODUCT	SERV	CAL	FAT (G)	% cal from fat	CHOL (mg)	SOD (mg)
Chicken, frozen, w/rice (Lean Cuisine, Chicken à l'Orange with Almond Rice)	8 oz	270	5	17	50	400

LITE PICK ○

COMMENTS: Very low in fat. Note small serving size. Most entrees are 9–11 ounces. Meets the healthful guidelines described on page 168.

PRODUCT	SERV	CAL	FAT (G)	% cal from fat	CHOL (mg)	SOD (mg)
Chicken, frozen, w/rice (Lean Cuisine, Glazed Chicken with Vegetable Rice)	8½ oz	270	8	27	60	710

LITE PICK ○

COMMENTS: Note small serving size. Most entrees are 9–11 ounces. Meets the healthful guidelines described on page 168.

PRODUCT	SERV	CAL	FAT (G)	% cal from fat	CHOL (mg)	SOD (mg)
Chicken, frozen (Right Course, Chicken Tenderloins in Barbecue Sauce with Rice Pilaf)	8¾ oz	270	6	20	40	590

LITE PICK ○

COMMENTS: Very low in fat. Note small serving size. Most entrees are 9–11 ounces. Meets the healthful guidelines described on page 168.

PRODUCT	SERV	CAL	FAT (G)	% cal from fat	CHOL (mg)	SOD (mg)
Chicken, frozen, w/rice (Weight Watchers, Sweet n' Sour Chicken Tenders with Rice)	10³⁄₁₆ oz	250	2	7	45	600

LITE PICK ○

COMMENTS: Very low in fat. Meets the healthful guidelines described on page 168.

PRODUCT	SERV	CAL	FAT (G)	% cal from fat	CHOL (mg)	SOD (mg)
Chicken, frozen, w/vegetables (Lean Cuisine, Breast of Chicken Marsala with Vegetables)	8⅛ oz	190	5	24	65	850

LITE PICK ○

COMMENTS: Note small serving size. Most entrees are 9–11 ounces. Meets the healthful guidelines described on page 168.

PRODUCT	SERV	CAL	FAT (G)	% cal from fat	CHOL (mg)	SOD (mg)
Chicken, frozen, w/rice (Sensible Chef, Glazed Chicken with Rice)	9 oz	210	3	13	na	1140

○

COMMENTS: Too high in sodium, but very low in fat.

PRODUCT	SERV	CAL	FAT (G)	% cal from fat	CHOL (mg)	SOD (mg)
Chicken, frozen, w/rice (Sensible Chef, Chicken à la King with Rice)	9 oz	250	8	29	19	990

LITE PICK ○◇◇

COMMENTS: Lower in cholesterol than most frozen entrees. Meets the healthful guidelines described on page 168.

PRODUCT	SERV	CAL	FAT (G)	% cal from fat	CHOL (mg)	SOD (mg)
Chicken, frozen, w/rice (Weight Watchers, Imperial Chicken Chicken Tenders and Mushrooms in Sauce with Rice and Broccoli)	9¼ oz	230	4	16	60	980

LITE PICK ○

COMMENTS: Very low in fat. Meets the healthful guidelines described on page 168.

PRODUCT	SERV	CAL	FAT (G)	% cal from fat	CHOL (mg)	SOD (mg)
Chicken, frozen, w/vegetables (Weight Watchers, Southern Fried Chicken Patty with Vegetable Medley)	6½ oz	270	16	53	70	610

COMMENTS: Note small serving size. Most entrees are 9–11 ounces. Very high in fat.

PRODUCT	SERV	CAL	FAT (G)	% cal from fat	CHOL (mg)	SOD (mg)
Chili, canned, w/beans (Estee)	7½ oz	390	28	65	0	130

□□□

COMMENTS: Light only in sodium. 95 calories and 14 grams fat, *more* than 7½ ounces regular canned chili with beans, but 944 milligrams less sodium. Very low in fat. Note small serving size. Most entrees are 9–11 ounces.

PRODUCT	SERV	CAL	FAT (G)	% cal from fat	CHOL (mg)	SOD (mg)
Chili, canned, w/beans (Featherweight, Low Sodium)	7½ oz	270	13	43	na	85

□□□

COMMENTS: 25 fewer calories, 2 grams less fat, 989 milligrams less sodium than 7½ ounces regular canned chili with beans. Very high in fat. Note small serving size. Most entrees are 9–11 ounces.

PRODUCT	SERV	CAL	FAT (G)	% cal from fat	CHOL (mg)	SOD (mg)
Chili, frozen (Right Course, Vegetarian Chili)	9¾ oz	280	7	23	0	590

LITE PICK ○

COMMENTS: Meets the healthful guidelines described on page 168.

PRODUCT	SERV	CAL	FAT (G)	% cal from fat	CHOL (mg)	SOD (mg)
Dumplings, canned, chicken (Featherweight, Low Sodium)	7½ oz	160	5	28	na	115

○□□□

COMMENTS: No direct comparison but low in fat and sodium. Note small serving size. Most entrees are 9–11 ounces.

PRODUCT	SERV	CAL	FAT (G)	% cal from fat	CHOL (mg)	SOD (mg)
Ham, frozen, w/vegetables (Budget Gourmet, Slim Selects, Ham and Asparagus au Gratin)	9 oz	280	10	32	40	1130

COMMENTS: Too high in fat and sodium.

PRODUCT	SERV	CAL	FAT (G)	% cal from fat	CHOL (mg)	SOD (mg)
Lamb, frozen, w/rice (Lean Cuisine, Herbed Lamb with Rice)	10⅜ oz	270	8	27	60	950

LITE PICK ○

COMMENTS: Meets the healthful guidelines described on page 168.

PRODUCT	SERV	CAL	FAT (G)	% cal from fat	CHOL (mg)	SOD (mg)
Mexican, frozen (El Charrito, Light Enchiladas Saltillo)	9½ oz	350	16	41	na	na

COMMENTS: Too high in calories and very high in fat.

PRODUCT	SERV	CAL	FAT (G)	% cal from fat	CHOL (mg)	SOD (mg)
Mexican, frozen, beef (Budget Gourmet, Slim Selects, Sirloin Enchilada Ranchero)	9 oz	290	15	47	35	770

COMMENTS: Too high in fat.

PRODUCT	SERV	CAL	FAT (G)	% cal from fat	CHOL (mg)	SOD (mg)
Mexican, frozen, beef (El Charrito, Light Beef Enchiladas Juarez)	9½ oz	300	12	36	na	na

COMMENTS: Too high in fat.

PRODUCT	SERV	CAL	FAT (G)	% cal from fat	CHOL (mg)	SOD (mg)
Mexican, frozen, beef (Weight Watchers, Beef Fajitas)	6¾ oz	270	7	23	30	720

LITE PICK ○

COMMENTS: Note small serving size. Most entrees are 9–11 ounces. Meets the healthful guidelines described on page 168.

PRODUCT	SERV	CAL	FAT (G)	% cal from fat	CHOL (mg)	SOD (mg)
Mexican, frozen, beef (Weight Watchers, Beef Enchilada Ranchero)	9⅛ oz	310	13	38	90	990

COMMENTS: Too high in calories and fat.

PRODUCT	SERV	CAL	FAT (G)	% cal from fat	CHOL (mg)	SOD (mg)
Mexican, frozen, beef (Weight Watchers, Beefsteak Burritos)	7⅜ oz	330	12	33	80	820

COMMENTS: Too high in calories and fat. Note small serving size. Most entrees are 9–11 ounces.

PRODUCT	SERV	CAL	FAT (G)	% cal from fat	CHOL (mg)	SOD (mg)

Mexican, frozen, cheese

(El Charrito, Light Cheese Enchiladas Ranchero)

	SERV	CAL	FAT (G)	% cal from fat	CHOL (mg)	SOD (mg)
	8⅞ oz	370	18	44	na	1530

COMMENTS: Too high in calories and very high in fat and sodium. Note small serving size. Most entrees are 9–11 ounces.

PRODUCT	SERV	CAL	FAT (G)	% cal from fat	CHOL (mg)	SOD (mg)

Mexican, frozen, cheese

(Weight Watchers, Cheese Enchiladas Ranchero)

	SERV	CAL	FAT (G)	% cal from fat	CHOL (mg)	SOD (mg)
	8⅞ oz	370	22	54	105	1100

COMMENTS: Too high in calories, fat, sodium, and cholesterol. Very high in fat. Note small serving size. Most entrees are 9–11 ounces.

PRODUCT	SERV	CAL	FAT (G)	% cal from fat	CHOL (mg)	SOD (mg)

Mexican, frozen, chicken

(Budget Gourmet, Slim Selects, Chicken Enchilada Suiza)

	SERV	CAL	FAT (G)	% cal from fat	CHOL (mg)	SOD (mg)
	9 oz	270	9	30	50	1080

○

COMMENTS: Too high in sodium.

PRODUCT	SERV	CAL	FAT (G)	% cal from fat	CHOL (mg)	SOD (mg)
Mexican, frozen, chicken (El Charrito, Light Chicken Enchiladas Con Chorizo)	9½ oz	310	11	32	na	na

COMMENTS: Too high in fat and calories.

PRODUCT	SERV	CAL	FAT (G)	% cal from fat	CHOL (mg)	SOD (mg)
Mexican, frozen, chicken (El Charrito, Light Chicken Enchiladas Suiza)	9½ oz	300	10	30	na	na

○

COMMENTS: Meets the healthful guidelines for calories and fat described on page 168. Cholesterol and sodium information not available.

PRODUCT	SERV	CAL	FAT (G)	% cal from fat	CHOL (mg)	SOD (mg)
Mexican, frozen, chicken (Weight Watchers, Chicken Burrito)	7⅝ oz	330	14	38	65	800

COMMENTS: Too high in calories and fat. Note small serving size. Most entrees are 9–11 ounces.

PRODUCT	SERV	CAL	FAT (G)	% cal from fat	CHOL (mg)	SOD (mg)

Mexican, frozen, chicken
(Weight Watchers, Chicken Fajitas)

	SERV	CAL	FAT (G)	% cal from fat	CHOL (mg)	SOD (mg)
	6¾ oz	260	6	21	30	640

LITE PICK ○

COMMENTS: Note small serving size. Most entrees are 9–11 ounces. Meets the healthful guidelines described on page 168.

PRODUCT	SERV	CAL	FAT (G)	% cal from fat	CHOL (mg)	SOD (mg)

Mexican, frozen, chicken
(Weight Watchers, Chicken Enchiladas Suiza)

	SERV	CAL	FAT (G)	% cal from fat	CHOL (mg)	SOD (mg)
	9⁹⁄₁₆ oz	360	17	43	70	980

COMMENTS: Too high in calories and very high in fat.

PRODUCT	SERV	CAL	FAT (G)	% cal from fat	CHOL (mg)	SOD (mg)

Mexican, frozen, tofu
(Legume, Mexican Enchiladas and Sauce)

	SERV	CAL	FAT (G)	% cal from fat	CHOL (mg)	SOD (mg)
	11 oz	270	8	27	0	390

LITE PICK ○◇

COMMENTS: One of the few cholesterol-free entrees. Lower in sodium than most entrees, as well. Meets the healthful guidelines described on page 168.

PRODUCT	SERV	CAL	FAT (G)	% cal from fat	CHOL (mg)	SOD (mg)
Oriental, frozen, beef (Benihana, Lite Beef and Mushrooms)	9 oz	270	6	20	na	960

LITE PICK ○

COMMENTS: Very low in fat. Meets the healthful guidelines described on page 168.

PRODUCT	SERV	CAL	FAT (G)	% cal from fat	CHOL (mg)	SOD (mg)
Oriental, frozen, beef (Budget Gourmet Slim Selects, Oriental Beef)	10 oz	290	9	28	25	810

LITE PICK ○

COMMENTS: Meets the healthful guidelines described on page 168.

PRODUCT	SERV	CAL	FAT (G)	% cal from fat	CHOL (mg)	SOD (mg)
Oriental, frozen, beef (Dining Lite, Oriental Pepper Steak with Rice)	9¼ oz	270	7	23	40	1150

○

COMMENTS: Too high in sodium.

PRODUCT	SERV	CAL	FAT (G)	% cal from fat	CHOL (mg)	SOD (mg)

Oriental, frozen, beef
(Healthy Choice, Oriental Pepper Steak Dinner)

PRODUCT	SERV	CAL	FAT (G)	% cal from fat	CHOL (mg)	SOD (mg)
	11¼ oz	270	5	17	70	530

LITE PICK ○

COMMENTS: Very low in fat. Meets the healthful guidelines described on page 168.

PRODUCT	SERV	CAL	FAT (G)	% cal from fat	CHOL (mg)	SOD (mg)

Oriental, frozen, beef
(LaChoy, Fresh and Lite Beef Broccoli)

	11 oz	290	7	22	na	970

LITE PICK ○

COMMENTS: Meets the healthful guidelines described on page 168. Cholesterol information not available.

PRODUCT	SERV	CAL	FAT (G)	% cal from fat	CHOL (mg)	SOD (mg)

Oriental, frozen, beef
(LaChoy, Fresh and Lite Beef Teriyaki)

	10 oz	280	7	23	na	900

LITE PICK ○

COMMENTS: Meets the healthful guidelines described on page 168. Cholesterol information not available.

PRODUCT	SERV	CAL	FAT (G)	% cal from fat	CHOL (mg)	SOD (mg)
Oriental, frozen, beef (LaChoy, Fresh and Lite Peppersteak)	10 oz	290	9	28	na	1170

○

COMMENTS: Too high in sodium.

PRODUCT	SERV	CAL	FAT (G)	% cal from fat	CHOL (mg)	SOD (mg)
Oriental, frozen, beef (Lean Cuisine, Oriental Beef with Vegetable Rice)	8⅝ oz	270	8	27	45	1090

○

COMMENTS: Too high in sodium. Note small serving size. Most entrees are 9–11 ounces.

PRODUCT	SERV	CAL	FAT (G)	% cal from fat	CHOL (mg)	SOD (mg)
Oriental, frozen, beef (Lean Cuisine, Szechwan Beef with Noodles and Vegetables)	9¼ oz	280	11	35	90	720

COMMENTS: Too high in fat.

PRODUCT	SERV	CAL	FAT (G)	% cal from fat	CHOL (mg)	SOD (mg)
Oriental, frozen, beef (Light & Elegant, Beef Teriyaki with Rice and Peppers)	8 oz	240	3	11	45	625

LITE PICK ○

COMMENTS: Very low in fat. Note small serving size. Most entrees are 9–11 ounces. Meets the healthful guidelines described on page 168.

PRODUCT	SERV	CAL	FAT (G)	% cal from fat	CHOL (mg)	SOD (mg)
Oriental, frozen, chicken (Armour Dinner Classics, Lite Chicken Oriental)	10 oz	230	2	8	na	880

LITE PICK ○

COMMENTS: Very low in fat. Meets the healthful guidelines described on page 168. Cholesterol information not available.

PRODUCT	SERV	CAL	FAT (G)	% cal from fat	CHOL (mg)	SOD (mg)
Oriental, frozen, chicken (Armour Dinner Classics, Lite Sweet and Sour Chicken)	10½ oz	240	2	8	na	500

LITE PICK ○

COMMENTS: Very low in fat. Meets the healthful guidelines described on page 168. Cholesterol information not available.

PRODUCT	SERV	CAL	FAT (G)	% cal from fat	CHOL (mg)	SOD (mg)
Oriental, frozen, chicken (Benihana, Lite Chicken and Broccoli)	9 oz	280	4	13	na	790

LITE PICK ○

COMMENTS: Very low in fat. Meets the healthful guidelines described on page 168. Cholesterol information not available.

PRODUCT	SERV	CAL	FAT (G)	% cal from fat	CHOL (mg)	SOD (mg)
Oriental, frozen, chicken (Benihana, Lite Chicken in Spicy Garlic Sauce)	9 oz	270	4	13	na	820

LITE PICK ○

COMMENTS: Very low in fat. Meets the healthful guidelines described on page 168. Cholesterol information not available.

PRODUCT	SERV	CAL	FAT (G)	% cal from fat	CHOL (mg)	SOD (mg)
Oriental, frozen, chicken (Benihana, Lite Grilled Chicken)	8½ oz	250	1	4	na	850

LITE PICK ○

COMMENTS: Very low in fat. Meets the healthful guidelines described on page 168. Cholesterol information not available.

PRODUCT	SERV	CAL	FAT (G)	% cal from fat	CHOL (mg)	SOD (mg)
Oriental, frozen, chicken (Budget Gourmet Slim Selects, Mandarin Chicken)	10 oz	290	6	19	25	690

LITE PICK ○

COMMENTS: Very low in fat. Meets the healthful guidelines described on page 168.

PRODUCT	SERV	CAL	FAT (G)	% cal from fat	CHOL (mg)	SOD (mg)
Oriental, frozen, chicken (Dining Lite, Chicken Chow Mein with Rice)	10 oz	220	2	8	30	1260

COMMENTS: Very low in fat. Too high in sodium.

PRODUCT	SERV	CAL	FAT (G)	% cal from fat	CHOL (mg)	SOD (mg)
Oriental, frozen, chicken (Healthy Choice, Chicken Oriental Dinner)	11¼ oz	210	1	4	45	410

LITE PICK ○

COMMENTS: Very low in fat and lower in sodium than most frozen entrees. Meets the healthful guidelines described on page 168.

PRODUCT	SERV	CAL	FAT (G)	% cal from fat	CHOL (mg)	SOD (mg)
Oriental, frozen, chicken (Healthy Choice, Sweet and Sour Chicken Dinner)	11½ oz	260	2	7	50	260

LITE PICK ○

COMMENTS: Very low in fat and lower in sodium than most frozen entrees. Meets the healthful guidelines described on page 168.

PRODUCT	SERV	CAL	FAT (G)	% cal from fat	CHOL (mg)	SOD (mg)
Oriental, frozen, chicken (LaChoy, Fresh and Lite Almond Chicken)	9¾ oz	290	12	37	na	820

COMMENTS: Too high in fat.

PRODUCT	SERV	CAL	FAT (G)	% cal from fat	CHOL (mg)	SOD (mg)
Oriental, frozen, chicken (LaChoy, Fresh and Lite Imperial Chicken Chow Mein)	11 oz	270	7	23	na	950

LITE PICK ○

COMMENTS: Meets the healthful guidelines described on page 168. Cholesterol information not available.

PRODUCT	SERV	CAL	FAT (G)	% cal from fat	CHOL (mg)	SOD (mg)
Oriental, frozen, chicken (LaChoy, Fresh and Lite Spicy Oriental Chicken)	9¾ oz	290	6	19	na	440

LITE PICK ○

COMMENTS: Very low in fat. Lower in sodium than most entrees. Meets the healthful guidelines described on page 168. Cholesterol information not available.

PRODUCT	SERV	CAL	FAT (G)	% cal from fat	CHOL (mg)	SOD (mg)
Oriental, frozen, chicken (LaChoy, Fresh and Lite Sweet and Sour Chicken)	10 oz	280	4	13	na	360

LITE PICK ○

COMMENTS: Very low in fat. Lower in sodium than most entrees. Meets the healthful guidelines described on page 168. Cholesterol information not available.

PRODUCT	SERV	CAL	FAT (G)	% cal from fat	CHOL (mg)	SOD (mg)
Oriental, frozen, chicken (Le Menu Lightstyle, Chicken Chow Mein)	10 oz	260	4	14	50	790

LITE PICK ○

COMMENTS: Very low in fat. Meets the healthful guidelines described on page 168.

PRODUCT	SERV	CAL	FAT (G)	% cal from fat	CHOL (mg)	SOD (mg)
Oriental, frozen, chicken (Lean Cuisine, Chicken Chow Mein with Rice)	11¼ oz	250	5	18	30	1160

○

COMMENTS: Too high in sodium, but very low in fat.

PRODUCT	SERV	CAL	FAT (G)	% cal from fat	CHOL (mg)	SOD (mg)
Oriental, frozen, seafood (Benihana, Lite Oriental Style Shrimp)	10 oz	230	2	8	na	1100

○

COMMENTS: Too high in sodium. No cholesterol information is available, but shrimp is higher in cholesterol than meat, poultry, and most other seafood.

PRODUCT	SERV	CAL	FAT (G)	% cal from fat	CHOL (mg)	SOD (mg)
Oriental, frozen, seafood (Benihana, Lite Seafood Supreme)	10 oz	255	3	11	na	1250

○

COMMENTS: Very low in fat, but too high in sodium.

PRODUCT	SERV	CAL	FAT (G)	% cal from fat	CHOL (mg)	SOD (mg)
Oriental, frozen, seafood (Benihana, Lite Shrimp and Cashews)	9 oz	260	6	21	na	1050

○

COMMENTS: Too high in sodium. No cholesterol information is available, but shrimp is higher in cholesterol than meat, poultry, and most other seafood.

PRODUCT	SERV	CAL	FAT (G)	% cal from fat	CHOL (mg)	SOD (mg)
Oriental, frozen, seafood (LaChoy, Fresh and Lite Shrimp with Lobster Sauce)	10 oz	210	7	30	na	960

○

COMMENTS: Cholesterol information isn't available for this product, but shrimp and lobster are higher in cholesterol than meat, poultry, and most other seafood.

PRODUCT	SERV	CAL	FAT (G)	% cal from fat	CHOL (mg)	SOD (mg)
Oriental, frozen, seafood (Lean Cuisine, Shrimp and Chicken Cantonese with Noodles)	10⅛ oz	260	9	31	105	970

COMMENTS: Too high in fat and cholesterol.

PRODUCT	SERV	CAL	FAT (G)	% cal from fat	CHOL (mg)	SOD (mg)
Pasta, canned, w/meat (Estee, Ravioli with Beef)	7½ oz	210	8	34	na	110

□□□

COMMENTS: Light only in sodium. 25 fewer calories, 1,133 milligrams less than 8 ounces regular canned beef ravioli, but 2 grams *more* fat, which makes this product too high in fat. Note small serving size. Most entrees are 9–11 ounces.

PRODUCT	SERV	CAL	FAT (G)	% cal from fat	CHOL (mg)	SOD (mg)
Pasta, canned, w/meat (Estee, Spaghetti with Meatballs)	7½ oz	240	15	56	na	130

□□□

COMMENTS: Light only in sodium; too high in fat. Note small serving size. Most entrees are 9–11 ounces.

PRODUCT	SERV	CAL	FAT (G)	% cal from fat	CHOL (mg)	SOD (mg)
Pasta, canned, w/meat (Featherweight, Low Sodium Beef Ravioli)	8 oz	220	4	16	na	75

○

COMMENTS: 15 fewer calories, 2 grams less, 1,168 milligrams less sodium than 8 ounces regular canned beef ravioli. Very low in fat. Note small serving size. Most entrees are 9–11 ounces. Cholesterol information not available.

PRODUCT	SERV	CAL	FAT (G)	% cal from fat	CHOL (mg)	SOD (mg)
Pasta, canned, w/meat (Featherweight, Low Sodium Spaghetti with Meatballs)	7½ oz	200	5	23	na	95

○□□□

COMMENTS: No direct comparison, but this product is low in fat and sodium. Note small serving size. Most entrees are 9–11 ounces.

PRODUCT	SERV	CAL	FAT (G)	% cal from fat	CHOL (mg)	SOD (mg)
Pasta, frozen, w/vegetables (Lean Cuisine, Vegetable and Pasta Mornay with Ham)	9⅜ oz	280	13	42	45	1190

COMMENTS: Too high in sodium, very high in fat.

PRODUCT	SERV	CAL	FAT (G)	% cal from fat	CHOL (mg)	SOD (mg)
Pasta, frozen, w/cheese (Budget Gourmet Slim Selects, Cheese Ravioli)	10 oz	260	7	24	45	960

LITE PICK ○

COMMENTS: Meets the healthful guidelines described on page 168.

PRODUCT	SERV	CAL	FAT (G)	% cal from fat	CHOL (mg)	SOD (mg)
Pasta, frozen, w/cheese (Dining Lite, Cheese Cannelloni with Tomato Sauce)	9 oz	270	10	33	na	760

COMMENTS: Too high in fat.

PRODUCT	SERV	CAL	FAT (G)	% cal from fat	CHOL (mg)	SOD (mg)
Pasta, frozen, w/cheese (Dining Lite, Zitis in Tomato Sauce with Cheese)	10 oz	220	3	12	na	880

LITE PICK ○

COMMENTS: Very low in fat. Cholesterol information is not available.

PRODUCT	SERV	CAL	FAT (G)	% cal from fat	CHOL (mg)	SOD (mg)
Pasta, frozen, w/cheese (Le Menu Lightstyle, Three-Cheese Stuffed Shells)	10 oz	280	8	26	25	720

LITE PICK ○

COMMENTS: Meets the healthful guidelines described on page 168.

PRODUCT	SERV	CAL	FAT (G)	% cal from fat	CHOL (mg)	SOD (mg)
Pasta, frozen, w/cheese (Lean Cuisine, Cheese Cannelloni with Tomato Sauce)	9⅛ oz	270	10	33	30	900

COMMENTS: Too high in fat.

PRODUCT	SERV	CAL	FAT (G)	% cal from fat	CHOL (mg)	SOD (mg)
Pasta, frozen, w/cheese (Weight Watchers, Baked Cheese Ravioli)	9 oz	310	12	35	50	600

COMMENTS: Too high in fat and calories.

PRODUCT	SERV	CAL	FAT (G)	% cal from fat	CHOL (mg)	SOD (mg)
Pasta, frozen, w/cheese (Weight Watchers, Cheese Manicotti)	9¼ oz	300	13	39	75	670

COMMENTS: Too high in fat.

PRODUCT	SERV	CAL	FAT (G)	% cal from fat	CHOL (mg)	SOD (mg)
Pasta, frozen, w/chicken (Le Menu Lightstyle, Chicken Cannelloni)	10¼ oz	250	5	18	65	600

LITE PICK ○

COMMENTS: Very low in fat. Meets the healthful guidelines described on page 168.

PRODUCT	SERV	CAL	FAT (G)	% cal from fat	CHOL (mg)	SOD (mg)
Pasta, frozen, w/chicken (Sensible Chef, Fetuccini Alfredo with Chicken)	9 oz	410	22	48	22	830

COMMENTS: Too high in calories, very high in fat.

PRODUCT	SERV	CAL	FAT (G)	% cal from fat	CHOL (mg)	SOD (mg)
Pasta, frozen, w/meat (Armour Dinner Classics, Lite Tortellini with Meat)	10 oz	250	9	32	na	850

COMMENTS: Too high in fat.

PRODUCT	SERV	CAL	FAT (G)	% cal from fat	CHOL (mg)	SOD (mg)
Pasta, frozen, w/meat (Budget Gourmet, Slim Selects, Fettucini with Meat Sauce)	10 oz	290	10	31	25	980

COMMENTS: Too high in fat.

PRODUCT	SERV	CAL	FAT (G)	% cal from fat	CHOL (mg)	SOD (mg)
Pasta, frozen, w/meat (Budget Gourmet, Slim Selects, Lasagna with Meat Sauce)	10 oz	290	10	31	25	890

COMMENTS: Too high in fat.

PRODUCT	SERV	CAL	FAT (G)	% cal from fat	CHOL (mg)	SOD (mg)
Pasta, frozen, w/meat (Dining Lite, Spaghetti with Beef and Mushroom Sauce)	9 oz	220	8	33	25	880

○

COMMENTS: Too high in fat.

PRODUCT	SERV	CAL	FAT (G)	% cal from fat	CHOL (mg)	SOD (mg)
Pasta, frozen, w/meat (Lean Cuisine, Beef and Port Cannelloni with Mornay Sauce)	9⅝ oz	270	10	33	45	940

COMMENTS: Too high in fat.

PRODUCT	SERV	CAL	FAT (G)	% cal from fat	CHOL (mg)	SOD (mg)
Pasta, frozen, w/meat (Lean Cuisine, Baked Rigatoni with Meat Sauce and Cheese)	9¾ oz	260	10	35	35	1040

COMMENTS: Too high in fat and sodium.

PRODUCT	SERV	CAL	FAT (G)	% cal from fat	CHOL (mg)	SOD (mg)
Pasta, frozen, w/meat (Lean Cuisine, Spaghetti with Beef and Mushroom Sauce)	11½ oz	280	7	23	25	1140

○

COMMENTS: Too high in sodium.

PRODUCT	SERV	CAL	FAT (G)	% cal from fat	CHOL (mg)	SOD (mg)
Pasta, frozen, w/meat (Lean Cuisine, Veal Lasagna)	10¼ oz	280	8	26	75	1000

LITE PICK ○

COMMENTS: Meets the healthful guidelines described on page 168.

PRODUCT	SERV	CAL	FAT (G)	% cal from fat	CHOL (mg)	SOD (mg)
Pasta, frozen, w/meat (Sensible Chef, Lasagna with Meat Sauce)	9 oz	390	19	44	126	1140

COMMENTS: Too high in calories, sodium, and cholesterol. Also very high in fat.

PRODUCT	SERV	CAL	FAT (G)	% cal from fat	CHOL (mg)	SOD (mg)
Pasta, frozen, w/meat (Weight Watchers, Lasagna with Meat Sauce)	11 oz	340	14	37	70	1060

COMMENTS: Too high in calories, fat, and sodium.

PRODUCT	SERV	CAL	FAT (G)	% cal from fat	CHOL (mg)	SOD (mg)
Pasta, frozen, w/meat (Weight Watchers, Pasta Rigati, Meat Sauce with Pasta and Cheese)	11 oz	290	8	25	45	800

LITE PICK ○

COMMENTS: Meets the healthful guidelines described on page 168.

PRODUCT	SERV	CAL	FAT (G)	% cal from fat	CHOL (mg)	SOD (mg)
Pasta, frozen, w/meat (Weight Watchers, Spaghetti with Meat Sauce)	10½ oz	280	7	23	20	920

LITE PICK ○◇◇

COMMENTS: Very low in fat. Lower in cholesterol than most frozen entrees.

PRODUCT	SERV	CAL	FAT (G)	% cal from fat	CHOL (mg)	SOD (mg)
Pasta, frozen, w/seafood (Budget Gourmet Slim Selects, Linguini with Scallops and Clams)	9½ oz	280	11	35	60	630

COMMENTS: Too high in fat.

PRODUCT	SERV	CAL	FAT (G)	% cal from fat	CHOL (mg)	SOD (mg)
Pasta, frozen, w/seafood (Lean Cuisine, Linguini with Clam Sauce)	9⅝ oz	260	7	24	30	800

LITE PICK ○

COMMENTS: Meets the healthful guidelines described on page 168.

PRODUCT	SERV	CAL	FAT (G)	% cal from fat	CHOL (mg)	SOD (mg)
Pasta, frozen, w/seafood (Lean Cuisine, Tuna Lasagna with Spinach Noodles and Vegetables)	9¾ oz	280	10	32	65	990

COMMENTS: Too high in fat.

PRODUCT	SERV	CAL	FAT (G)	% cal from fat	CHOL (mg)	SOD (mg)
Pasta, frozen, w/seafood (Sensible Chef, Linguini with Shrimp and Clams)	9 oz	190	3	14	18	1230

○◇◇

COMMENTS: Very low in fat but too high in sodium. Lower in cholesterol than most frozen entrees.

PRODUCT	SERV	CAL	FAT (G)	% cal from fat	CHOL (mg)	SOD (mg)
Pasta, frozen, w/seafood (Weight Watchers, Seafood Linguini)	9 oz	220	8	33	5	770

◇◇

COMMENTS: Too high in fat. Lower in cholesterol than most frozen entrees.

PRODUCT	SERV	CAL	FAT (G)	% cal from fat	CHOL (mg)	SOD (mg)
Pasta, frozen, w/tofu (Legume, Cannelloni and Florentine Sauce)	11 oz	260	7	24	0	650

LITE PICK ○◇

COMMENTS: Low in fat and one of the few entrees that is cholesterol free. Meets the healthful guidelines described on page 168.

PRODUCT	SERV	CAL	FAT (G)	% cal from fat	CHOL (mg)	SOD (mg)
Pasta, frozen, w/tofu (Legume, Ravioli, round)	4 pc	220	5	20	0	220

LITE PICK ○◇

COMMENTS: Very low in fat. Lower in sodium than most entrees and one of the few that is cholesterol free. Meets the healthful guidelines described on page 168.

PRODUCT	SERV	CAL	FAT (G)	% cal from fat	CHOL (mg)	SOD (mg)
Pasta, frozen, w/tofu (Legume, Vegetable Lasagna and Sauce)	12 oz	240	8	30	0	520

LITE PICK ○◇

COMMENTS: One of the few entrees that is cholesterol free. Meets the healthful guidelines described on page 168.

PRODUCT	SERV	CAL	FAT (G)	% cal from fat	CHOL (mg)	SOD (mg)
Pasta, frozen, w/vegetables (Dining Lite, Fettuccini and Broccoli with Alfredo Sauce)	9½ oz	290	13	40	na	550

COMMENTS: Very high in fat. Cholesterol information is not available.

PRODUCT	SERV	CAL	FAT (G)	% cal from fat	CHOL (mg)	SOD (mg)
Pasta, frozen, w/vegetables (Dining Lite, Zucchini Lasagna)	10 oz	240	6	23	20	840

LITE PICK ○◇◇

COMMENTS: Lower in cholesterol than most frozen entrees. Meets the healthful guidelines described on page 168.

PRODUCT	SERV	CAL	FAT (G)	% cal from fat	CHOL (mg)	SOD (mg)
Pasta, frozen, w/vegetables (Lean Cuisine, Zucchini Lasagna)	11 oz	260	7	24	20	975

LITE PICK ○◇◇

COMMENTS: Lower in cholesterol than most frozen entrees. Meets the healthful guidelines described on page 168.

PRODUCT	SERV	CAL	FAT (G)	% cal from fat	CHOL (mg)	SOD (mg)
Pasta, frozen, w/vegetables (Weight Watchers, Pasta Primavera)	8½ oz	290	13	40	15	880

◇◇

COMMENTS: Very high in fat, but lower in cholesterol than most frozen entrees. Note small serving size. Most entrees are 9–11 ounces.

PRODUCT	SERV	CAL	FAT (G)	% cal from fat	CHOL (mg)	SOD (mg)
Pasta, frozen, w/cheese (Weight Watchers, Italian Cheese Lasagna with Ricotta, Mozzarella, and Romano Cheeses)	12 oz	370	14	34	60	970

COMMENTS: Too high in fat and calories.

PRODUCT	SERV	CAL	FAT (G)	% cal from fat	CHOL (mg)	SOD (mg)
Pizza, frozen (Lean Cuisine, Cheese French Bread)	5⅛ oz	310	9	26	10	830

○

COMMENTS: 30 fewer calories, 4 grams less fat, and 10 milligrams less sodium than 5⅛ oz Stouffer's regular French Bread Cheese Pizza.

PRODUCT	SERV	CAL	FAT (G)	% cal from fat	CHOL (mg)	SOD (mg)
Pizza, frozen (Lean Cuisine, Deluxe French Bread)	6⅛ oz	340	12	32	30	1080

COMMENTS: 90 fewer calories, 9 grams less fat, 50 milligrams less sodium than 6⅛ ounces Stouffer's regular Deluxe French Bread Pizza.

PRODUCT	SERV	CAL	FAT (G)	% cal from fat	CHOL (mg)	SOD (mg)
Pizza, frozen (Weight Watchers, Cheese French Bread)	5⅛ oz	320	11	31	45	730

COMMENTS: 20 fewer calories, 2 grams less fat, 110 milligrams less sodium than one piece of Stouffer's regular cheese French Bread pizza.

PRODUCT	SERV	CAL	FAT (G)	% cal from fat	CHOL (mg)	SOD (mg)
Pizza, frozen (Weight Watchers, Cheese)	5¾ oz	320	8	23	45	920

○

COMMENTS: No direct comparison, but is low in fat and high in sodium.

PRODUCT	SERV	CAL	FAT (G)	% cal from fat	CHOL (mg)	SOD (mg)
Pizza, frozen (Weight Watchers, Deluxe French Bread)	6⅛ oz	330	12	33	30	880

COMMENTS: 100 fewer calories, 9 grams less fat, 250 milligrams less sodium than an equal piece of regular Deluxe French Bread Pizza.

PRODUCT	SERV	CAL	FAT (G)	% cal from fat	CHOL (mg)	SOD (mg)
Pizza, frozen, combination (Weight Watchers, Deluxe Combination with Sausage, Mushrooms, Olives, and Peppers)	6¾ oz	300	8	24	35	750

○

COMMENTS: No direct comparison, but has 130 fewer calories, 13 grams less fat, 380 milligrams less sodium than an equal slice of Stouffer's regular Deluxe French Bread pizza.

PRODUCT	SERV	CAL	FAT (G)	% cal from fat	CHOL (mg)	SOD (mg)
Pizza, frozen, w/pepperoni (Weight Watchers, Pepperoni French Bread)	5¼ oz	330	13	35	50	860

COMMENTS: 80 fewer calories, 7 grams less fat, 260 milligrams less sodium than 5½ ounces regular Stouffer's Pepperoni French Bread Pizza.

PRODUCT	SERV	CAL	FAT (G)	% cal from fat	CHOL (mg)	SOD (mg)
Pizza, frozen, w/pepperoni (Lean Cuisine, Pepperoni French Bread)	5¼ oz	340	12	32	25	970

COMMENTS: 70 fewer calories, 8 grams less fat, 150 milligrams less sodium than 5½ ounces Stouffer's regular Pepperoni French Bread Pizza.

PRODUCT	SERV	CAL	FAT (G)	% cal from fat	CHOL (mg)	SOD (mg)
Pizza, frozen, w/pepperoni (Weight Watchers, Pepperoni)	5⅞ oz	320	9	25	50	880

○

COMMENTS: 105 fewer calories, 13 grams less fat than an equal size slice of regular pepperoni pizza. (No information available for cholesterol and sodium comparison.)

PRODUCT	SERV	CAL	FAT (G)	% cal from fat	CHOL (mg)	SOD (mg)
Pizza, frozen, w/sausage (Lean Cuisine, Sausage French Bread)	6 oz	330	10	27	30	1040

○

COMMENTS: 90 fewer calories, 10 grams less fat, 150 milligrams less sodium than 6 ounces Stouffer's regular Sausage French Bread Pizza.

PRODUCT	SERV	CAL	FAT (G)	% cal from fat	CHOL (mg)	SOD (mg)
Pizza, frozen, w/sausage (Weight Watchers, Sausage)	6¼ oz	310	8	23	40	820

○

COMMENTS: No direct comparison, but this product is low in fat.

PRODUCT	SERV	CAL	FAT (G)	% cal from fat	CHOL (mg)	SOD (mg)

Potato, frozen, w/cheese
(Weight Watchers, Broccoli and Cheese Baked Potato)

| | 10½ oz | 280 | 7 | 23 | 30 | 700 |

LITE PICK ○

COMMENTS: Meets the healthful guidelines described on page 168.

PRODUCT	SERV	CAL	FAT (G)	% cal from fat	CHOL (mg)	SOD (mg)

Potato, frozen, w/chicken
(Weight Watchers, Chicken Divan Baked Potato)

| | 11 oz | 300 | 6 | 18 | 30 | 840 |

LITE PICK ○

COMMENTS: Very low in fat. Meets the healthful guidelines described on page 168.

PRODUCT	SERV	CAL	FAT (G)	% cal from fat	CHOL (mg)	SOD (mg)

Seafood, frozen
(Armour Dinner Classics, Lite Baby Bay Shrimp)

| | 10½ oz | 260 | 6 | 21 | na | 1100 |

○

COMMENTS: Too high in sodium. No cholesterol information is available for this product, but shrimp is higher in cholesterol than meat, poultry, and most other seafood.

PRODUCT	SERV	CAL	FAT (G)	% cal from fat	CHOL (mg)	SOD (mg)
Seafood, frozen (Armour Dinner Classics, Lite Seafood with Natural Herbs)	10½ oz	220	4	16	na	960

○

COMMENTS: Very low in fat. No cholesterol information is available for this product, but shrimp is higher in cholesterol than meat, poultry, and most other seafood.

PRODUCT	SERV	CAL	FAT (G)	% cal from fat	CHOL (mg)	SOD (mg)
Seafood, frozen (Healthy Choice, Shrimp Creole Dinner)	11¼ oz	230	2	9	90	420

LITE PICK ○

COMMENTS: Very low in fat and lower in sodium than most frozen entrees. Meets the healthful guidelines described on page 168.

PRODUCT	SERV	CAL	FAT (G)	% cal from fat	CHOL (mg)	SOD (mg)
Seafood, frozen (Healthy Choice, Sole au Gratin Dinner)	11¼ oz	280	5	16	40	490

LITE PICK ○

COMMENTS: Very low in fat and lower in sodium than most frozen entrees. Meets the healthful guidelines described on page 168.

PRODUCT	SERV	CAL	FAT (G)	% cal from fat	CHOL (mg)	SOD (mg)
Seafood, frozen (Le Menu LightStyle, Flounder vin Blanc)	10 oz	220	9	21	70	640

LITE PICK ○

COMMENTS: Meets the healthful guidelines described on page 168.

PRODUCT	SERV	CAL	FAT (G)	% cal from fat	CHOL (mg)	SOD (mg)
Seafood, frozen (Lean Cuisine, Fillet of Fish Divan)	12⅜ oz	270	9	30	90	700

LITE PICK ○

COMMENTS: Meets the healthful guidelines described on page 168.

PRODUCT	SERV	CAL	FAT (G)	% cal from fat	CHOL (mg)	SOD (mg)
Seafood, frozen (Lean Cuisine, Fillet of Fish Florentine)	9 oz	240	9	34	100	700

COMMENTS: Too high in fat.

PRODUCT	SERV	CAL	FAT (G)	% cal from fat	CHOL (mg)	SOD (mg)
Seafood, frozen (Lean Cuisine, Fillet of Fish Jardinere with Souffléed Potatoes)	11¼ oz	280	10	32	95	840

COMMENTS: Too high in fat.

PRODUCT	SERV	CAL	FAT (G)	% cal from fat	CHOL (mg)	SOD (mg)
Seafood, frozen (Mrs. Paul's, Light Fish au Gratin)	9 oz	270	9	30	na	1100

LITE PICK ○

COMMENTS: Too high in sodium. Cholesterol information is not available.

PRODUCT	SERV	CAL	FAT (G)	% cal from fat	CHOL (mg)	SOD (mg)
Seafood, frozen (Mrs. Paul's, Light Fish Dijon)	8¾ oz	210	9	39	na	430

COMMENTS: Too high in fat. Lower in sodium than most entrees. Note small serving size. Most entrees are 9–11 ounces.

PRODUCT	SERV	CAL	FAT (G)	% cal from fat	CHOL (mg)	SOD (mg)
Seafood, frozen (Mrs. Paul's, Light Fish Florentine)	8 oz	200	9	41	na	430

COMMENTS: Very high in fat. Lower in sodium than most entrees. Note small serving size. Most entrees are 9–11 ounces.

PRODUCT	SERV	CAL	FAT (G)	% cal from fat	CHOL (mg)	SOD (mg)
Seafood, frozen (Mrs. Paul's, Light Fish Mornay)	9 oz	250	10	36	na	660

COMMENTS: Too high in fat.

PRODUCT	SERV	CAL	FAT (G)	% cal from fat	CHOL (mg)	SOD (mg)
Seafood, frozen (Mrs. Paul's, Light Fish and Pasta)	9 oz	230	8	27	na	870

○

COMMENTS: Too high in fat.

PRODUCT	SERV	CAL	FAT (G)	% cal from fat	CHOL (mg)	SOD (mg)
Seafood, frozen (Mrs. Paul's, Light Shrimp Cajun Style)	9 oz	200	3	14	na	860

○

COMMENTS: Very low in fat. No cholesterol information is available for this product, but shrimp is higher in cholesterol than meat, poultry, and most other seafood.

PRODUCT	SERV	CAL	FAT (G)	% cal from fat	CHOL (mg)	SOD (mg)
Seafood, frozen (Weight Watchers, Stuffed Sole with Newburg Sauce)	10½ oz	310	9	26	5	880

LITE PICK ○◇◇

COMMENTS: Lower in cholesterol than most frozen entrees. Meets the healthful guidelines described on page 168.

PRODUCT	SERV	CAL	FAT (G)	% cal from fat	CHOL (mg)	SOD (mg)
Seafood, frozen, w/vegetables (Mrs. Paul's, Light Shrimp Primavera)	9½ oz	190	4	19	na	980

○

COMMENTS: Very low in fat. No cholesterol information is available for this product, but shrimp is higher in cholesterol than meat, poultry, and most other seafood.

PRODUCT	SERV	CAL	FAT (G)	% cal from fat	CHOL (mg)	SOD (mg)
Seafood, frozen w/vegetables (Right Course, Shrimp Primavera)	9⅝ oz	240	7	26	50	590

LITE PICK ○

COMMENTS: Meets the healthful guidelines described on page 168.

PRODUCT	SERV	CAL	FAT (G)	% cal from fat	CHOL (mg)	SOD (mg)
Seafood, frozen, w/pasta (Mrs. Paul's, Light Shrimp and Clams with Linguini)	10 oz	280	9	29	na	790

○

COMMENTS: No cholesterol information is available for this product, but shrimp is higher in cholesterol than meat, poultry, and most other seafood.

PRODUCT	SERV	CAL	FAT (G)	% cal from fat	CHOL (mg)	SOD (mg)
Seafood, frozen, w/pasta (Mrs. Paul's, Light Tuna Pasta Casserole)	10 oz	270	7	23	na	960

LITE PICK ○

COMMENTS: Meets the healthful guidelines described on page 168. Cholesterol information is not available.

PRODUCT	SERV	CAL	FAT (G)	% cal from fat	CHOL (mg)	SOD (mg)

Seafood, frozen, w/vegetables
(Weight Watchers, Filet of Fish au Gratin with Broccoli)

	9¼ oz	210	6	26	85	700

LITE PICK ○

COMMENTS: Meets the healthful guidelines described on page 168.

PRODUCT	SERV	CAL	FAT (G)	% cal from fat	CHOL (mg)	SOD (mg)

Seafood, frozen, w/vegetables
(Weight Watchers, Oven Fried Fish with Vegetable Medley)

	6⅞ oz	220	12	49	50	350

COMMENTS: Very high in fat. Note small serving size. Most entrees are 9–11 ounces.

PRODUCT	SERV	CAL	FAT (G)	% cal from fat	CHOL (mg)	SOD (mg)

Stew, canned, w/chicken
(Featherweight, Low Sodium Chicken)

	7½ oz	170	6	32	na	55

□□□

COMMENTS: No direct comparison, but this product is too high in fat. Note small serving size. Most entrees are 9–11 ounces.

PRODUCT	SERV	CAL	FAT (G)	% cal from fat	CHOL (mg)	SOD (mg)
Stew, canned, w/meat						
(Estee, Beef)	7½ oz	210	9	39	na	110

□□□

COMMENTS: Light only in sodium. 65 calories and 5 grams fat, *more* than 7½ ounces regular canned beef stew, and 720 milligrams less sodium. Note small serving size. Most entrees are 9–11 ounces.

PRODUCT	SERV	CAL	FAT (G)	% cal from fat	CHOL (mg)	SOD (mg)
Stew, canned, w/meat						
(Featherweight, Low Sodium Beef)	7½ oz	220	8	33	na	95

COMMENTS: Light only in sodium. 75 calories and 4 grams fat *more* than 7½ ounces regular canned vegetable beef stew, but 735 milligrams less sodium. Too high in fat.

PRODUCT	SERV	CAL	FAT (G)	% cal from fat	CHOL (mg)	SOD (mg)
Stew, frozen, w/meat						
(Lean Cuisine, Meatball Stew)	10 oz	250	10	36	80	1120

COMMENTS: Too high in fat and sodium.

PRODUCT	SERV	CAL	FAT (G)	% cal from fat	CHOL (mg)	SOD (mg)
Turkey, frozen (Budget Gourmet, Slim Selects Glazed Turkey)	9 oz	270	5	17	50	760

LITE PICK ○

COMMENTS: Very low in fat. Meets the healthful guidelines described on page 168.

PRODUCT	SERV	CAL	FAT (G)	% cal from fat	CHOL (mg)	SOD (mg)
Turkey, frozen (Healthy Choice, Turkey Breast Dinner)	11¼ oz	270	5	17	55	450

LITE PICK ○

COMMENTS: Very low in fat and lower in sodium than most frozen entrees. Meets the healthful guidelines described on page 168.

PRODUCT	SERV	CAL	FAT (G)	% cal from fat	CHOL (mg)	SOD (mg)
Turkey, frozen (Le Menu Lightstyle, Turkey Divan)	10 oz	280	9	29	40	820

LITE PICK ○

COMMENTS: Meets the healthful guidelines described on page 168.

PRODUCT	SERV	CAL	FAT (G)	% cal from fat	CHOL (mg)	SOD (mg)
Turkey, frozen (Lean Cuisine, Turkey Dijon)	9½ oz	280	10	32	75	820

COMMENTS: Too high in fat.

PRODUCT	SERV	CAL	FAT (G)	% cal from fat	CHOL (mg)	SOD (mg)
Turkey, frozen (Lean Cuisine, Sliced Turkey Breast with Mushroom Sauce)	8 oz	220	5	20	50	750

LITE PICK ○

COMMENTS: Very low in fat. Note small serving size. Most entrees are 9–11 ounces. Meets the healthful guidelines described on page 168.

PRODUCT	SERV	CAL	FAT (G)	% cal from fat	CHOL (mg)	SOD (mg)
Turkey, frozen (Weight Watchers, Stuffed Turkey Breast with Gravy and Vegetable Medley)	8½ oz	270	10	33	90	960

COMMENTS: Too high in fat. Note small serving size. Most entrees are 9–11 ounces.

PRODUCT	SERV	CAL	FAT (G)	% cal from fat	CHOL (mg)	SOD (mg)
Turkey, frozen, w/rice (Right Course, Sliced Turkey in Curry Sauce with Rice Pilaf)	8¾ oz	320	8	23	50	570

LITE PICK ○

COMMENTS: Meets the healthful guidelines described on page 168.

PRODUCT	SERV	CAL	FAT (G)	% cal from fat	CHOL (mg)	SOD (mg)
Veal, frozen (Le Menu Lightstyle, Veal Marsala)	10 oz	260	6	21	100	800

LITE PICK ○

COMMENTS: Meets the healthful guidelines described on page 168.

PRODUCT	SERV	CAL	FAT (G)	% cal from fat	CHOL (mg)	SOD (mg)
Veal, frozen (Weight Watchers, Veal Patty Parmigiana with Vegetable Medley)	8⁷⁄₁₆ oz	240	11	41	55	780

COMMENTS: Very high in fat. Note small serving size. Most entrees are 9–11 ounces.

PRODUCT	SERV	CAL	FAT (G)	% cal from fat	CHOL (mg)	SOD (mg)
Veal, frozen, w/vegetables (Lean Cuisine, Veal Primavera)	9⅛ oz	250	9	32	80	790

COMMENTS: Too high in fat.

FISH

PRODUCT	SERV	CAL	FAT (G)	% cal from fat	CHOL (mg)	SOD (mg)
Catfish, frozen (Mrs. Paul's, Light Breaded Fillets)	4½ oz	250	10	36	na	389

COMMENTS: 30 fewer calories, 6 grams less fat, 161 milligrams less sodium than one 4 ounce Mrs. Paul's Crispy Crunchy Fish Fillet. Too high in fat.

PRODUCT	SERV	CAL	FAT (G)	% cal from fat	CHOL (mg)	SOD (mg)
Cod, frozen (Mrs. Paul's, Light Breaded Fillets)	4½ oz	220	7	29	na	412

○

COMMENTS: 60 fewer calories, 9 grams less fat, 138 milligrams less sodium than one 4 ounce Mrs. Paul's Crispy Crunchy Fish Fillet.

PRODUCT	SERV	CAL	FAT (G)	% cal from fat	CHOL (mg)	SOD (mg)
Fish Fillets, frozen (Gorton's, Light Recipe Lightly Breaded)	1 fillet	170	7	37	na	380

COMMENTS: No direct comparison, but this product is too high in fat.

PRODUCT	SERV	CAL	FAT (G)	% cal from fat	CHOL (mg)	SOD (mg)
Fish Fillets, frozen (Gorton's, Light Recipe Tempura Batter)	1 fillet	190	12	57	na	400

COMMENTS: No direct comparison, but this product is very high in fat.

PRODUCT	SERV	CAL	FAT (G)	% cal from fat	CHOL (mg)	SOD (mg)
Fish fillets, frozen (Mrs. Paul's, Supreme Light Batter)	3⅜ oz	210	12	51	na	540

NO LITE BARGAIN

COMMENTS: This product has a higher percentage of calories from fat and 10 calories *more* per ounce than Mrs. Paul's regular Batter Dipped Fish Fillets! Very high in fat, and high in sodium. Note the small size of the fillet.

PRODUCT	SERV	CAL	FAT (G)	% cal from fat	CHOL (mg)	SOD (mg)
Flounder, frozen (Gorton's, Light Recipe Stuffed Flounder)	6½ oz	260	14	48	na	880

COMMENTS: No direct comparison, but this product is very high in fat.

PRODUCT	SERV	CAL	FAT (G)	% cal from fat	CHOL (mg)	SOD (mg)
Flounder, frozen (Mrs. Paul's, Light Breaded Fillets)	4½ oz	260	11	38	na	536

COMMENTS: 10 calories, 4 grams less fat than 4 ounces Mrs. Paul's Crispy Crunchy Flounder Fillet, but 36 milligrams *more* sodium. High in fat and sodium.

PRODUCT	SERV	CAL	FAT (G)	% cal from fat	CHOL (mg)	SOD (mg)
Haddock, frozen (Gorton's, Light Recipe Haddock Fillets with Lemon Butter sauce)	6 oz	250	13	47	na	660

COMMENTS: No direct comparison, but this product is very high in fat.

PRODUCT	SERV	CAL	FAT (G)	% cal from fat	CHOL (mg)	SOD (mg)
Haddock, frozen (Mrs. Paul's, Light Breaded Fillets)	4½ oz	220	5	20	na	456

○

COMMENTS: 80 fewer calories, 8 grams less fat than one 4 ounce Mrs. Paul's Crispy Crunchy Breaded Haddock Fillet, but 46 milligrams more sodium. Very low in fat.

PRODUCT	SERV	CAL	FAT (G)	% cal from fat	CHOL (mg)	SOD (mg)
Perch, frozen (Mrs. Paul's, Light Breaded Fillets)	4½ oz	270	13	43	na	391

COMMENTS: 50 fewer calories, 6 grams less fat, 69 milligrams less sodium than one 4 ounce Mrs. Paul's Crispy Crunchy Ocean Perch Fillet. Very high in fat.

PRODUCT	SERV	CAL	FAT (G)	% cal from fat	CHOL (mg)	SOD (mg)
Pollock, frozen (Mrs. Paul's, Light Breaded Fillets)	4½ oz	240	11	41	na	530

COMMENTS: 40 fewer calories, 5 grams less fat, 20 milligrams less sodium than one 4 ounce Mrs. Paul's Crispy Crunchy Fillet. Very high in fat and high in sodium.

PRODUCT	SERV	CAL	FAT (G)	% cal from fat	CHOL (mg)	SOD (mg)
Salmon, pink, canned (Featherweight, Low Sodium)	3⅞ oz	140	6	39	na	90

□□□

COMMENTS: 15 fewer calories, 336 milligrams less sodium than 3⅞ ounces regular canned pink salmon. High in fat. Note that the serving size for salmon is much smaller than that of tuna (see page 243).

PRODUCT	SERV	CAL	FAT (G)	% cal from fat	CHOL (mg)	SOD (mg)
Scrod, frozen (Gorton's, Light Recipe Baked Stuffed Scrod)	6 oz	250	14	50	na	490

COMMENTS: No direct comparison, but this product is very high in fat.

PRODUCT	SERV	CAL	FAT (G)	% cal from fat	CHOL (mg)	SOD (mg)
Shrimp, frozen (Gorton's, Light Recipe Shrimp Scampi)	6 oz	350	24	62	na	520

COMMENTS: No direct comparison, but this product is very high in fat.

PRODUCT	SERV	CAL	FAT (G)	% cal from fat	CHOL (mg)	SOD (mg)
Sole, frozen (Gorton's, Light Recipe Filet of Sole with Lemon Butter Sauce)	6 oz	250	14	50	na	650

COMMENTS: No direct comparison, but this product is very high in fat.

PRODUCT	SERV	CAL	FAT (G)	% cal from fat	CHOL (mg)	SOD (mg)
Sole, frozen (Mrs. Paul's, Light Breaded Fillets)	4½ oz	260	11	38	na	536

COMMENTS: 20 fewer calories, 5 grams less fat than 4 ounces Mrs. Paul's Crispy Crunchy Fillet, but 14 milligrams *more* sodium. High in fat and sodium.

PRODUCT	SERV	CAL	FAT (G)	% cal from fat	CHOL (mg)	SOD (mg)
Tuna, canned (Featherweight, Chunk Light Low Sodium)	2 oz	60	1	15	30	30

COMMENTS: 3 fewer calories, 4 milligrams less sodium, .5 gram fat more than 2 oz regular light tuna in water, but 199 milligrams less sodium. Very low in fat.

PRODUCT	SERV	CAL	FAT (G)	% cal from fat	CHOL (mg)	SOD (mg)
Tuna, canned (Star-Kist, Chunk Light In Spring Water)	2 oz	65	<1	<14	na	310

○

COMMENTS: 85 fewer calories, 12 grams less fat than 2 ounces Star-Kist Chunk Light Tuna in Oil. Very low in fat.

PRODUCT	SERV	CAL	FAT (G)	% cal from fat	CHOL (mg)	SOD (mg)
Tuna, canned (Star-Kist, Chunk Light In Spring Water Reduced Sodium)	2 oz	65	<1	<14	na	135

○□□□

COMMENTS: 5 *more* calories than, same fat as 2 ounces regular Star-Kist Chunk Light Tuna in Spring Water, but 175 milligrams less sodium. Very low in fat.

PRODUCT	SERV	CAL	FAT (G)	% cal from fat	CHOL (mg)	SOD (mg)
Tuna, canned (Star-Kist, Solid Light In Oil)	2 oz	150	13	78	na	310

NO LITE BARGAIN

COMMENTS: Same amount of sodium as, but 10 *more* calories and 3 grams *more* fat than 2 ounces Star-Kist white tuna in oil. Very high in fat.

PRODUCT	SERV	CAL	FAT (G)	% cal from fat	CHOL (mg)	SOD (mg)
Tuna, canned (Star-Kist, Solid Light In Spring Water)	2 oz	60	<1	<15	na	310

○

COMMENTS: Same amount of sodium as, but 90 fewer calories and 12 grams less fat than 2 ounces Star-Kist Solid Light Tuna in Oil. Very low in fat.

PRODUCT	SERV	CAL	FAT (G)	% cal from fat	CHOL (mg)	SOD (mg)
Tuna, canned (Star-Kist, Imported Chunk White In Spring Water Reduced Sodium)	2 oz	70	1	13	na	30

LITE PICK ○□□

COMMENTS: 280 milligrams sodium less than 2 ounces Star-Kist Solid White Tuna in Spring Water. Very low in fat.

FROZEN DESSERTS

PRODUCT	SERV	CAL	FAT (G)	% cal from fat	CHOL (mg)	SOD (mg)
Frozen bars (Borden, Light Dream Pops, all flavors)	1¾ oz	30	2	60	na	50

□□□

COMMENTS: No direct comparison. The high percentage of calories from fat is deceiving; with only 2 grams of fat it is actually low in fat. Sweetened with sorbitol and aspartame.

PRODUCT	SERV	CAL	FAT (G)	% cal from fat	CHOL (mg)	SOD (mg)
Frozen bars (Borden, Light Fudge)	1¾ oz	60	3	45	na	50

□□□

COMMENTS: 31 fewer calories, 5 milligrams less sodium, but almost 3 grams more fat than a regular fudgesicle. This product is very high in fat. Sweetened with sorbitol and aspartame.

PRODUCT	SERV	CAL	FAT (G)	% cal from fat	CHOL (mg)	SOD (mg)
Frozen bars (Borden, Light Ice Pops, all flavors)	1¾ oz	20	0	0	0	10

LITE PICK ○◇□□

COMMENTS: No direct comparison, but this product is fat and cholesterol free. Sweetened with sorbitol and aspartame.

PRODUCT	SERV	CAL	FAT (G)	% cal from fat	CHOL (mg)	SOD (mg)
Frozen bars (Carnation, Creamy Lites Ice Cream Bars, Chocolate)	1 bar	50	2	36	na	30

□□

COMMENTS: No direct comparison. The high percentage of calories from fat is deceiving; with only 2 grams of fat, it is actually low in fat.

PRODUCT	SERV	CAL	FAT (G)	% cal from fat	CHOL (mg)	SOD (mg)
Frozen bars (Carnation, Creamy Lites Ice Cream Bars, Strawberry)	1 bar	50	2	36	na	30

□□

COMMENTS: No direct comparison. The high percentage of calories from fat is deceiving; with only 2 grams of fat, it is actually low in fat.

PRODUCT	SERV	CAL	FAT (G)	% cal from fat	CHOL (mg)	SOD (mg)
Frozen bars (Chilly Things, Light Pops, all flavors)	1 bar	12	0	0	0	5

LITE PICK ○◇□□

COMMENTS: No direct comparison, but this product is fat free. Sweetened with aspartame.

PRODUCT	SERV	CAL	FAT (G)	% cal from fat	CHOL (mg)	SOD (mg)
Frozen bars (Crystal Light Pops, Berry Blend Flavor)	1 bar	13	0	0	0	2

LITE PICK ○◇□

COMMENTS: No direct comparison, but this product is fat free. Sweetened with aspartame.

PRODUCT	SERV	CAL	FAT (G)	% cal from fat	CHOL (mg)	SOD (mg)
Frozen bars (Crystal Light Pops, Fruit Punch Flavor)	1 bar	14	0	0	0	2

LITE PICK ○◇□

COMMENTS: No direct comparison, but this product is fat free. Sweetened with aspartame.

PRODUCT	SERV	CAL	FAT (G)	% cal from fat	CHOL (mg)	SOD (mg)
Frozen bars (Crystal Light Pops, Orange Flavor)	1 bar	13	0	0	0	3

LITE PICK ○◇□

COMMENTS: No direct comparison, but this product is fat free. Sweetened with aspartame.

PRODUCT	SERV	CAL	FAT (G)	% cal from fat	CHOL (mg)	SOD (mg)
Frozen bars (Crystal Light Pops, Pina Colada Flavor)	1 bar	14	0	0	0	2

LITE PICK ○◇□

COMMENTS: No direct comparison, but this product is fat free. Sweetened with aspartame.

PRODUCT	SERV	CAL	FAT (G)	% cal from fat	CHOL (mg)	SOD (mg)
Frozen bars (Crystal Light Pops, Pineapple Flavor)	1 bar	14	0	0	0	2

LITE PICK ○◇□

COMMENTS: No direct comparison, but this product is fat free. Sweetened with aspartame.

PRODUCT	SERV	CAL	FAT (G)	% cal from fat	CHOL (mg)	SOD (mg)
Frozen bars (Crystal Light Pops, Pink Lemonade Flavor)	1 bar	14	0	0	0	2

LITE PICK ○◇□

COMMENTS: No direct comparison, but this product is fat free. Sweetened with aspartame.

PRODUCT	SERV	CAL	FAT (G)	% cal from fat	CHOL (mg)	SOD (mg)
Frozen bars (Crystal Light Pops, Raspberry Flavor)	1 bar	13	0	0	0	4

LITE PICK ○◇□

COMMENTS: No direct comparison, but this product is fat free. Sweetened with aspartame.

PRODUCT	SERV	CAL	FAT (G)	% cal from fat	CHOL (mg)	SOD (mg)
Frozen bars (Crystal Light Pops, Strawberry Daquiri Flavor)	1 bar	14	0	0	0	2

LITE PICK ○◇□

COMMENTS: No direct comparison, but this product is fat free. Sweetened with aspartame.

PRODUCT	SERV	CAL	FAT (G)	% cal from fat	CHOL (mg)	SOD (mg)
Frozen bars (Dole, Fresh Lites, Cherry)	1 bar	25	0	0	0	6

LITE PICK ○◇□□

COMMENTS: No direct comparison, but this product is fat free. Sweetened with aspartame.

PRODUCT	SERV	CAL	FAT (G)	% cal from fat	CHOL (mg)	SOD (mg)
Frozen bars (Dole, Fresh Lites, Lemon)	1 bar	25	0	0	0	16

LITE PICK ○◇□□

COMMENTS: No direct comparison, but this product is fat free. Sweetened with aspartame.

PRODUCT	SERV	CAL	FAT (G)	% cal from fat	CHOL (mg)	SOD (mg)
Frozen bars (Dole, Fresh Lites, Orange)	1 bar	25	0	0	0	7

LITE PICK ○◇□□

COMMENTS: No direct comparison, but this product is fat free. Sweetened with aspartame.

PRODUCT	SERV	CAL	FAT (G)	% cal from fat	CHOL (mg)	SOD (mg)
Frozen bars (Dole, Fresh Lites, Pineapple	1 bar	25	0	0	0	7

LITE PICK ○◇□□

COMMENTS: No direct comparison, but this product is fat free. Sweetened with aspartame.

PRODUCT	SERV	CAL	FAT (G)	% cal from fat	CHOL (mg)	SOD (mg)
Frozen bars (Dole, Fresh Lites, Raspberry)	1 bar	25	0	0	0	6

LITE PICK ○◇□□

COMMENTS: No direct comparison, but this product is fat free. Sweetened with aspartame.

PRODUCT	SERV	CAL	FAT (G)	% cal from fat	CHOL (mg)	SOD (mg)
Frozen bars (Frozfruit, Cantaloupe)	1 bar	70	0	0	0	na

LITE PICK ○◇

COMMENTS: No direct comparison, but this product is fat free. Sweetened with fructose and sucrose. Sodium information is not available, but most frozen fruit bars are very low in sodium.

PRODUCT	SERV	CAL	FAT (G)	% cal from fat	CHOL (mg)	SOD (mg)
Frozen bars (Frozfruit, Cherry)	1 bar	70	0	0	0	na

LITE PICK ○◇

COMMENTS: No direct comparison, but this product is fat free. Sweetened with fructose and sucrose. Sodium information is not available, but most frozen fruit bars are very low in sodium.

PRODUCT	SERV	CAL	FAT (G)	% cal from fat	CHOL (mg)	SOD (mg)
Frozen bars (Frozfruit, Cream Base Banana)	1 bar	120	4	30	na	na

○

COMMENTS: No direct comparison. Although higher in fat than fruit-based bars, this product is still low in fat for a cream-based bar. Since cream is an ingredient in this product, it may contain some cholesterol.

PRODUCT	SERV	CAL	FAT (G)	% cal from fat	CHOL (mg)	SOD (mg)
Frozen bars (Frozfruit, Cream Base Raspberry)	1 bar	120	4	30	na	na

COMMENTS: No direct comparison. Although higher in fat than fruit-based bars, this product is still low in fat for a cream-based bar. Since cream is an ingredient in this product, it may contain some cholesterol.

PRODUCT	SERV	CAL	FAT (G)	% cal from fat	CHOL (mg)	SOD (mg)
Frozen bars (Frozfruit Cream Base Strawberry)	1 bar	120	4	30	na	na

○

COMMENTS: Although higher in fat than fruit-based bars, this product is still low in fat for a cream-based bar. Since cream is an ingredient in this product, it may contain some cholesterol.

PRODUCT	SERV	CAL	FAT (G)	% cal from fat	CHOL (mg)	SOD (mg)
Frozen bars (Frozfruit, Lemon)	1 bar	70	0	0	0	na

LITE PICK ○◇

COMMENTS: No direct comparison, but this product is fat free. Sweetened with fructose and sucrose. Sodium information is not available, but most frozen fruit bars are very low in sodium.

PRODUCT	SERV	CAL	FAT (G)	% cal from fat	CHOL (mg)	SOD (mg)
Frozen bars (Frozfruit, Lime)	1 bar	70	0	0	0	na

LITE PICK ○◇

COMMENTS: No direct comparison, but this product is fat free. Sweetened with fructose and sucrose. Sodium information is not available, but most frozen fruit bars are very low in sodium.

PRODUCT	SERV	CAL	FAT (G)	% cal from fat	CHOL (mg)	SOD (mg)
Frozen bars (Frozfruit Mango)	1 bar	70	0	0	0	na

LITE PICK ○◇

COMMENTS: No direct comparison, but this product is fat free. Sweetened with fructose and sucrose. Sodium information is not available, but most frozen fruit bars are very low in sodium.

PRODUCT	SERV	CAL	FAT (G)	% cal from fat	CHOL (mg)	SOD (mg)
Frozen bars (Frozfruit, Orange)	1 bar	70	0	0	0	na

LITE PICK ○◇

COMMENTS: No direct comparison, but this product is fat free. Sweetened with fructose and sucrose. No sodium information is available, but most frozen fruit bars are very low in sodium.

PRODUCT	SERV	CAL	FAT (G)	% cal from fat	CHOL (mg)	SOD (mg)
Frozen bars (Frozfruit, Peach)	1 bar	70	0	0	0	na

LITE PICK ○◇

COMMENTS: No direct comparison, but this product is fat free. Sweetened with fructose and sucrose. No sodium information is available, but most frozen fruit bars are very low in sodium.

PRODUCT	SERV	CAL	FAT (G)	% cal from fat	CHOL (mg)	SOD (mg)
Frozen bars (Frozfruit, Pineapple)	1 bar	70	0	0	0	na

LITE PICK ○◇

COMMENTS: No direct comparison, but this product is fat free. Sweetened with fructose and sucrose. No sodium information is available, but most frozen fruit bars are very low in sodium.

PRODUCT	SERV	CAL	FAT (G)	% cal from fat	CHOL (mg)	SOD (mg)
Frozen bars (Frozfruit, Raspberry)	1 bar	70	0	0	0	na

LITE PICK ○◇

COMMENTS: No direct comparison, but this product is fat free. Sweetened with fructose and sucrose. Sodium information is not available, but most frozen fruit bars are very low in sodium.

PRODUCT	SERV	CAL	FAT (G)	% cal from fat	CHOL (mg)	SOD (mg)
Frozen bars (Frozfruit, Strawberry)	1 bar	70	0	0	0	na

LITE PICK ○◇

COMMENTS: No direct comparison, but this product is fat free. Sweetened with fructose and sucrose. Sodium information is not available, but most frozen fruit bars are very low in sodium.

PRODUCT	SERV	CAL	FAT (G)	% cal from fat	CHOL (mg)	SOD (mg)
Frozen bars (Frozfruit, Watermelon)	1 bar	70	0	0	0	na

LITE PICK ○◇

COMMENTS: No direct comparison, but this product is fat free. Sweetened with fructose and sucrose. Sodium information is not available, but most frozen fruit bars are very low in sodium.

PRODUCT	SERV	CAL	FAT (G)	% cal from fat	CHOL (mg)	SOD (mg)
Frozen bars (Fruit-A-Freeze, Coconut)	1 bar	110	1	8	na	30

○□□

COMMENTS: Very low in fat. Since cream is an ingredient in this product, it may contain some cholesterol.

PRODUCT	SERV	CAL	FAT (G)	% cal from fat	CHOL (mg)	SOD (mg)
Frozen bars (Fruit-A-Freeze, Pineapple)	1 bar	70	0	0	0	3

LITE PICK ○◇□

COMMENTS: No direct comparison, but this product is fat free.

PRODUCT	SERV	CAL	FAT (G)	% cal from fat	CHOL (mg)	SOD (mg)
Frozen bars (Fruit-A-Freeze, Strawberry)	1 bar	90	1	10	0	25

LITE PICK ○□□

COMMENTS: No direct comparison, but this product is very low in fat. Since cream is an ingredient in this product, it may contain some cholesterol.

PRODUCT	SERV	CAL	FAT (G)	% cal from fat	CHOL (mg)	SOD (mg)
Frozen bars (Fruit-A-Freeze, Watermelon)	1 bar	50	0	0	0	4

LITE PICK ○◇□

COMMENTS: No direct comparison, but this product is fat free.

PRODUCT	SERV	CAL	FAT (G)	% cal from fat	CHOL (mg)	SOD (mg)
Frozen bars (Weight Watchers, Chocolate Mousse)	1¾ oz	35	<1	<26	na	30

○□□

COMMENTS: No direct comparison, but this product is low in fat and sodium. It is not a lite pick because cholesterol information is not available.

PRODUCT	SERV	CAL	FAT (G)	% cal from fat	CHOL (mg)	SOD (mg)
Frozen bars (Weight Watchers, Chocolate Treat)	2¾ oz	100	1	9	na	75

○☐☐☐

COMMENTS: No direct comparison, but this product is very low in fat. It is not a lite pick because cholesterol information is not available.

PRODUCT	SERV	CAL	FAT (G)	% cal from fat	CHOL (mg)	SOD (mg)
Frozen bars (Weight Watchers, Chocolate Dip)	1¾ oz	110	7	57	na	35

☐☐

COMMENTS: No direct comparison, but this product is very high in fat, and low in sodium.

PRODUCT	SERV	CAL	FAT (G)	% cal from fat	CHOL (mg)	SOD (mg)
Frozen bars (Weight Watchers, Chocolate Mint Treat)	1¾ oz	60	1	15	na	50

○☐☐☐

COMMENTS: No direct comparison, but this product is very low in fat. It is not a lite pick because cholesterol information is not available.

PRODUCT	SERV	CAL	FAT (G)	% cal from fat	CHOL (mg)	SOD (mg)
Frozen bars (Weight Watchers, Double Fudge Treat)	1¾ oz	60	1	15	na	50

○□□□

COMMENTS: No direct comparison, but this product is very low in fat. It is not a lite pick because cholesterol information is not available.

PRODUCT	SERV	CAL	FAT (G)	% cal from fat	CHOL (mg)	SOD (mg)
Frozen bars (Weight Watchers, Fruit Juice)	1 bar	35	0	0	0	10

LITE PICK ○◇□□

COMMENTS: No direct comparison, but this product is fat free and low in sodium.

PRODUCT	SERV	CAL	FAT (G)	% cal from fat	CHOL (mg)	SOD (mg)
Frozen bars (Weight Watchers, Orange-Vanilla Treat)	1¾ oz	60	1	15	na	50

○□□□

COMMENTS: No direct comparison, but this product is very low in fat.

Frozen bars
(Weight Watchers,
Vanilla Ice Milk

PRODUCT	SERV	CAL	FAT (G)	% cal from fat	CHOL (mg)	SOD (mg)
Sandwich)	1 bar	150	3	18	na	170

○

COMMENTS: 17 fewer calories, 3 grams less fat than one regular ice cream sandwich bar, but 76 milligrams *more* sodium. Very low in fat.

Frozen dairy dessert
(Baskin Robbins,
Low, Lite n' Luscious

PRODUCT	SERV	CAL	FAT (G)	% cal from fat	CHOL (mg)	SOD (mg)
Chunky Banana)	4 oz	100	2	18	3	47

LITE PICK ○◇◇□□□

COMMENTS: No direct comparison, but this product is very low in fat.

Frozen dairy dessert
(Baskin Robbins,
Low, Lite n' Luscious

PRODUCT	SERV	CAL	FAT (G)	% cal from fat	CHOL (mg)	SOD (mg)
Jamocha(r) Chip)	4 oz	110	2	16	na	48

LITE PICK ○◇◇□□□

COMMENTS: No direct comparison, but this product is very low in fat.

PRODUCT	SERV	CAL	FAT (G)	% cal from fat	CHOL (mg)	SOD (mg)
Frozen dairy dessert (Baskin Robbins, Low, Lite n' Luscious Pineapple Coconut)	4 oz	110	2	16	3	50

LITE PICK ○◇◇□□□

COMMENTS: No direct comparison, but this product is very low in fat.

PRODUCT	SERV	CAL	FAT (G)	% cal from fat	CHOL (mg)	SOD (mg)
Frozen dairy dessert (Dreyer's, Grand Light Berry Wonderful)	4 oz	110	4	33	30	50

□□□

COMMENTS: No direct comparison, but this product is lower in fat than most ice cream.

PRODUCT	SERV	CAL	FAT (G)	% cal from fat	CHOL (mg)	SOD (mg)
Frozen dairy dessert (Dreyer's, Grand Light Chocolate Chip)	4 oz	120	5	38	30	50

□□□

COMMENTS: 30 fewer calories, 4 grams less fat than 4 ounces regular Dreyer's Grand Chocolate Chip Ice Cream, with the same amount of cholesterol, but 10 milligrams *more* sodium.

PRODUCT	SERV	CAL	FAT (G)	% cal from fat	CHOL (mg)	SOD (mg)
Frozen dairy dessert (Dreyer's, Grand Light Chocolate Fudge Mousse)	4 oz	130	5	35	30	60

□□□

COMMENTS: No direct comparison. Though lower in fat than most regular ice cream, it is still high in fat.

PRODUCT	SERV	CAL	FAT (G)	% cal from fat	CHOL (mg)	SOD (mg)
Frozen dairy dessert (Dreyer's, Grand Light Chocolate)	4 oz	110	4	33	30	50

□□□

COMMENTS: No direct comparison, but this product is lower in fat than most chocolate ice cream.

PRODUCT	SERV	CAL	FAT (G)	% cal from fat	CHOL (mg)	SOD (mg)
Frozen dairy dessert (Dreyer's, Grand Light Coffee)	4 oz	100	4	36	30	50

□□□

COMMENTS: No direct comparison, but this product is lower in fat than most ice cream.

PRODUCT	SERV	CAL	FAT (G)	% cal from fat	CHOL (mg)	SOD (mg)
Frozen dairy dessert (Dreyer's, Grand Light Cookies n' Cream)	4 oz	120	5	38	30	60

□□□

COMMENTS: 40 fewer calories, 4 grams less fat, 20 milligrams less sodium than 4 ounces regular Dreyer's Cookies n' Cream Ice Cream, but 2 milligrams *more* cholesterol.

PRODUCT	SERV	CAL	FAT (G)	% cal from fat	CHOL (mg)	SOD (mg)
Frozen dairy dessert (Dreyer's, Grand Light Marble Fudge)	4 oz	120	4	30	30	60

○□□□

COMMENTS: 30 fewer calories, 4 grams less fat than 4 ounces regular Dreyer's Grand Marble Fudge Ice Cream, but 2 milligrams cholesterol and 10 milligrams *more* sodium.

PRODUCT	SERV	CAL	FAT (G)	% cal from fat	CHOL (mg)	SOD (mg)
Frozen dairy dessert (Dreyer's, Grand Light Mint Chocolate Chip)	4 oz	120	5	38	30	50

□□□

COMMENTS: No direct comparison. Though lower in fat than most ice cream, this product is still high in fat.

PRODUCT	SERV	CAL	FAT (G)	% cal from fat	CHOL (mg)	SOD (mg)
Frozen dairy dessert (Dreyer's, Grand Light New York Blueberry Cheesecake)	4 oz	110	4	33	30	50

□□□

COMMENTS: No direct comparison, but this product is lower in fat than most ice cream.

PRODUCT	SERV	CAL	FAT (G)	% cal from fat	CHOL (mg)	SOD (mg)
Frozen dairy dessert (Dreyer's, Grand Light Rocky Road)	4 oz	130	5	35	30	50

COMMENTS: 40 fewer calories, 5 grams less fat than 4 ounces regular Dreyer's Grand Rocky Road Ice Cream, but 20 milligrams *more* sodium.

PRODUCT	SERV	CAL	FAT (G)	% cal from fat	CHOL (mg)	SOD (mg)
Frozen dairy dessert (Dreyer's, Grand Light Strawberries n' Cream)	4 oz	100	4	36	30	40

□ □ □

COMMENTS: 30 fewer calories, 3 grams less fat than 4 ounces regular Dreyer's Grand Strawberries n' Cream Ice Cream, with the same amount of sodium but 4 milligrams *more* cholesterol.

PRODUCT	SERV	CAL	FAT (G)	% cal from fat	CHOL (mg)	SOD (mg)
Frozen dairy dessert (Dreyer's, Grand Light Strawberry)	4 oz	110	4	33	30	50

□ □ □

COMMENTS: No direct comparison, but this product is lower in fat than most strawberry ice cream.

PRODUCT	SERV	CAL	FAT (G)	% cal from fat	CHOL (mg)	SOD (mg)
Frozen dairy dessert (Dreyer's, Grand Light Tempting Toffee Crunch)	4 oz	120	5	38	30	80

□ □ □

COMMENTS: No direct comparison. Though lower in fat than regular ice cream, this product is still high in fat.

PRODUCT	SERV	CAL	FAT (G)	% cal from fat	CHOL (mg)	SOD (mg)
Frozen dairy dessert (Dreyer's, Grand Light Vanilla)	4 oz	100	4	36	30	50

□□□

COMMENTS: 60 fewer calories, 6 grams less fat, 10 milligrams less cholesterol than 4 ounces regular Dreyer's Vanilla Grand Ice Cream.

PRODUCT	SERV	CAL	FAT (G)	% cal from fat	CHOL (mg)	SOD (mg)
Frozen nondairy dessert (American Glacé, Soft Serve, California Chocolate)	4 oz	48	0	0	0	<35

LITE PICK ○◇□□

COMMENTS: No direct comparison, but this product is fat free.

PRODUCT	SERV	CAL	FAT (G)	% cal from fat	CHOL (mg)	SOD (mg)
Frozen nondairy dessert (American Glacé, Soft Serve, Dutch Chocolate)	4 oz	48	0	0	0	<35

LITE PICK ○◇□□

COMMENTS: No direct comparison, but this product is fat free.

PRODUCT	SERV	CAL	FAT (G)	% cal from fat	CHOL (mg)	SOD (mg)
Frozen nondairy dessert (American Glacé, Soft Serve, Kona Coffee)	4 oz	48	0	0	0	<35

LITE PICK ○◇□□

COMMENTS: No direct comparison, but this product is fat free.

PRODUCT	SERV	CAL	FAT (G)	% cal from fat	CHOL (mg)	SOD (mg)
Frozen nondairy dessert (American Glacé, Soft Serve, Red Raspberry)	4 oz	48	0	0	0	<35

LITE PICK ○◇□□

COMMENTS: No direct comparison, but this product is fat free.

PRODUCT	SERV	CAL	FAT (G)	% cal from fat	CHOL (mg)	SOD (mg)
Frozen nondairy dessert (American Glacé, Soft Serve, Strawberry)	4 oz	48	0	0	0	<35

LITE PICK ○◇□□

COMMENTS: No direct comparison, but this product is fat free.

PRODUCT	SERV	CAL	FAT (G)	% cal from fat	CHOL (mg)	SOD (mg)
Frozen nondairy dessert (American Glacé, Soft Serve, Tahitian Vanilla)	4 oz	48	0	0	0	<35

LITE PICK ○◇□□

COMMENTS: No direct comparison, but this product is fat free.

PRODUCT	SERV	CAL	FAT (G)	% cal from fat	CHOL (mg)	SOD (mg)
Frozen nondairy dessert (Tofutti Cuties, Frutti)	2 oz	55	<1	<16	0	20

LITE PICK ○◇□□

COMMENTS: No direct comparison. Very low in fat.

PRODUCT	SERV	CAL	FAT (G)	% cal from fat	CHOL (mg)	SOD (mg)
Frozen nondairy dessert (Tofutti Cuties, Key Lime)	2 oz	55	<1	<16	0	20

LITE PICK ○◇□□

COMMENTS: No direct comparison. Very low in fat.

PRODUCT	SERV	CAL	FAT (G)	% cal from fat	CHOL (mg)	SOD (mg)
Frozen nondairy dessert (Tofutti Cuties, Raspberry)	2 oz	55	<1	<16	0	20
LITE PICK ○◇□□						

COMMENTS: No direct comparison. Very low in fat.

PRODUCT	SERV	CAL	FAT (G)	% cal from fat	CHOL (mg)	SOD (mg)
Frozen nondairy dessert (Tofutti Cuties, Strawberry)	2 oz	55	<1	<16	0	20
LITE PICK ○◇□□						

COMMENTS: No direct comparison. Very low in fat.

PRODUCT	SERV	CAL	FAT (G)	% cal from fat	CHOL (mg)	SOD (mg)
Frozen nondairy dessert (Tofutti Cuties, Tutti-Frutti)	2 oz	55	<1	<16	0	20
LITE PICK ○◇□□						

COMMENTS: No direct comparison. Very low in fat.

PRODUCT	SERV	CAL	FAT (G)	% cal from fat	CHOL (mg)	SOD (mg)
Frozen nondairy dessert (Tofutti, Lite-lite Hard Pack, all flavors)	4 oz	90	<1	<10	0	80

LITE PICK ○◇□□□

COMMENTS: 110 fewer calories, 10 grams less fat, 10 milligrams less sodium than 4 ounces regular Tofutti. Very low in fat.

PRODUCT	SERV	CAL	FAT (G)	% cal from fat	CHOL (mg)	SOD (mg)
Frozen nondairy dessert (Tofutti, Lite-lite Soft Serve, all flavors)	4 oz	90	<1	<10	0	80

LITE PICK ○◇□□□

COMMENTS: 110 fewer calories, 10 grams less fat, 10 milligrams less sodium than 4 ounces regular vanilla Tofutti. Very low in fat.

PRODUCT	SERV	CAL	FAT (G)	% cal from fat	CHOL (mg)	SOD (mg)
Frozen cakes and pies (Formagg, Amaretto Almond le Creame Cake)	2 oz	120	7	53	0	0

◇□

COMMENTS: 43 fewer calories, 1 gram less fat, 108 milligrams less sodium than 2 ounces regular cheesecake, but still very high in fat. Note the small serving size.

PRODUCT	SERV	CAL	FAT (G)	% cal from fat	CHOL (mg)	SOD (mg)
Frozen cakes and pies (Formagg, Pineapple le Creame Cake)	2 oz	120	7	53	0	0

◇□

COMMENTS: 43 fewer calories, 1 gram less fat, 108 milligrams less sodium than 2 ounces regular cheesecake, but still very high in fat. Note the small serving size.

PRODUCT	SERV	CAL	FAT (G)	% cal from fat	CHOL (mg)	SOD (mg)
Frozen cakes and pies (Formagg, Plain le Creame Cake)	2 oz	120	7	53	0	0

◇□

COMMENTS: 43 fewer calories, 1 gram less fat, 108 milligrams less sodium than 2 ounces regular cheesecake, but still very high in fat. Note the small serving size.

PRODUCT	SERV	CAL	FAT (G)	% cal from fat	CHOL (mg)	SOD (mg)
Frozen cakes and pies (Formagg, Strawberry le Creame Cake)	2 oz	120	7	53	0	0

◇□

COMMENTS: 43 fewer calories, 1 gram less fat, 108 milligrams less sodium than 2 ounces regular cheesecake, but still very high in fat. Note the small serving size.

PRODUCT	SERV	CAL	FAT (G)	% cal from fat	CHOL (mg)	SOD (mg)
Frozen cakes and pies (Pepperidge Farm, Cholesterol-Free Pound Cake)	1 oz	110	6	49	0	90

◇☐☐☐

COMMENTS: 20 fewer calories, 1 gram less fat, 50 milligrams less cholesterol, 60 milligrams less sodium than 1 ounce regular Pepperidge Farm Pound Cake. Note the small serving size.

PRODUCT	SERV	CAL	FAT (G)	% cal from fat	CHOL (mg)	SOD (mg)
Frozen cakes and pies (Weight Watchers, Apple Pie)	3½ oz	190	5	24	10	270

○◇◇

COMMENTS: 49 fewer calories, 5 grams less fat, 4 milligrams less cholesterol, 88 milligrams less sodium than an equal slice of regular frozen apple pie. However, Weight Watchers slices are about 40% smaller than a regular slice of apple pie.

PRODUCT	SERV	CAL	FAT (G)	% cal from fat	CHOL (mg)	SOD (mg)
Frozen cakes and pies (Weight Watchers, Apple Sweet Roll)	2½ oz	190	5	24	15	160

○◇◇

COMMENTS: 42 fewer calories, 4 grams less fat, 51 milligrams less sodium than an equal amount of regular apple Danish.

PRODUCT	SERV	CAL	FAT (G)	% cal from fat	CHOL (mg)	SOD (mg)
Frozen cakes and pies (Weight Watchers, Boston Cream Pie)	3 oz	170	4	21	5	290

○◇◇

COMMENTS: 14 fewer calories, 3 grams less fat, 9 milligrams less cholesterol than an equal amount of regular frozen Boston cream pie, but 131 milligrams *more* sodium.

PRODUCT	SERV	CAL	FAT (G)	% cal from fat	CHOL (mg)	SOD (mg)
Frozen cakes and pies (Weight Watchers, Cheesecake)	3.9 oz	220	7	29	25	290

○

COMMENTS: 98 fewer calories, 9 grams less fat than an equal serving of regular frozen cheesecake, but 78 milligrams *more* sodium.

PRODUCT	SERV	CAL	FAT (G)	% cal from fat	CHOL (mg)	SOD (mg)
Frozen cakes and pies (Weight Watchers, Chocolate Brownie)	1¼ oz	100	4	36	10	150

◇◇

COMMENTS: 46 fewer calories, 3 grams less fat than an equal serving of a regular frozen brownie, but 68 milligrams *more* sodium. Note small serving size.

PRODUCT	SERV	CAL	FAT (G)	% cal from fat	CHOL (mg)	SOD (mg)
Frozen cakes and pies (Weight Watchers, Chocolate Cake)	2½ oz	180	5	25	5	320

○◇◇

COMMENTS: 99 fewer calories, 8 grams less fat than an equal serving of regular frozen chocolate cake, but 117 milligrams *more* sodium. Note small serving size.

PRODUCT	SERV	CAL	FAT (G)	% cal from fat	CHOL (mg)	SOD (mg)
Frozen cakes and pies (Weight Watchers, German Chocolate Cake)	2½ oz	190	7	33	10	350

◇◇

COMMENTS: 91 fewer calories, 9 grams less fat than an equal amount of regular frozen German chocolate cake, but 133 milligrams *more* sodium. Note the small serving size.

PRODUCT	SERV	CAL	FAT (G)	% cal from fat	CHOL (mg)	SOD (mg)
Frozen cakes and pies (Weight Watchers Pound Cake with Blueberry Topping)	2½ oz	180	6	30	15	200

◇◇◇

COMMENTS: 102 fewer calories, 11 grams less fat, 35 milligrams less sodium than a 2½ ounce slice of regular frozen pound cake. Note the small serving size.

PRODUCT	SERV	CAL	FAT (G)	% cal from fat	CHOL (mg)	SOD (mg)
Frozen cakes and pies (Weight Watchers, Strawberry Cheesecake)	3.9 oz	180	5	25	20	240

○◇◇

COMMENTS: 94 fewer calories, 5 grams less fat than an equal amount of regular frozen strawberry cheesecake, but 29 milligrams *more* sodium.

PRODUCT	SERV	CAL	FAT (G)	% cal from fat	CHOL (mg)	SOD (mg)
Frozen cakes and pies (Weight Watchers, Strawberry Shortcake)	3 oz	160	4	23	0	180

○◇

COMMENTS: 7 fewer calories than an equal amount of strawberry shortcake. However, Weight Watchers serving size is one half the size of regular strawberry shortcake.

PRODUCT	SERV	CAL	FAT (G)	% cal from fat	CHOL (mg)	SOD (mg)
Frozen mousse (Weight Watchers, Chocolate Mousse)	2½ oz	170	6	32	10	180

◇◇

COMMENTS: 32 more calories, 6 grams less fat, 74 milligrams less cholesterol and 137 milligrams *more* sodium than an equal serving of regular chocolate mousse. Note the small serving size.

PRODUCT	SERV	CAL	FAT (G)	% cal from fat	CHOL (mg)	SOD (mg)
Frozen mousse (Weight Watchers, Raspberry Mousse)	2½ oz	160	6	34	20	160

◇◇

COMMENTS: No direct comparison.

PRODUCT	SERV	CAL	FAT (G)	% cal from fat	CHOL (mg)	SOD (mg)
Frozen yogurt (Baskin Robbins, Apple Cinnamon)	4 oz	124	2	15	8	54

LITE PICK ○◇◇□□□

COMMENTS: No direct comparison. Very low in fat.

PRODUCT	SERV	CAL	FAT (G)	% cal from fat	CHOL (mg)	SOD (mg)
Frozen yogurt (Baskin Robbins, Banana)	4 oz	124	2	15	8	54

LITE PICK ○◇◇□□□

COMMENTS: No direct comparison. Very low in fat.

PRODUCT	SERV	CAL	FAT (G)	% cal from fat	CHOL (mg)	SOD (mg)
Frozen yogurt (Baskin Robbins, Black Cherry)	4 oz	124	2	15	8	54

LITE PICK ○◇◇□□□

COMMENTS: No direct comparison. Very low in fat.

PRODUCT	SERV	CAL	FAT (G)	% cal from fat	CHOL (mg)	SOD (mg)
Frozen yogurt (Baskin Robbins, Blueberry	4 oz	124	2	15	8	54

LITE PICK ○◇◇□□□

COMMENTS: No direct comparison. Very low in fat.

PRODUCT	SERV	CAL	FAT (G)	% cal from fat	CHOL (mg)	SOD (mg)
Frozen yogurt (Baskin Robbins, Cappuccino)	4 oz	124	2	15	8	54

LITE PICK ○◇◇□□□

COMMENTS: No direct comparison. Very low in fat.

PRODUCT	SERV	CAL	FAT (G)	% cal from fat	CHOL (mg)	SOD (mg)
Frozen yogurt (Baskin Robbins, Cheesecake)	4 oz	124	2	15	8	54

LITE PICK ○◇◇□□□

COMMENTS: No direct comparison. Very low in fat.

PRODUCT	SERV	CAL	FAT (G)	% cal from fat	CHOL (mg)	SOD (mg)
Frozen yogurt (Baskin Robbins, Chocolate Mint)	4 oz	124	2	15	8	54

LITE PICK ○◇◇□□□

COMMENTS: No direct comparison. Very low in fat.

PRODUCT	SERV	CAL	FAT (G)	% cal from fat	CHOL (mg)	SOD (mg)
Frozen yogurt (Baskin Robbins, Chocolate Raspberry)	4 oz	124	2	15	8	54

LITE PICK ○◇◇□□□

COMMENTS: No direct comparison. Very low in fat.

PRODUCT	SERV	CAL	FAT (G)	% cal from fat	CHOL (mg)	SOD (mg)
Frozen yogurt (Baskin Robbins, Chocolate)	4 oz	124	2	15	8	54

LITE PICK ○◇◇□□□

COMMENTS: No direct comparison. Very low in fat.

PRODUCT	SERV	CAL	FAT (G)	% cal from fat	CHOL (mg)	SOD (mg)
Frozen yogurt (Baskin Robbins, Coconut)	4 oz	124	2	15	8	54

LITE PICK ○◇◇□□□

COMMENTS: No direct comparison. Very low in fat.

PRODUCT	SERV	CAL	FAT (G)	% cal from fat	CHOL (mg)	SOD (mg)
Frozen yogurt (Baskin Robbins, Grand Marnier®)	4 oz	124	2	15	8	54

LITE PICK ○◇◇□□□

COMMENTS: No direct comparison. Very low in fat.

PRODUCT	SERV	CAL	FAT (G)	% cal from fat	CHOL (mg)	SOD (mg)

Frozen yogurt
(Baskin Robbins, Jamoca®)

| | 4 oz | 124 | 2 | 15 | 8 | 54 |

LITE PICK ○◇◇□□□

COMMENTS: No direct comparison. Very low in fat.

PRODUCT	SERV	CAL	FAT (G)	% cal from fat	CHOL (mg)	SOD (mg)

Frozen yogurt
(Baskin Robbins, Kahlua®)

| | 4 oz | 124 | 2 | 15 | 8 | 54 |

LITE PICK ○◇◇□□□

COMMENTS: No direct comparison. Very low in fat.

PRODUCT	SERV	CAL	FAT (G)	% cal from fat	CHOL (mg)	SOD (mg)

Frozen yogurt
(Baskin Robbins, Mandarin Chocolate)

| | 4 oz | 124 | 2 | 15 | 8 | 54 |

LITE PICK ○◇◇□□□

COMMENTS: No direct comparison. Very low in fat.

PRODUCT	SERV	CAL	FAT (G)	% cal from fat	CHOL (mg)	SOD (mg)
Frozen yogurt (Baskin Robbins, Mixed Berry)	4 oz	124	2	15	8	54

LITE PICK ○◇◇□□□

COMMENTS: No direct comparison. Very low in fat.

PRODUCT	SERV	CAL	FAT (G)	% cal from fat	CHOL (mg)	SOD (mg)
Frozen yogurt (Baskin Robbins, Peach)	4 oz	124	2	15	8	54

LITE PICK ○◇◇□□□

COMMENTS: No direct comparison. Very low in fat.

PRODUCT	SERV	CAL	FAT (G)	% cal from fat	CHOL (mg)	SOD (mg)
Frozen yogurt (Baskin Robbins, Peanut Butter)	4 oz	124	2	15	8	54

LITE PICK ○◇◇□□□

COMMENTS: No direct comparison. Very low in fat.

PRODUCT	SERV	CAL	FAT (G)	% cal from fat	CHOL (mg)	SOD (mg)
Frozen yogurt (Baskin Robbins, Raspberry)	4 oz	124	2	15	8	54

LITE PICK ○◇◇□□□

COMMENTS: No direct comparison. Very low in fat.

PRODUCT	SERV	CAL	FAT (G)	% cal from fat	CHOL (mg)	SOD (mg)
Frozen yogurt (Baskin Robbins, Strawberry)	4 oz	124	2	15	8	54

LITE PICK ○◇◇□□□

COMMENTS: No direct comparison. Very low in fat.

PRODUCT	SERV	CAL	FAT (G)	% cal from fat	CHOL (mg)	SOD (mg)
Frozen yogurt (Baskin Robbins, Sunny Orange)	4 oz	124	2	15	8	54

LITE PICK ○◇◇□□□

COMMENTS: No direct comparison. Very low in fat.

PRODUCT	SERV	CAL	FAT (G)	% cal from fat	CHOL (mg)	SOD (mg)
Frozen yogurt (Baskin Robbins, Vanilla)	4 oz	124	2	15	8	54

LITE PICK ○◇◇□□□

COMMENTS: No direct comparison. Very low in fat.

PRODUCT	SERV	CAL	FAT (G)	% cal from fat	CHOL (mg)	SOD (mg)
Frozen yogurt (Baskin Robbins, White Chocolate)	4 oz	124	2	15	8	54

LITE PICK ○◇◇□□□

COMMENTS: No direct comparison. Very low in fat.

PRODUCT	SERV	CAL	FAT (G)	% cal from fat	CHOL (mg)	SOD (mg)
Frozen yogurt (Colombo, Lite Nonfat)	4 oz	95	0	0	0	70

LITE PICK ○◇□□□

COMMENTS: 4 fewer calories, 2 grams less fat, 10 milligrams less cholesterol, 35 milligrams less sodium than 4 ounces regular Colombo Lowfat Frozen Yogurt.

PRODUCT	SERV	CAL	FAT (G)	% cal from fat	CHOL (mg)	SOD (mg)
Frozen yogurt (Tuscan, Lowfat Hard Pack, Chocolate)	4 fl oz	120	2	15	3.77	110

LITE PICK ○◇◇□□□

COMMENTS: No direct comparison. Very low in fat.

PRODUCT	SERV	CAL	FAT (G)	% cal from fat	CHOL (mg)	SOD (mg)
Frozen yogurt (Tuscan, Lowfat Hard Pack, Coffee)	4 fl oz	110	1	8	3.80	100

LITE PICK ○◇◇□□□

COMMENTS: No direct comparison. Very low in fat.

PRODUCT	SERV	CAL	FAT (G)	% cal from fat	CHOL (mg)	SOD (mg)
Frozen yogurt (Tuscan, Lowfat Hard Pack, Strawberry)	4 fl oz	115	1	8	3.82	100

LITE PICK ○◇◇□□□

COMMENTS: No direct comparison. Very low in fat.

PRODUCT	SERV	CAL	FAT (G)	% cal from fat	CHOL (mg)	SOD (mg)
Frozen yogurt (Tuscan, Lowfat Hard Pack, Vanilla)	4 fl oz	110	1	8	3.80	100

LITE PICK ○◇◇□□□

COMMENTS: No direct comparison. Very low in fat.

PRODUCT	SERV	CAL	FAT (G)	% cal from fat	CHOL (mg)	SOD (mg)
Frozen yogurt (Tuscan, Lowfat On a Stick, Chocolate coated Chocolate)	1 bar	150	8	48	3.14	65

◇◇□□□

COMMENTS: Only the yogurt is low fat. Adding the chocolate coating makes this product very high in fat.

PRODUCT	SERV	CAL	FAT (G)	% cal from fat	CHOL (mg)	SOD (mg)
Frozen yogurt (Tuscan, Lowfat On a Stick, Chocolate Coated Coffee)	1 bar	130	6	42	2.47	60

◇◇□□□

COMMENTS: Only the yogurt is low fat. Adding the chocolate coating makes this product very high in fat.

PRODUCT	SERV	CAL	FAT (G)	% cal from fat	CHOL (mg)	SOD (mg)

Frozen yogurt
(Tuscan, Lowfat On a Stick, Chocolate Coated Strawberry)

| | 1 bar | 130 | 7 | 48 | 2.47 | 60 |

◇◇□□□

COMMENTS: Only the yogurt is low fat. Adding the chocolate coating makes this product very high in fat.

PRODUCT	SERV	CAL	FAT (G)	% cal from fat	CHOL (mg)	SOD (mg)

Frozen yogurt
(Tuscan, Lowfat On A Stick, Chocolate Coated Vanilla)

| | 1 bar | 130 | 6 | 42 | 2.47 | 75 |

◇◇□□□

COMMENTS: Only the yogurt is low fat. Adding the chocolate coating makes this product very high in fat.

PRODUCT	SERV	CAL	FAT (G)	% cal from fat	CHOL (mg)	SOD (mg)

Frozen yogurt
(Tuscan, Lowfat On a Stick, Chocolate)

| | 2½ oz | 85 | 1 | 11 | 2.85 | 65 |

LITE PICK ○◇◇□□□

COMMENTS: No direct comparison. Very low in fat.

PRODUCT	SERV	CAL	FAT (G)	% cal from fat	CHOL (mg)	SOD (mg)
Frozen yogurt (Tuscan, Lowfat On a Stick, Honey Granola Coated Vanilla)	1 bar	160	8	45	na	100

□□□

COMMENTS: Only the yogurt is low fat. Adding the honey granola coating makes this product very high in fat.

PRODUCT	SERV	CAL	FAT (G)	% cal from fat	CHOL (mg)	SOD (mg)
Frozen yogurt (Tuscan, Lowfat On a Stick, Strawberry)	1 bar	70	1	13	2.18	40

LITE PICK ○○◇□□□

COMMENTS: Very low in fat.

PRODUCT	SERV	CAL	FAT (G)	% cal from fat	CHOL (mg)	SOD (mg)
Frozen yogurt (The Yogurt Lover's Yogurt, Soft Serve Chocolate)	4 oz	84	1.9	20	6	73

LITE PICK ○○◇□□□

COMMENTS: No direct comparison. Very low in fat.

PRODUCT	SERV	CAL	FAT (G)	% cal from fat	CHOL (mg)	SOD (mg)
Frozen yogurt (The Yogurt Lover's Yogurt, Soft Serve Vanilla)	4 oz	86	1.7	18	6.5	67

LITE PICK ○◇◇□□□

COMMENTS: No direct comparison. Very low in fat.

PRODUCT	SERV	CAL	FAT (G)	% cal from fat	CHOL (mg)	SOD (mg)
Frozen yogurt (Yoplait, Lowfat, Chocolate)	3 oz	90	3	30	10	50

LITE PICK ○◇◇□□□

COMMENTS: No direct comparison, but is low in fat.

PRODUCT	SERV	CAL	FAT (G)	% cal from fat	CHOL (mg)	SOD (mg)
Frozen yogurt (Yoplait, Lowfat, Coffee)	3 oz	90	3	30	10	50

LITE PICK ○◇◇□□□

COMMENTS: No direct comparison, but is low in fat.

PRODUCT	SERV	CAL	FAT (G)	% cal from fat	CHOL (mg)	SOD (mg)
Frozen yogurt (Yoplait Lowfat, Fruit Flavors)	3 oz	90	3	30	10	50

LITE PICK ○◇◇□□□

COMMENTS: No direct comparison, but is low in fat.

PRODUCT	SERV	CAL	FAT (G)	% cal from fat	CHOL (mg)	SOD (mg)
Frozen yogurt (Yoplait Lowfat, Vanilla Chocolate Chip)	3 oz	110	5	41	na	50

□□□

COMMENTS: No direct comparison. Very high in fat.

PRODUCT	SERV	CAL	FAT (G)	% cal from fat	CHOL (mg)	SOD (mg)
Frozen yogurt (Yoplait Lowfat, Vanilla)	3 oz	90	3	30	10	50

LITE PICK ○◇◇□□□

COMMENTS: No direct comparison, but is low in fat.

PRODUCT	SERV	CAL	FAT (G)	% cal from fat	CHOL (mg)	SOD (mg)
Ice milk (Borden, Light Chocolate)	½ c	100	2	18	na	80

LITE PICK ○□□□

COMMENTS: 30 fewer calories, 4 grams less fat than ½ cup regular Borden's Olde Fashioned Recipe Dutch Chocolate Ice Cream. Very low in fat. (No cholesterol information is available for this product, but most ice milk falls within the low cholesterol category.)

PRODUCT	SERV	CAL	FAT (G)	% cal from fat	CHOL (mg)	SOD (mg)
Ice milk (Borden, Light ''Chippety'' Chocolate chip)	½ c	120	4	30	na	55

LITE PICK ○□□□

COMMENTS: No direct comparison. (No cholesterol information is available for this product, but most ice milk falls within the low cholesterol category.)

PRODUCT	SERV	CAL	FAT (G)	% cal from fat	CHOL (mg)	SOD (mg)
Ice milk (Borden, Light Cookies 'n Cream)	½ c	110	3	25	na	140

LITE PICK ○□□□

COMMENTS: No direct comparison. (No cholesterol information is available for this product, but most ice milk falls within the low cholesterol category.)

PRODUCT	SERV	CAL	FAT (G)	% cal from fat	CHOL (mg)	SOD (mg)
Ice milk (Borden, Light Honey Roasted Maple Walnut)	½ c	130	5	35	na	55

□□□

COMMENTS: No direct comparison. (No cholesterol information is available, but most ice milk falls within the low cholesterol category.)

PRODUCT	SERV	CAL	FAT (G)	% cal from fat	CHOL (mg)	SOD (mg)
Ice milk (Borden, Light Mocha Almond Fudge)	½ c	130	5	35	na	150

COMMENTS: No direct comparison. (No cholesterol information is available, but most ice milk falls within the low cholesterol category.)

PRODUCT	SERV	CAL	FAT (G)	% cal from fat	CHOL (mg)	SOD (mg)
Ice milk (Borden, Light Pralines 'n Cream)	½ c	110	3	25	na	140

LITE PICK ○□□□

COMMENTS: No direct comparison. (No cholesterol information is available, but most ice milk falls within the low cholesterol category.)

PRODUCT	SERV	CAL	FAT (G)	% cal from fat	CHOL (mg)	SOD (mg)
Ice milk (Borden, Light Raspberry Parfait)	½ c	110	3	25	na	140

LITE PICK ○□□□

COMMENTS: No direct comparison. (No cholesterol information is available, but most ice milk falls within the low cholesterol category.)

PRODUCT	SERV	CAL	FAT (G)	% cal from fat	CHOL (mg)	SOD (mg)
Ice milk (Borden, Light Strawberries 'n Cream)	½ c	110	3	25	na	140

LITE PICK ○□□□

COMMENTS: 20 fewer calories, 2 grams less fat than ½ cup regular Borden's Olde Fashioned Recipe Strawberries 'n Cream, but 85 milligrams *more* sodium.

PRODUCT	SERV	CAL	FAT (G)	% cal from fat	CHOL (mg)	SOD (mg)
Ice milk (Borden, Light Strawberry)	½ c	90	2	20	na	65

LITE PICK ○□□□

COMMENTS: 40 fewer calories, 4 grams less fat than ½ cup regular Borden strawberry ice cream, but 10 milligrams *more* sodium. Very low in fat. (No cholesterol information is available, but most ice milk falls within the low cholesterol category.)

PRODUCT	SERV	CAL	FAT (G)	% cal from fat	CHOL (mg)	SOD (mg)
Ice milk (Borden, Light Vanilla flavored)	½ c	110	3	25	na	55

LITE PICK ○□□□

COMMENTS: 20 fewer calories, 4 grams less fat than ½ cup regular Borden vanilla ice cream. (No cholesterol information is available, but most ice milk falls within the low cholesterol category.)

PRODUCT	SERV	CAL	FAT (G)	% cal from fat	CHOL (mg)	SOD (mg)
Ice milk (Breyer's Light Chocolate Fudge Twirl)	½ c	120	4	30	13	60

LITE PICK ○◇□□□

COMMENTS: No direct comparison, but much lower in fat than regular ice cream.

PRODUCT	SERV	CAL	FAT (G)	% cal from fat	CHOL (mg)	SOD (mg)
Ice milk (Breyer's, Light Chocolate Malt)	½ c	120	4	30	13	55

LITE PICK ○◇◇□□□

COMMENTS: No direct comparison, but much lower in fat than regular ice cream.

PRODUCT	SERV	CAL	FAT (G)	% cal from fat	CHOL (mg)	SOD (mg)

Ice milk
(Breyer's, Light
Praline Almond)

	½ c	130	5	35	15	70

◇◇□□□

COMMENTS: No direct comparison. Though lower in fat than regular ice cream, it is still high in fat.

PRODUCT	SERV	CAL	FAT (G)	% cal from fat	CHOL (mg)	SOD (mg)

Ice milk
(Breyer's, Light
Strawberry)

	½ c	110	3	25	13	50

LITE PICK ○◇◇□□□

COMMENTS: 20 fewer calories, 3 grams less fat, 2 milligrams less cholesterol but 10 milligrams *more* sodium than ½ cup regular Breyer's strawberry ice cream.

PRODUCT	SERV	CAL	FAT (G)	% cal from fat	CHOL (mg)	SOD (mg)

Ice milk
(Breyer's, Light
Toffee Fudge Parfait)

	½ c	140	5	32	15	90

LITE PICK ○◇◇□□□

COMMENTS: No direct comparison. Though lower in fat than regular ice cream, it is still high in fat.

PRODUCT	SERV	CAL	FAT (G)	% cal from fat	CHOL (mg)	SOD (mg)
Ice milk (Breyer's, Light Vanilla)	½ c	120	4	30	15	60

LITE PICK ○◇◇□□□

COMMENTS: 30 fewer calories, 4 grams less fat, 10 milligrams less cholesterol but 10 milligrams *more* sodium than ½ cup Breyer's regular vanilla ice cream.

PRODUCT	SERV	CAL	FAT (G)	% cal from fat	CHOL (mg)	SOD (mg)
Ice milk (Lite n' Lively, Caramel Nut)	½ c	120	4	30	5	100

LITE PICK ○◇◇□□□

COMMENTS: No direct comparison, but much lower in fat than regular ice cream.

PRODUCT	SERV	CAL	FAT (G)	% cal from fat	CHOL (mg)	SOD (mg)
Ice milk (Lite n' Lively, Chocolate)	½ c	110	3	25	5	65

LITE PICK ○◇◇□□□

COMMENTS: 30 fewer calories, 4 grams less fat, 10 milligrams less cholesterol, but 5 milligrams *more* sodium than ½ cup regular Sealtest chocolate ice cream. (Both Sealtest and Lite n' Lively are Borden's brands.)

PRODUCT	SERV	CAL	FAT (G)	% cal from fat	CHOL (mg)	SOD (mg)
Ice milk (Lite n' Lively, Chocolate Chip)	½ c	120	4	30	5	50

LITE PICK ○◇◇□□□

COMMENTS: 30 fewer calories, 4 grams less fat, 10 milligrams less cholesterol than ½ cup regular Sealtest chocolate chip ice cream. (Both Sealtest and Lite n' Lively are Borden's brands.)

PRODUCT	SERV	CAL	FAT (G)	% cal from fat	CHOL (mg)	SOD (mg)
Ice milk (Lite n' Lively, Coffee)	½ c	100	3	27	5	55

LITE PICK ○◇◇□□□

COMMENTS: 40 fewer calories, 4 grams less fat, 10 milligrams less cholesterol but 5 milligrams *more* sodium than ½ cup regular Sealtest coffee ice cream. (Both Sealtest and Lite n' Lively are Borden's brands.)

PRODUCT	SERV	CAL	FAT (G)	% cal from fat	CHOL (mg)	SOD (mg)
Ice milk (Lite n' Lively, Cookies n' Cream)	½ c	120	3	23	5	80

LITE PICK ○◇◇□□□

COMMENTS: 30 fewer calories, 5 grams less fat, 10 milligrams less cholesterol but 15 milligrams *more* sodium than ½ cup regular Sealtest Cookies n' Cream ice cream. (Both Sealtest and Lite n' Lively are Borden's brands.)

PRODUCT	SERV	CAL	FAT (G)	% cal from fat	CHOL (mg)	SOD (mg)
Ice milk (Lite n' Lively, Heavenly Hash)	½ c	120	4	30	14	55

LITE PICK ○◇◇□□□

COMMENTS: 30 fewer calories, 3 grams less fat, 11 milligrams less cholesterol but 15 milligrams *more* sodium than ½ cup regular Sealtest Heavenly Hash ice cream. (Both Sealtest and Lite n' Lively are Borden's brands.)

PRODUCT	SERV	CAL	FAT (G)	% cal from fat	CHOL (mg)	SOD (mg)
Ice milk (Lite n' Lively, Neapolitan)	½ c	110	3	25	5	55

LITE PICK ○◇◇□□□

COMMENTS: 30 fewer calories, 3 grams less fat, 10 milligrams less cholesterol but 15 milligrams *more* sodium than ½ cup regular Sealtest vanilla/strawberry/chocolate ice cream. (Both Sealtest and Lite n' Lively are Borden's brands.)

PRODUCT	SERV	CAL	FAT (G)	% cal from fat	CHOL (mg)	SOD (mg)
Ice milk (Lite n' Lively, Vanilla Fudge Swirl)	½ c	110	3	25	5	55

LITE PICK ○◇◇□□□

COMMENTS: 40 fewer calories, 4 grams less fat, 10 milligrams less cholesterol but 15 milligrams *more* sodium than ½ cup regular Sealtest Fudge Royale ice cream. (Both Sealtest and Lite n' Lively are Borden's brands.)

PRODUCT	SERV	CAL	FAT (G)	% cal from fat	CHOL (mg)	SOD (mg)
Ice milk (Lite n' Lively, Vanilla)	½ c	100	3	27	5	55

LITE PICK ○◇◇□□□

COMMENTS: 40 fewer calories, 4 grams less fat, 10 milligrams less cholesterol but 5 milligrams *more* sodium than ½ cup regular Sealtest vanilla ice cream. (Both Sealtest and Lite n' Lively are Borden's brands.)

PRODUCT	SERV	CAL	FAT (G)	% cal from fat	CHOL (mg)	SOD (mg)
Ice milk (Weight Watchers, Chocolate)	4 fl oz	110	3	25	na	75

LITE PICK ○□□□

COMMENTS: 38 fewer calories, 5 grams less fat than 4 ounces regular chocolate ice cream, but 37 milligrams *more* sodium. (No cholesterol information is available for this product, but most ice milk falls within the low cholesterol category.)

PRODUCT	SERV	CAL	FAT (G)	% cal from fat	CHOL (mg)	SOD (mg)
Ice milk (Weight Watchers, Fudge Marble)	4 fl oz	120	3	23	na	75

LITE PICK ○□□□

COMMENTS: No direct comparison, but is much lower in fat than ice cream. (No cholesterol information is available for this product, but most ice milk falls within the low cholesterol category.)

PRODUCT	SERV	CAL	FAT (G)	% cal from fat	CHOL (mg)	SOD (mg)
Ice milk (Weight Watchers, Fudge Marble)	4 fl oz	120	3	23	na	75

LITE PICK ○□□□

COMMENTS: No direct comparison, but is much lower in fat than ice cream. (No cholesterol information is available for this product, but most ice milk falls within the low cholesterol category.)

PRODUCT	SERV	CAL	FAT (G)	% cal from fat	CHOL (mg)	SOD (mg)
Ice milk (Weight Watchers, Neapolitan)	4 fl oz	110	3	25	na	75

LITE PICK ○□□□

COMMENTS: No direct comparison, but is much lower in fat than ice cream. (No cholesterol information is available for this product, but most ice milk falls within the low cholesterol category.)

PRODUCT	SERV	CAL	FAT (G)	% cal from fat	CHOL (mg)	SOD (mg)
Ice milk (Weight Watchers, Peaches n' Creme)	4 fl oz	120	3	23	na	75

LITE PICK ○□□□

COMMENTS: No direct comparison, but much lower in fat than ice cream. (No cholesterol information is available for this product, but most ice milk falls within the low cholesterol category.)

PRODUCT	SERV	CAL	FAT (G)	% cal from fat	CHOL (mg)	SOD (mg)
Ice milk (Weight Watchers, Strawberries n' Creme)	4 fl oz	120	3	23	na	75

LITE PICK ○□□□

COMMENTS: No direct comparison, but much lower in fat than ice cream. (No cholesterol information is available for this product, but most ice milk falls within the low cholesterol category.)

PRODUCT	SERV	CAL	FAT (G)	% cal from fat	CHOL (mg)	SOD (mg)
Ice milk (Weight Watchers, Vanilla)	4 fl oz	100	3	27	na	75

LITE PICK ○◇◇◇

COMMENTS: 35 fewer calories, 4 grams less fat than 4 ounces regular 10% butterfat vanilla ice cream, but 17 milligrams *more* sodium. (No cholesterol information is available for this product, but most ice milk falls within the low cholesterol category.)

PRODUCT	SERV	CAL	FAT (G)	% cal from fat	CHOL (mg)	SOD (mg)
Shake (Vitari, Peach)	12 oz	150	0	0	0	400

○◇

COMMENTS: High in sodium, but fat free.

PRODUCT	SERV	CAL	FAT (G)	% cal from fat	CHOL (mg)	SOD (mg)
Shake (Vitari, Strawberry)	12 oz	150	0	0	0	380

○◇

COMMENTS: High in sodium, but fat free.

FRUIT

PRODUCT	SERV	CAL	FAT (G)	% cal from fat	CHOL (mg)	SOD (mg)
Applesauce, canned (Del Monte, Lite Fruits)	½ c	50	0	0	0	<10

LITE PICK ○◇☐☐

COMMENTS: 40 fewer calories than ½ cup regular Del Monte applesauce.

PRODUCT	SERV	CAL	FAT (G)	% cal from fat	CHOL (mg)	SOD (mg)
Applesauce, canned (Featherweight, Water Packed)	½ c	50	0	0	0	<3

LITE PICK ○◇☐

COMMENTS: 47 fewer calories, about 1 milligram less sodium than ½ cup regular sweetened applesauce.

PRODUCT	SERV	CAL	FAT (G)	% cal from fat	CHOL (mg)	SOD (mg)
Apricots, canned (Del Monte, Lite Fruits, Halves)	½ c	60	0	0	0	<10

LITE PICK ○◇□□

COMMENTS: 40 fewer calories than ½ cup regular Del Monte apricot halves.

PRODUCT	SERV	CAL	FAT (G)	% cal from fat	CHOL (mg)	SOD (mg)
Apricots, canned (Featherweight, Juice Packed, Halves)	½ c	50	0	0	0	<10

LITE PICK ○◇□

COMMENTS: 57 fewer calories than ½ cup apricot halves packed in syrup.

PRODUCT	SERV	CAL	FAT (G)	% cal from fat	CHOL (mg)	SOD (mg)
Fruit, chunky mixed, canned (Del Monte, Lite Fruits)	½ c	50	0	0	0	<10

LITE PICK ○◇□□

COMMENTS: 30 fewer calories than ½ cup regular Del Monte Chunky Mixed Fruits.

PRODUCT	SERV	CAL	FAT (G)	% cal from fat	CHOL (mg)	SOD (mg)
Fruit Cocktail, canned (Del Monte, Lite Fruits)	½ c	50	0	0	0	<10

LITE PICK ○◇□□

COMMENTS: 30 fewer calories than ½ cup regular Del Monte fruit cocktail.

PRODUCT	SERV	CAL	FAT (G)	% cal from fat	CHOL (mg)	SOD (mg)
Fruit cocktail, canned (Featherweight, Juice Packed)	½ c	50	0	0	0	<10

LITE PICK ○◇□□

COMMENTS: 43 fewer calories than ½ cup regular fruit cocktail packed in syrup, and about 3 milligrams *more* sodium.

PRODUCT	SERV	CAL	FAT (G)	% cal from fat	CHOL (mg)	SOD (mg)
Fruit salad, canned (Featherweight, Juice Packed)	½ c	50	0	0	0	<10

LITE PICK ○◇□□

COMMENTS: 44 fewer calories than ½ cup regular fruit salad in heavy syrup, and about 3 milligrams *more* sodium.

PRODUCT	SERV	CAL	FAT (G)	% cal from fat	CHOL (mg)	SOD (mg)
Grapefruit, canned (Featherweight, Juice Packed, Segments)	½ c	40	0	0	0	<10

LITE PICK ○◇□

COMMENTS: 36 fewer calories than ½ cup regular grapefruit segments packed in light syrup, and about 8 milligrams *more* sodium.

PRODUCT	SERV	CAL	FAT (G)	% cal from fat	CHOL (mg)	SOD (mg)
Oranges, mandarin, canned (Dole, In Light Syrup)	½ c	76	.13	2	0	8

LITE PICK ○◇□□

COMMENTS: No direct comparison, but this product is naturally low in fat, cholesterol, and sodium.

PRODUCT	SERV	CAL	FAT (G)	% cal from fat	CHOL (mg)	SOD (mg)
Oranges, mandarin, canned (Featherweight, Water Packed)	½ c	35	0	0	0	<10

LITE PICK ○◇□□

COMMENTS: 41 fewer calories than ½ cup regular mandarin oranges in light syrup, and about 2 milligrams *more* sodium.

PRODUCT	SERV	CAL	FAT (G)	% cal from fat	CHOL (mg)	SOD (mg)
Peaches, canned (Del Monte, Lite Fruits, Freestone)	½ c	60	0	0	0	<10

LITE PICK ○◇□□

COMMENTS: 30 fewer calories than ½ cup regular Del Monte freestone peaches.

PRODUCT	SERV	CAL	FAT (G)	% cal from fat	CHOL (mg)	SOD (mg)
Peaches, canned (Del Monte, Lite Fruits, Yellow Cling)	½ c	50	0	0	0	<10

LITE PICK ○◇□□

COMMENTS: 30 fewer calories than ½ cup regular Del Monte yellow cling peaches.

PRODUCT	SERV	CAL	FAT (G)	% cal from fat	CHOL (mg)	SOD (mg)
Peaches, canned (Featherweight, Juice Packed Halves or Slices)	½ c	50	0	0	0	<10

LITE PICK ○◇□□

COMMENTS: 45 fewer calories than ½ cup peaches in heavy syrup, and about 2 milligrams *more* sodium.

PRODUCT	SERV	CAL	FAT (G)	% cal from fat	CHOL (mg)	SOD (mg)
Pears, canned (Del Monte, Lite Fruits)	½ c	50	0	0	0	<10

LITE PICK ○◇□□

COMMENTS: 30 fewer calories than ½ cup regular Del Monte pears.

PRODUCT	SERV	CAL	FAT (G)	% cal from fat	CHOL (mg)	SOD (mg)
Pears, canned (Featherweight, Juice Packed, Halves)	½ c	60	0	0	0	<10

LITE PICK ○◇□□

COMMENTS: 34 calories less than ½ cup regular pears packed in syrup, and only about 3 milligrams *more* sodium.

PRODUCT	SERV	CAL	FAT (G)	% cal from fat	CHOL (mg)	SOD (mg)
Pineapple, canned (Dole, In Juice)	½ c	70	.5	6	0	1

LITE PICK ○◇□

COMMENTS: 25 fewer calories than ½ cup regular Dole pineapple in syrup.

PRODUCT	SERV	CAL	FAT (G)	% cal from fat	CHOL (mg)	SOD (mg)
Pineapple, canned (Featherweight, Juice Packed, Slices)	½ c	70	0	0	0	<10

LITE PICK ○◇□□

COMMENTS: 29 fewer calories, 8 milligrams less sodium than ½ cup pineapple packed in syrup.

PRODUCT	SERV	CAL	FAT (G)	% cal from fat	CHOL (mg)	SOD (mg)
Plums, canned (Featherweight, Juice Packed, Whole Purple)	½ c	80	0	0	0	<10

LITE PICK ○◇□□

COMMENTS: 35 fewer calories, 15 milligrams less sodium than ½ cup plums in heavy syrup.

PRODUCT	SERV	CAL	FAT (G)	% cal from fat	CHOL (mg)	SOD (mg)
Raspberries, frozen (Birds Eye, In Lite Syrup)	5 oz	100	1	9	0	0

LITE PICK ○◇□

COMMENTS: No direct comparison, but this product is naturally low in fat, cholesterol, and sodium.

PRODUCT	SERV	CAL	FAT (G)	% cal from fat	CHOL (mg)	SOD (mg)
Strawberries, frozen (Birds Eye, In Light Syrup, Halves)	5 oz	90	0	0	0	5

LITE PICK ○◇□□

COMMENTS: 30 fewer calories than regular Birds Eye strawberry halves in syrup, and 5 milligrams *more* sodium.

PRODUCT	SERV	CAL	FAT (G)	% cal from fat	CHOL (mg)	SOD (mg)
Strawberries, frozen (Birds Eye, In Light Syrup, Whole)	4 oz	80	0	0	0	0

LITE PICK ○◇□

COMMENTS: 40 fewer calories than 4 ounces regular Birds Eye strawberry halves in syrup.

LUNCHEON MEAT

PRODUCT	SERV	CAL	FAT (G)	% cal from fat	CHOL (mg)	SOD (mg)
Bacon, Canadian (Hormel, Light n' Lean Slices, Canadian Bacon Style)	½ oz	17	.5	26	na	na

○

COMMENTS: 3 fewer calories, .5 grams less fat than ½ ounce regular Canadian bacon.

PRODUCT	SERV	CAL	FAT (G)	% cal from fat	CHOL (mg)	SOD (mg)
Beef (Eckrich, Slender Sliced)	1 oz	35	1	26	na	270

○

COMMENTS: No direct comparison, but is low in fat and high in sodium.

PRODUCT	SERV	CAL	FAT (G)	% cal from fat	CHOL (mg)	SOD (mg)
Beef (Oscar Mayer, Lean Cold Cut Slices, Smoked)	½ oz	19	.3	14	7	179

○◇◇

COMMENTS: No direct comparison, but this product is very low in fat and high in sodium.

PRODUCT	SERV	CAL	FAT (G)	% cal from fat	CHOL (mg)	SOD (mg)
Beef, corned (Eckrich, Slender Sliced)	1 oz	40	1	23	na	270

○

COMMENTS: No direct comparison, but is low in fat and high in sodium.

PRODUCT	SERV	CAL	FAT (G)	% cal from fat	CHOL (mg)	SOD (mg)
Beef, corned (Oscar Mayer, Lean Cold Cut Slices)	1 oz	16	.4	23	10	208

○◇◇

COMMENTS: No direct comparison, but this product is low in fat and high in sodium.

PRODUCT	SERV	CAL	FAT (G)	% cal from fat	CHOL (mg)	SOD (mg)
Bologna (Armour, Slices, Lower Salt) ◇◇	½ oz	90	8	80	15	200

COMMENTS: 10 fewer calories, 1 gram less fat, 110 milligrams less sodium than one slice regular Armour Star Bologna. Very high in fat and sodium.

PRODUCT	SERV	CAL	FAT (G)	% cal from fat	CHOL (mg)	SOD (mg)
Bologna (Armour Slices, Lower Salt Beef) ◇◇	1 oz	90	8	80	15	190

COMMENTS: 10 fewer calories, 1 gram less fat, 110 milligrams less sodium than 1 slice regular beef bologna. Very high in fat, but lower in sodium than most luncheon meats.

PRODUCT	SERV	CAL	FAT (G)	% cal from fat	CHOL (mg)	SOD (mg)
Bologna (Eckrich, Lean Supreme)	1 oz	70	6	77	na	240

COMMENTS: 30 fewer calories, 3 grams less fat than 1 ounce regular Eckrich beef bologna. Very high in fat and sodium.

PRODUCT	SERV	CAL	FAT (G)	% cal from fat	CHOL (mg)	SOD (mg)
Bologna (Hormel, Light n' Lean Slices)	1 oz	70	6	77	na	na

COMMENTS: 19 fewer calories, 2 grams less fat than by regular bologna. Very high in fat.

PRODUCT	SERV	CAL	FAT (G)	% cal from fat	CHOL (mg)	SOD (mg)
Bologna (Hormel, Light n' Lean Slices, Thin sliced)	½ oz	35	3	77	na	na

COMMENTS: 9 fewer calories, 1 gram less fat than ½ ounce regular bologna. Very high in fat.

PRODUCT	SERV	CAL	FAT (G)	% cal from fat	CHOL (mg)	SOD (mg)
Chicken (Oscar Mayer, Lean Cold Cut Slices, Oven Roasted Breast)	1 oz	29	.7	22	13	361

○◇◇

COMMENTS: No direct comparison, but this product is low in fat and high in sodium.

PRODUCT	SERV	CAL	FAT (G)	% cal from fat	CHOL (mg)	SOD (mg)
Chicken (Oscar Mayer, Lean Cold Cut Slices, Smoked Breast)	1 oz	26	.4	14	15	405

○◇◇

COMMENTS: No direct comparison, but this product is very low in fat and very high in sodium.

PRODUCT	SERV	CAL	FAT (G)	% cal from fat	CHOL (mg)	SOD (mg)
Franks (Armour, Lower Salt Jumbo Hot Dogs)	2 oz	170	15	79	30	380

COMMENTS: 20 fewer calories, 3 grams less fat, 210 milligrams less sodium than a 2 ounce regular Armour Star Jumbo Hot Dog. Very high in fat and high in sodium.

PRODUCT	SERV	CAL	FAT (G)	% cal from fat	CHOL (mg)	SOD (mg)
Franks (Eckrich, Lean Supreme Jumbo)	1 pc	140	12	77	na	490

COMMENTS: No direct comparison, but this product is very high in fat and sodium.

PRODUCT	SERV	CAL	FAT (G)	% cal from fat	CHOL (mg)	SOD (mg)
Franks, beef (Armour, Lower Salt Jumbo Hot Dogs)	2 oz	170	15	79	30	390

COMMENTS: 20 fewer calories, 3 grams less fat, 210 milligrams less sodium than a 2 ounce regular Armour Star Jumbo Beef Hot Dog. Very high in fat and high in sodium.

PRODUCT	SERV	CAL	FAT (G)	% cal from fat	CHOL (mg)	SOD (mg)
Ham (Eckrich, Lean Supreme, Chopped)	1 oz	35	2	51	na	350

COMMENTS: Same fat and sodium as, but 10 fewer calories than 1 ounce regular Eckrich chopped ham. The high percentage of calories from fat is deceiving; since it contains only 2 grams of fat, this product is actually low in fat. High in sodium.

PRODUCT	SERV	CAL	FAT (G)	% cal from fat	CHOL (mg)	SOD (mg)
Ham (Eckrich, Slender Sliced, Smoked)	1 oz	40	2	45	na	360

COMMENTS: No direct comparison. The high percentage of calories from fat is deceiving; since it contains only 2 grams of fat per serving, this product is actually low in fat. High in sodium.

PRODUCT	SERV	CAL	FAT (G)	% cal from fat	CHOL (mg)	SOD (mg)

Ham
(Hormel, Light n'
Lean Slices,
Barbecue) | .8 oz | 25 | 1 | 36 | na | na |

COMMENTS: No direct comparison. The high percentage of calories from fat is deceiving; since it contains only 1 gram of fat per serving, this product is actually low in fat.

PRODUCT	SERV	CAL	FAT (G)	% cal from fat	CHOL (mg)	SOD (mg)

Ham
(Hormel, Light n'
Lean Slices, Black
Peppered) | .8 oz | 25 | 1 | 36 | na | na |

COMMENTS: No direct comparison. The high percentage of calories from fat is deceiving; since it contains only 1 gram of fat per serving, this product is actually low in fat.

PRODUCT	SERV	CAL	FAT (G)	% cal from fat	CHOL (mg)	SOD (mg)

Ham
(Hormel, Light n'
Lean Slices,
Boneless, Water
Added) | 1 oz | 30 | 1 | 30 | na | na |

○

COMMENTS: 22 fewer calories, 2 grams less fat than regular sliced ham. Low in fat.

PRODUCT	SERV	CAL	FAT (G)	% cal from fat	CHOL (mg)	SOD (mg)
Ham (Hormel, Light n' Lean Slices, Chopped)	.8 oz	35	2	51	na	na

COMMENTS: 17 fewer calories, 2 grams less fat than .8 ounces regular chopped ham. The high percentage of calories from fat is deceiving; since it contains only 2 grams of fat per serving, this product is actually low in fat.

PRODUCT	SERV	CAL	FAT (G)	% cal from fat	CHOL (mg)	SOD (mg)
Ham (Hormel, Light n' Lean Slices, Cooked, Smoked)	.8 oz	25	1	36	na	na

COMMENTS: No direct comparison. The high percentage of calories from fat is deceiving; since it contains only 1 gram of fat per serving, this product is actually low in fat.

PRODUCT	SERV	CAL	FAT (G)	% cal from fat	CHOL (mg)	SOD (mg)
Ham (Hormel, Light n' Lean Slices, Cooked)	.8 oz	25	1	36	na	na

COMMENTS: No direct comparison. The high percentage of calories from fat is deceiving; since it contains only 1 gram of fat per serving, this product is actually low in fat.

PRODUCT	SERV	CAL	FAT (G)	% cal from fat	CHOL (mg)	SOD (mg)
Ham (Hormel, Light n' Lean Slices, Glazed)	.8 oz	25	1	36	na	na

COMMENTS: No direct comparison. The high percentage of calories from fat is deceiving; since it contains only 1 gram of fat per serving, this product is actually low in fat.

PRODUCT	SERV	CAL	FAT (G)	% cal from fat	CHOL (mg)	SOD (mg)
Ham (Hormel, Light n' Lean Slices, Red Peppered)	.8 oz	25	1	36	na	na

COMMENTS: No direct comparison. The high percentage of calories from fat is deceiving; since it contains only 1 gram of fat per serving, this product is actually low in fat.

PRODUCT	SERV	CAL	FAT (G)	% cal from fat	CHOL (mg)	SOD (mg)
Ham (Oscar Mayer, Lean Cold Cut Slices, Boiled with Natural Juices)	.75 oz	23	.7	27	12	290

◇◇◇

COMMENTS: No direct comparison, but this product is low in fat and high in sodium.

PRODUCT	SERV	CAL	FAT (G)	% cal from fat	CHOL (mg)	SOD (mg)
Ham (Oscar Mayer, Lean Cold Cut Slices, Cooked Italian Style)	.75 oz	25	1	36	10	265

◇◇

COMMENTS: No direct comparison. The high percentage of calories from fat is deceiving; since it contains only 1 gram of fat per serving, this product is actually low in fat. High in sodium.

PRODUCT	SERV	CAL	FAT (G)	% cal from fat	CHOL (mg)	SOD (mg)
Ham (Oscar Mayer, Lean Cold Cut Slices, Cracked Black Pepper)	.75 oz	24	.8	30	11	296

○◇◇

COMMENTS: No direct comparison, but this product is low in fat and high in sodium.

PRODUCT	SERV	CAL	FAT (G)	% cal from fat	CHOL (mg)	SOD (mg)
Loaf, ham w/cheese (Hormel, Light n' Lean Slices, Ham and Cheese)	.8 oz	45	3	60	na	na

COMMENTS: No direct comparison, but very high in fat.

PRODUCT	SERV	CAL	FAT (G)	% cal from fat	CHOL (mg)	SOD (mg)
Loaf, pickle (Hormel, Light n' Lean Slices)	1 oz	50	3.5	63	na	na

COMMENTS: No direct comparison, but this product is very high in fat.

PRODUCT	SERV	CAL	FAT (G)	% cal from fat	CHOL (mg)	SOD (mg)
Lunch meat (Hormel, Light n' Lean Slices, New England Brand)	1 oz	45	3	60	na	na

COMMENTS: No direct comparison, but this product is very high in fat.

PRODUCT	SERV	CAL	FAT (G)	% cal from fat	CHOL (mg)	SOD (mg)
Lunch meat (Hormel, Light n' Lean Slices, Spiced Luncheon)	1 oz	60	4.5	68	na	na

COMMENTS: No direct comparison, but this product is very high in fat.

PRODUCT	SERV	CAL	FAT (G)	% cal from fat	CHOL (mg)	SOD (mg)
Pastrami (Oscar Mayer, Lean Cold Cut Slices)	.6 oz	16	.3	17	7	219

○◇◇

COMMENTS: No direct comparison, but this product is very low in fat and high in sodium.

PRODUCT	SERV	CAL	FAT (G)	% cal from fat	CHOL (mg)	SOD (mg)
Pork (Eckrich, Slender Sliced)	1 oz	45	2	40	na	320

COMMENTS: No direct comparison. The high percentage of calories from fat is deceiving; since it contains only 2 grams of fat per serving, this product is actually low in fat, but high in sodium.

PRODUCT	SERV	CAL	FAT (G)	% cal from fat	CHOL (mg)	SOD (mg)
Salami (Hormel, Light n' Lean Slices, Cotto)	.75 oz	40	2.5	56	na	na

COMMENTS: No direct comparison, but this product is very high in fat.

PRODUCT	SERV	CAL	FAT (G)	% cal from fat	CHOL (mg)	SOD (mg)
Sausage, summer (Hormel, Light n' Lean)	.75 oz	50	4	72	na	na

COMMENTS: No direct comparison, but this product is very high in fat.

PRODUCT	SERV	CAL	FAT (G)	% cal from fat	CHOL (mg)	SOD (mg)
Turkey (Butterball Deli, No Salt Added, Breast)	1 oz	45	2	40	na	15

□□

COMMENTS: 20 calories and 2 grams *more* fat than 1 ounce regular Butterball Oven Prepared Skinless Deli Turkey Breast, but 255 milligrams less sodium. The high percentage of calories from fat is deceiving; since it contains only 2 grams of fat, this product is actually low in fat.

PRODUCT	SERV	CAL	FAT (G)	% cal from fat	CHOL (mg)	SOD (mg)
Turkey (Eckrich, Slender Sliced)	1 oz	45	2	40	na	290

COMMENTS: No direct comparison. The high percentage of calories from fat is deceiving; since it contains only 2 grams of fat, this product is actually low in fat, but high in sodium.

PRODUCT	SERV	CAL	FAT (G)	% cal from fat	CHOL (mg)	SOD (mg)
Turkey (Hormel, Light n' Lean Slices, Breast)	.8 oz	30	1	30	na	na

○

COMMENTS: No direct comparison, but is low in fat.

PRODUCT	SERV	CAL	FAT (G)	% cal from fat	CHOL (mg)	SOD (mg)
Turkey (Oscar Mayer, Lean Cold Cut Slices, Smoked Breast)	.75 oz	20	.3	14	9	317

○◇◇

COMMENTS: No direct comparison, but this product is very low in fat and high in sodium.

PRODUCT	SERV	CAL	FAT (G)	% cal from fat	CHOL (mg)	SOD (mg)
Turkey (Wampler Longacre, Smoked Breast)	1 oz	34	.7	19	16	168

○◇◇

COMMENTS: No direct comparison, but this product is very low in fat and lower in sodium than most luncheon meats.

PRODUCT	SERV	CAL	FAT (G)	% cal from fat	CHOL (mg)	SOD (mg)
Turkey (Wampler Longacre, Lean-Lite Deli Sliced Oven Roast Breast)	1 oz	34	.7	19	14	155

○◇◇

COMMENTS: No direct comparison, but this product is very low in fat and lower in sodium than most luncheon meats.

PRODUCT	SERV	CAL	FAT (G)	% cal from fat	CHOL (mg)	SOD (mg)
Turkey (Wampler Longacre, Lean-Lite Deli Sliced Oven Roasted Skinless Breast)	1 oz	34	.3	8	16	168

○◇◇

COMMENTS: No direct comparison, but this product is very low in fat and lower in sodium than most luncheon meats.

PRODUCT	SERV	CAL	FAT (G)	% cal from fat	CHOL (mg)	SOD (mg)
Turkey ham (Butterball, Deli, Thin Sliced)	1 oz	35	1	26	na	390

○

COMMENTS: No direct comparison, but this product is low in fat and high in sodium.

PRODUCT	SERV	CAL	FAT (G)	% cal from fat	CHOL (mg)	SOD (mg)
Turkey ham (Wampler Longacre, Lean-Lite Deli Sliced Smokehouse)	1 oz	37	1.6	39	28	158

COMMENTS: No direct comparison. The high percentage of calories from fat is deceiving; since it contains only 1.6 grams of fat per serving, this product is actually low in fat. Lower in sodium than most luncheon meats.

PASTA
AND
GRAINS

PRODUCT	SERV	CAL	FAT (G)	% cal from fat	CHOL (mg)	SOD (mg)
Noodles, egg (Foulds, No Yolks)	2 oz	210	2	9	0	40

LITE PICK ○◇□□□

COMMENTS: This product has approximately the same calories, fat, and sodium as regular egg noodles, and 55–70 milligrams less cholesterol. Very low in fat.

PRODUCT	SERV	CAL	FAT (G)	% cal from fat	CHOL (mg)	SOD (mg)
Noodles, egg (Hershey, Light & Fluffy)	2 oz	220	3	12	na	5

○□□

COMMENTS: Lighter only in texture.

PRODUCT	SERV	CAL	FAT (G)	% cal from fat	CHOL (mg)	SOD (mg)
Pasta, ribbon, whole wheat (Pritikin)	2 oz	220	2	8	0	40

LITE PICK ○◇□□□

COMMENTS: No direct comparison, but this product is very low in fat.

PRODUCT	SERV	CAL	FAT (G)	% cal from fat	CHOL (mg)	SOD (mg)
Rice, pilaf, brown (Pritikin)	½ c	90	<1	<10	0	25

LITE PICK ○◇□□

COMMENTS: No direct comparison, but this product is very low in fat.

PRODUCT	SERV	CAL	FAT (G)	% cal from fat	CHOL (mg)	SOD (mg)
Rice, Spanish (Featherweight, Low Sodium)	7½ oz	140	0	0	na	32

○□□

COMMENTS: No direct comparison, but this product is fat free.

PRODUCT	SERV	CAL	FAT (G)	% cal from fat	CHOL (mg)	SOD (mg)
Rice, Spanish, brown						
(Pritikin)	½ c	100	<1	<9	0	15

LITE PICK ○◇◇□□

COMMENTS: No direct comparison, but this product is very low in fat.

PRODUCT	SERV	CAL	FAT (G)	% cal from fat	CHOL (mg)	SOD (mg)
Spaghetti, whole wheat						
(Pritikin)	2 oz	220	2	8	0	40

LITE PICK ○◇□□□

COMMENTS: No direct comparison, but this product is very low in fat.

PACKAGED MIXES AND BAKING INGREDIENTS

PRODUCT	SERV	CAL	FAT (G)	% cal from fat	CHOL (mg)	SOD (mg)
Baking powder (Featherweight, Low Sodium)	1 tsp	0	0	0	0	2

LITE PICK ○◇□

COMMENTS: 819 milligrams sodium less than 1 teaspoon regular baking powder.

PRODUCT	SERV	CAL	FAT (G)	% cal from fat	CHOL (mg)	SOD (mg)
Biscuits, buttermilk (Pillsbury, Extra Light Flaky)	2 pc	110	4	33	na	340

COMMENTS: Same fat and sodium as, but 10 fewer calories than two regular Pillsbury Tender Layer Buttermilk Biscuits.

PRODUCT	SERV	CAL	FAT (G)	% cal from fat	CHOL (mg)	SOD (mg)
Brownie mix						
(Estee)	2"x2" pc	45	2	40	30	15

□□

COMMENTS: 62 fewer calories, 13 grams less fat, 34 milligrams less sodium than a regular brownie about the same size. The high percentage of calories from fat is deceiving; since it contains only 2 grams of fat per serving, this product is actually low in fat.

PRODUCT	SERV	CAL	FAT (G)	% cal from fat	CHOL (mg)	SOD (mg)
Cake mix						
(Batter Lite, Cake and Frosting mix, Chocolate)	⅑th cake	110	2	16	0	43

LITE PICK ○○◇□□□

COMMENTS: No direct comparison, but this product is lower in calories, fat, and sodium than most regular cake mixes. Very low in fat. Sweetened with fructose.

PRODUCT	SERV	CAL	FAT (G)	% cal from fat	CHOL (mg)	SOD (mg)
Cake mix						
(Batter Lite, Cake and Frosting mix, White)	⅑th cake	110	2	16	0	36

LITE PICK ○○◇□□□

COMMENTS: No direct comparison, but this product is lower in calories, fat, and sodium than most regular cake mixes. Very low in fat. Sweetened with fructose.

PRODUCT	SERV	CAL	FAT (G)	% cal from fat	CHOL (mg)	SOD (mg)
Cake mix						60–
(Estee, all flavors)	⅒th cake	100	2	18	0	75

LITE PICK ○◇□□□

COMMENTS: No direct comparison, but this product is lower in calories, fat, and sodium than most regular cake mixes. Very low in fat. Sweetened with fructose.

PRODUCT	SERV	CAL	FAT (G)	% cal from fat	CHOL (mg)	SOD (mg)
Frosting mix						
(Batter Lite, Frost						
Lite)	.35 oz	22	0	0	0	13

LITE PICK ○◇□□

COMMENTS: 17 fewer calories, 34 milligrams less sodium than an equal amount of regular white fluffy frosting. Sweetened with fructose. Fat free.

PRODUCT	SERV	CAL	FAT (G)	% cal from fat	CHOL (mg)	SOD (mg)
Frosting mix		50–		18–		
(Estee)	1½ T	60	1–2	30	0	0

LITE PICK ○◇□

COMMENTS: No direct comparison, but this product is low in fat. Sweetened with sorbitol.

PRODUCT	SERV	CAL	FAT (G)	% cal from fat	CHOL (mg)	SOD (mg)
Pancake mix (Estee)	3 (3″)	100	0	0	0	135

LITE PICK ○◇□□□

COMMENTS: 87 fewer calories, 7 grams less fat, 405 milligrams less sodium than three 3″ regular buttermilk pancakes from a mix. Fat free.

PRODUCT	SERV	CAL	FAT (G)	% cal from fat	CHOL (mg)	SOD (mg)
Pancake mix (Featherweight)	3 (4″)	140	2	13	5	90

LITE PICK ○◇◇□□□

COMMENTS: 140 fewer calories, 8 grams less fat, 720 milligrams less sodium than three 4″ regular buttermilk pancakes from a mix. Very low in fat.

PRODUCT	SERV	CAL	FAT (G)	% cal from fat	CHOL (mg)	SOD (mg)
Pancake mix Hungry Jack, Extra Lights)	3 (4″)	210	7	30	na	490

○

COMMENTS: 30 fewer calories, 1 gram less fat, 80 milligrams less sodium than three 4″ Hungry Jack Buttermilk Pancakes. High in sodium.

PRODUCT	SERV	CAL	FAT (G)	% cal from fat	CHOL (mg)	SOD (mg)
Pancake mix (Hungry Jack, Extra Lights Complete)	3 (4″)	190	2	9	na	700

○

COMMENTS: 10 calories and 1 gram fat *more* than three 4″ Hungry Jack Buttermilk Complete Pancakes, but 10 milligrams less sodium. Very low in fat, but high in sodium.

PRODUCT	SERV	CAL	FAT (G)	% cal from fat	CHOL (mg)	SOD (mg)
Pancakes, buttermilk (Aunt Jemima, Lite Microwave Buttermilk)	3 (4″)	140	3	19	na	660

○

COMMENTS: 160 fewer calories, 8 grams less fat, 330 milligrams less sodium than three 4″ Aunt Jemima Buttermilk Pancakes. Very low in fat, but high in sodium.

PRODUCT	SERV	CAL	FAT (G)	% cal from fat	CHOL (mg)	SOD (mg)
Pancakes, buttermilk (Aunt Jemima, Lite Buttermilk Complete)	3 (4″)	130	2	14	na	570

○

COMMENTS: 130 fewer calories, 1 gram less fat, 390 milligrams less sodium than three 4″ Aunt Jemima Buttermilk Complete Pancakes and Waffle Mix pancakes. Very low in fat, but high in sodium.

PUDDINGS
AND
GELATINS

PRODUCT	SERV	CAL	FAT (G)	% cal from fat	CHOL (mg)	SOD (mg)
Custard, lemon						
(Featherweight)	½ c	40	0	0	na	40

○□□□

COMMENTS: 103 fewer calories, 5 grams less fat, 88 milligrams less sodium than ½ cup regular lemon custard pudding. Fat free. Sweetened with aspartame.

PRODUCT	SERV	CAL	FAT (G)	% cal from fat	CHOL (mg)	SOD (mg)
Custard, vanilla						
(Featherweight)	½ c	80	0	0	5	105

LITE PICK ○◇◇□□□

COMMENTS: 63 fewer calories, 5 grams less fat, 74 milligrams less sodium than ½ cup regular vanilla custard. Fat free. Sweetened with aspartame and fructose.

PRODUCT	SERV	CAL	FAT (G)	% cal from fat	CHOL (mg)	SOD (mg)
Gelatin, apple (Estee, Golden Apple)	½ c	8	0	0	0	10

LITE PICK ○◇□□

COMMENTS: 72 fewer calories, 45 milligrams less sodium than ½ cup regular gelatin. Fat free.

PRODUCT	SERV	CAL	FAT (G)	% cal from fat	CHOL (mg)	SOD (mg)
Gelatin, berry (Jell-O, Sugar Free Triple Berry)	½ c	8	0	0	0	52

LITE PICK ○◇□□□

COMMENTS: 72 fewer calories, 3 milligrams less sodium than ½ cup regular gelatin. Fat free. Sweetened with aspartame.

PRODUCT	SERV	CAL	FAT (G)	% cal from fat	CHOL (mg)	SOD (mg)
Gelatin, cherry (D-Zerta, Low Calorie)	½ c	8	0	0	0	0

LITE PICK ○◇□□□

COMMENTS: 72 fewer calories than ½ cup regular Jell-O gelatin. Fat free. Sweetened with aspartame.

PRODUCT	SERV	CAL	FAT (G)	% cal from fat	CHOL (mg)	SOD (mg)
Gelatin, cherry (Estee)	½ c	8	0	0	0	10

LITE PICK ○◇□□

COMMENTS: 72 fewer calories, 45 milligrams less sodium than ½ cup regular gelatin. Fat free. Sweetened with aspartame.

PRODUCT	SERV	CAL	FAT (G)	% cal from fat	CHOL (mg)	SOD (mg)
Gelatin, cherry (Featherweight)	½ c	10	0	0	na	4

LITE PICK ○◇□

COMMENTS: 71 fewer calories, 51 milligrams less sodium than ½ cup regular gelatin. Fat free. Sweetened with aspartame.

PRODUCT	SERV	CAL	FAT (G)	% cal from fat	CHOL (mg)	SOD (mg)
Gelatin, cherry (Jell-O, Sugar Free)	½ c	8	0	0	0	80

LITE PICK ○◇□□□

COMMENTS: 72 fewer calories than ½ cup regular gelatin, but 10 milligrams *more* sodium. Fat free. Sweetened with aspartame.

PRODUCT	SERV	CAL	FAT (G)	% cal from fat	CHOL (mg)	SOD (mg)
Gelatin, cherry (Royal, Sugar Free)	½ c	6	0	0	0	75

LITE PICK ○◇□□□

COMMENTS: 72 fewer calories, 25 milligrams less sodium than ½ cup regular Royal cherry gelatin. Fat free. Sweetened with aspartame.

PRODUCT	SERV	CAL	FAT (G)	% cal from fat	CHOL (mg)	SOD (mg)
Gelatin, lemon (Featherweight)	½ c	10	0	0	0	4

LITE PICK ○◇□

COMMENTS: 71 fewer calories, 51 milligrams less sodium than ½ cup regular gelatin. Fat free. Sweetened with aspartame.

PRODUCT	SERV	CAL	FAT (G)	% cal from fat	CHOL (mg)	SOD (mg)
Gelatin, lemon (Jell-O, Sugar Free)	½ c	8	0	0	0	55

LITE PICK ○◇□□□

COMMENTS: 72 fewer calories, 20 milligrams less sodium than ½ cup regular gelatin. Fat free. Sweetened with aspartame.

PRODUCT	SERV	CAL	FAT (G)	% cal from fat	CHOL (mg)	SOD (mg)
Gelatin, lemon/ lime (Estee)	½ c	8	0	0	0	10

LITE PICK ○◇□□

COMMENTS: 72 fewer calories, 45 milligrams less sodium than ½ cup regular gelatin. Fat free. Sweetened with aspartame.

PRODUCT	SERV	CAL	FAT (G)	% cal from fat	CHOL (mg)	SOD (mg)
Gelatin, lime (D-Zerta, Low Calorie)	½ c	8	0	0	0	0

LITE PICK ○◇□□□

COMMENTS: 72 fewer calories than ½ cup regular Jell-O gelatin. Fat free. Sweetened with aspartame.

PRODUCT	SERV	CAL	FAT (G)	% cal from fat	CHOL (mg)	SOD (mg)
Gelatin, lime (Featherweight)	½ c	10	0	0	0	5

LITE PICK ○◇□

COMMENTS: 71 fewer calories, 50 milligrams less sodium than ½ cup regular gelatin. Fat free. Sweetened with aspartame.

PRODUCT	SERV	CAL	FAT (G)	% cal from fat	CHOL (mg)	SOD (mg)
Gelatin, lime (Jell-O, Sugar Free)	½ c	8	0	0	0	60

LITE PICK ○◇□□□

COMMENTS: 72 fewer calories than ½ cup regular gelatin, but 10 milligrams *more* sodium. Fat free. Sweetened with aspartame.

PRODUCT	SERV	CAL	FAT (G)	% cal from fat	CHOL (mg)	SOD (mg)
Gelatin, lime (Royal, Sugar Free)	½ c	6	0	0	0	75

LITE PICK ○◇□□□

COMMENTS: 74 fewer calories, 15 milligrams less sodium than ½ cup regular Royal lime gelatin. Fat free. Sweetened with aspartame.

PRODUCT	SERV	CAL	FAT (G)	% cal from fat	CHOL (mg)	SOD (mg)
Gelatin, mixed fruit (Jell-O, Sugar Free)	½ c	8	0	0	0	52

LITE PICK ○◇□□□

COMMENTS: 72 fewer calories, 3 milligrams less sodium than ½ cup regular gelatin. Fat free. Sweetened with aspartame.

PRODUCT	SERV	CAL	FAT (G)	% cal from fat	CHOL (mg)	SOD (mg)
Gelatin, orange (Featherweight)	½ c	10	0	0	0	5

LITE PICK ○◇□

COMMENTS: 71 fewer calories, 50 milligrams less sodium than ½ cup regular gelatin. Fat free. Sweetened with aspartame.

PRODUCT	SERV	CAL	FAT (G)	% cal from fat	CHOL (mg)	SOD (mg)
Gelatin, orange (Jell-O, Sugar Free)	½ c	8	0	0	0	52

LITE PICK ○◇□□□

COMMENTS: 72 fewer calories, 3 milligrams less sodium than ½ cup regular gelatin. Fat free. Sweetened with aspartame.

PRODUCT	SERV	CAL	FAT (G)	% cal from fat	CHOL (mg)	SOD (mg)
Gelatin, orange (Royal, Sugar Free)	½ c	6	0	0	0	75

LITE PICK ○◇□□□

COMMENTS: 74 fewer calories, 25 milligrams less sodium than ½ cup regular Royal orange gelatin. Fat free. Sweetened with aspartame.

PRODUCT	SERV	CAL	FAT (G)	% cal from fat	CHOL (mg)	SOD (mg)
Gelatin, peach (Estee, Peach Melba)	½ c	8	0	0	0	10

LITE PICK ○◇□□

COMMENTS: 72 fewer calories, 45 milligrams less sodium than ½ cup regular gelatin. Fat free. Sweetened with aspartame.

PRODUCT	SERV	CAL	FAT (G)	% cal from fat	CHOL (mg)	SOD (mg)
Gelatin, pineapple (Jell-O, Sugar Free Hawaiian Pineapple)	½ c	8	0	0	0	52

LITE PICK ○◇□□□

COMMENTS: 72 fewer calories, 3 milligrams less sodium than ½ cup regular gelatin. Fat free. Sweetened with aspartame.

PRODUCT	SERV	CAL	FAT (G)	% cal from fat	CHOL (mg)	SOD (mg)
Gelatin, raspberry (D-Zerta, Low Calorie)	½ c	8	0	0	0	0

LITE PICK ○◇□□□

COMMENTS: 72 fewer calories than ½ cup regular Jell-O gelatin. Fat free. Sweetened with aspartame.

PRODUCT	SERV	CAL	FAT (G)	% cal from fat	CHOL (mg)	SOD (mg)
Gelatin, raspberry (Featherweight)	½ c	10	0	0	0	3

LITE PICK ○◇□

COMMENTS: 71 fewer calories, 52 milligrams less sodium than ½ cup regular gelatin. Fat free. Sweetened with aspartame.

PRODUCT	SERV	CAL	FAT (G)	% cal from fat	CHOL (mg)	SOD (mg)
Gelatin, raspberry (Jell-O, Sugar Free)	½ c	8	0	0	0	52

LITE PICK ○◇□□□

COMMENTS: 72 fewer calories, 3 milligrams less sodium than ½ cup regular gelatin. Fat free. Sweetened with aspartame.

PRODUCT	SERV	CAL	FAT (G)	% cal from fat	CHOL (mg)	SOD (mg)
Gelatin, raspberry (Royal, Sugar Free)	½ c	6	0	0	0	75

LITE PICK ○◇□□□

COMMENTS: 74 fewer calories, 25 milligrams less sodium than ½ cup regular Royal raspberry gelatin. Fat free. Sweetened with aspartame.

PRODUCT	SERV	CAL	FAT (G)	% cal from fat	CHOL (mg)	SOD (mg)
Gelatin, strawberry (D-Zerta, Low Calorie)	½ c	8	0	0	0	0

LITE PICK ○◇□□□

COMMENTS: 72 fewer calories than ½ cup regular Jell-O gelatin. Fat free. Sweetened with aspartame.

PRODUCT	SERV	CAL	FAT (G)	% cal from fat	CHOL (mg)	SOD (mg)
Gelatin, strawberry (Estee)	½ c	8	0	0	0	10

LITE PICK ○◇□□

COMMENTS: 72 fewer calories, 45 milligrams less sodium than ½ cup regular gelatin. Fat free. Sweetened with aspartame.

PRODUCT	SERV	CAL	FAT (G)	% cal from fat	CHOL (mg)	SOD (mg)
Gelatin, strawberry (Featherweight)	½ c	10	0	0	0	3

LITE PICK ○◇□

COMMENTS: 71 fewer calories, 52 milligrams less sodium than ½ cup regular gelatin. Fat free. Sweetened with aspartame.

PRODUCT	SERV	CAL	FAT (G)	% cal from fat	CHOL (mg)	SOD (mg)
Gelatin, strawberry (Jell-O, Sugar Free)	½ c	8	0	0	0	65

LITE PICK ○◇□□□

COMMENTS: 72 fewer calories, 10 milligrams less sodium than ½ cup regular Jell-O Wild Strawberry gelatin. Fat free. Sweetened with aspartame.

PRODUCT	SERV	CAL	FAT (G)	% cal from fat	CHOL (mg)	SOD (mg)
Gelatin, strawberry (Royal, Sugar Free)	½ c	6	0	0	0	75

LITE PICK ○◇□□□

COMMENTS: 74 fewer calories, 30 milligrams less sodium than ½ cup regular Royal strawberry gelatin. Fat free. Sweetened with aspartame.

PRODUCT	SERV	CAL	FAT (G)	% cal from fat	CHOL (mg)	SOD (mg)
Gelatin, strawberry-banana (Jell-O, Sugar Free)	½ c	8	0	0	0	52

LITE PICK ○◇□□□

COMMENTS: 72 fewer calories, 3 milligrams less sodium than ½ cup regular gelatin. Fat free. Sweetened with aspartame.

PRODUCT	SERV	CAL	FAT (G)	% cal from fat	CHOL (mg)	SOD (mg)
Gelatin, w/fruit (All-Ready Maid, Diet Gelatine With Fruit)	4 oz	16	0	0	0	<60

LITE PICK ○◇□□□

COMMENTS: No direct comparison, but this product has about 50 calories fewer per 4 ounce serving than regular gelatin. Fat free. Sweetened with saccharin.

PRODUCT	SERV	CAL	FAT (G)	% cal from fat	CHOL (mg)	SOD (mg)
Mousse, cheesecake (Weight Watchers, Dry Mix)	½ c	60	2	30	na	75

○□□□

COMMENTS: No direct comparison. The high percentage of calories from fat is deceiving; since it contains only 2 grams of fat per ½ cup serving, this product is actually low in fat. Sweetened with aspartame.

PRODUCT	SERV	CAL	FAT (G)	% cal from fat	CHOL (mg)	SOD (mg)
Mousse, chocolate (Featherweight)	½ c	100	3	27	5	65

LITE PICK ○◇□□

COMMENTS: No direct comparison. Sweetened with aspartame.

PRODUCT	SERV	CAL	FAT (G)	% cal from fat	CHOL (mg)	SOD (mg)
Mousse, chocolate (San Sucre, Dessert Mix)	3 oz	50	<1	18	<5	93

LITE PICK ○◇◇□□□

COMMENTS: No direct comparison, but this product is very low in fat. Sweetened with aspartame.

PRODUCT	SERV	CAL	FAT (G)	% cal from fat	CHOL (mg)	SOD (mg)
Mousse, chocolate (Weight Watchers, Dry Mix)	½ c	60	3	45	na	45

□□□

COMMENTS: No direct comparison. Sweetened with aspartame.

PRODUCT	SERV	CAL	FAT (G)	% cal from fat	CHOL (mg)	SOD (mg)
Mousse, lemon (San Sucre, Dessert Mix)	3 oz	50	<1	18	<5	93

LITE PICK ○◇◇□□□

COMMENTS: No direct comparison, but this product is very low in fat. Sweetened with aspartame.

PRODUCT	SERV	CAL	FAT (G)	% cal from fat	CHOL (mg)	SOD (mg)
Mousse, raspberry (Weight Watchers, Dry Mix)	½ c	60	3	45	na	75

□□□

COMMENTS: No direct comparison. Sweetened with aspartame.

PRODUCT	SERV	CAL	FAT (G)	% cal from fat	CHOL (mg)	SOD (mg)
Mousse, strawberry (San Sucre, Dessert Mix)	3 oz	50	<1	18	<5	93

LITE PICK ○◇◇○□□

COMMENTS: No direct comparison, but this product is very low in fat. Sweetened with aspartame.

PRODUCT	SERV	CAL	FAT (G)	% cal from fat	CHOL (mg)	SOD (mg)
Pudding, banana (Jell-O, Sugar Free Instant)	½ c	90	2	20	10	430

○◇◇

COMMENTS: Prepared with 2% low-fat milk, this product has 70 fewer calories, 2 grams less fat, 5 milligrams less cholesterol, 10 milligrams less sodium than ½ cup regular Jell-O Banana Instant Pudding made with whole milk. High in sodium. Sweetened with aspartame.

PRODUCT	SERV	CAL	FAT (G)	% cal from fat	CHOL (mg)	SOD (mg)
Pudding, butterscotch (D-Zerta Reduced Calorie)	½ c	70	0	0	0	65

LITE PICK ○◇□□□

COMMENTS: Prepared with skim milk, product has 90 fewer calories, 4 grams less fat, 15 milligrams less cholesterol, 415 milligrams less sodium than ½ cup regular butterscotch Jell-O Instant Pudding prepared with whole milk. Fat free. Sweetened with aspartame.

PRODUCT	SERV	CAL	FAT (G)	% cal from fat	CHOL (mg)	SOD (mg)
Pudding, butterscotch (Estee)	½ c	70	<1	13	2	80

LITE PICK ○◇□□□

COMMENTS: 101 fewer calories, 4 grams less fat, 15 milligrams less cholesterol, 398 milligrams less sodium than ½ cup regular butterscotch pudding from a mix. Very low in fat. Sweetened with aspartame.

PRODUCT	SERV	CAL	FAT (G)	% cal from fat	CHOL (mg)	SOD (mg)
Pudding, butterscotch (Featherweight)	½ c	12	0	0	na	6

○□□

COMMENTS: 159 fewer calories, 4 grams less fat, 472 milligrams less sodium than ½ cup regular instant butterscotch pudding. Fat free. Sweetened with aspartame.

PRODUCT	SERV	CAL	FAT (G)	% cal from fat	CHOL (mg)	SOD (mg)
Pudding, butterscotch (Jell-O, Sugar Free Instant)	½ c	90	2	20	10	420

○◇◇

COMMENTS: Prepared with 2% low-fat milk, product has 70 fewer calories, 2 grams less fat, 5 milligrams less cholesterol, 60 milligrams less sodium than ½ cup regular Jell-O butterscotch instant pudding made with whole milk. High in sodium. Very low in fat. Sweetened with aspartame.

PRODUCT	SERV	CAL	FAT (G)	% cal from fat	CHOL (mg)	SOD (mg)
Pudding, butterscotch (Royal, Sugar Free)	½ c	100	2	8	na	470

○

COMMENTS: Prepared with skim milk, product has 80 fewer calories, 3 grams less fat, 80 milligrams less sodium than ½ cup regular Royal sugar-free vanilla instant pudding made with whole milk. High in sodium. Very low in fat. Sweetened with aspartame.

PRODUCT	SERV	CAL	FAT (G)	% cal from fat	CHOL (mg)	SOD (mg)
Pudding, butterscotch (Weight Watchers, Dry Mix)	½ c	90	0	0	na	460

○

COMMENTS: 81 fewer calories, 4 grams less fat, 18 milligrams less sodium than ½ cup regular instant butterscotch pudding. Fat free, but high in sodium. Sweetened with aspartame.

PRODUCT	SERV	CAL	FAT (G)	% cal from fat	CHOL (mg)	SOD (mg)
Pudding, chocolate (D-Zerta, Reduced Calorie)	½ c	60	0	0	0	70

LITE PICK ○◇□□□

COMMENTS: Prepared with skim milk, product has 100 fewer calories, 4 grams less fat, 15 milligrams less cholesterol, 100 milligrams less sodium than ½ cup regular Jell-O chocolate pudding made with whole milk. Fat free. Sweetened with aspartame.

PRODUCT	SERV	CAL	FAT (G)	% cal from fat	CHOL (mg)	SOD (mg)
Pudding, chocolate (Estee)	½ c	70	<1	<13	2	75

LITE PICK ○◇□□□

COMMENTS: 109 fewer calories, 4 grams less fat, 15 milligrams less cholesterol, 452 milligrams less sodium than ½ cup regular instant chocolate pudding. Very low in fat. Sweetened with aspartame.

PRODUCT	SERV	CAL	FAT (G)	% cal from fat	CHOL (mg)	SOD (mg)
Pudding, chocolate (Featherweight)	½ c	12	0	0	na	15

○□□

COMMENTS: 167 fewer calories, 4 grams less fat, 512 milligrams less sodium than ½ cup regular instant chocolate pudding. Fat free. Sweetened with aspartame.

PRODUCT	SERV	CAL	FAT (G)	% cal from fat	CHOL (mg)	SOD (mg)
Pudding, chocolate (Jell-O, Sugar Free Instant Chocolate Fudge)	½ c	100	3	27	10	370

◇◇◇

COMMENTS: Prepared with 2% low-fat milk, product has 80 fewer calories, 2 grams less fat, 5 milligrams less cholesterol, 10 milligrams less sodium than ½ cup regular Jell-O Chocolate Fudge instant pudding made with whole milk. High in sodium. Sweetened with aspartame.

PRODUCT	SERV	CAL	FAT (G)	% cal from fat	CHOL (mg)	SOD (mg)
Pudding, chocolate (Jell-O, Sugar Free)	½ c	90	3	30	10	170

◇◇◇

COMMENTS: Prepared with 2% low-fat milk, product has 70 fewer calories, 1 gram less fat, 5 milligrams less cholesterol than ½ cup regular Jell-O chocolate pudding made with whole milk. Sweetened with aspartame.

PRODUCT	SERV	CAL	FAT (G)	% cal from fat	CHOL (mg)	SOD (mg)
Pudding, chocolate (Jell-O, Sugar Free Instant)	½ c	100	3	27	10	410

○◇◇

COMMENTS: Prepared with 2% low-fat milk, product has 80 fewer calories, 1 gram less fat, 5 milligrams less cholesterol, 110 milligrams less sodium than ½ cup regular chocolate Jell-O instant pudding made with whole milk. Sweetened with aspartame.

PRODUCT	SERV	CAL	FAT (G)	% cal from fat	CHOL (mg)	SOD (mg)
Pudding, chocolate (Royal, Sugar Free Instant)	½ c	110	3	25	na	480

○

COMMENTS: 80 fewer calories, 1 gram less fat than ½ cup regular Royal sugar-free chocolate instant pudding, but 90 milligrams *more* sodium, making it high in sodium. Sweetened with aspartame.

PRODUCT	SERV	CAL	FAT (G)	% cal from fat	CHOL (mg)	SOD (mg)
Pudding, chocolate (Weight Watchers, Dry Mix)	½ c	90	1	10	na	420

○

COMMENTS: 89 fewer calories, 4 grams less fat, 107 milligrams less sodium than ½ cup regular instant chocolate pudding. Very low in fat, but high in sodium. Sweetened with aspartame.

PRODUCT	SERV	CAL	FAT (G)	% cal from fat	CHOL (mg)	SOD (mg)
Pudding, lemon (Estee)	½ c	70	<1	<13	2	75

LITE PICK ○◇□□□

COMMENTS: 108 fewer calories, 4 grams less fat, 15 milligrams less cholesterol, 312 milligrams less sodium than ½ cup regular lemon pudding from a mix. Sweetened with aspartame.

PRODUCT	SERV	CAL	FAT (G)	% cal from fat	CHOL (mg)	SOD (mg)
Pudding, pistachio (Jell-O, Sugar Free Instant)	½ c	100	3	27	10	430

○◇◇

COMMENTS: Prepared with 2% low-fat milk, product has 70 fewer calories, 2 grams less fat, 5 milligrams less cholesterol, 10 milligrams less sodium than ½ cup regular pistachio Jell-O instant pudding made with whole milk. High in sodium. Sweetened with aspartame.

PRODUCT	SERV	CAL	FAT (G)	% cal from fat	CHOL (mg)	SOD (mg)
Pudding, vanilla (D-Zerta, Reduced Calorie Vanilla)	½ c	70	0	0	0	65

LITE PICK ○◇□□□

COMMENTS: Prepared with skim milk, product has 100 fewer calories, 4 grams less fat, 15 milligrams less cholesterol, 375 milligrams less sodium than ½ cup regular vanilla Jell-O Instant Pudding & Pie Filling prepared with whole milk. Fat free. Sweetened with aspartame.

PRODUCT	SERV	CAL	FAT (G)	% cal from fat	CHOL (mg)	SOD (mg)
Pudding, vanilla (Estee)	½ c	70	<1	<13	2	75

LITE PICK ○◇□□□

COMMENTS: 107 fewer calories, 4 grams less fat, 15 milligrams less cholesterol, 347 milligrams less sodium than ½ cup regular instant vanilla pudding. Very low in fat. Sweetened with aspartame.

PRODUCT	SERV	CAL	FAT (G)	% cal from fat	CHOL (mg)	SOD (mg)
Pudding, vanilla (Featherweight)	½ c	12	0	0	na	6

○□□

COMMENTS: 165 fewer calories, 4 grams less fat, 416 milligrams less sodium than ½ cup regular instant vanilla pudding. Fat free. Sweetened with aspartame.

PRODUCT	SERV	CAL	FAT (G)	% cal from fat	CHOL (mg)	SOD (mg)
Pudding, vanilla (Jell-O, Sugar Free)	½ c	80	2	23	10	200

○◇◇

COMMENTS: Prepared with 2% low-fat milk, product has 80 fewer calories, 2 grams less fat, 5 milligrams less cholesterol than ½ cup regular Jell-O vanilla pudding made with whole milk. Lower in sodium than Jell-O sugar-free instant pudding. Sweetened with aspartame.

PRODUCT	SERV	CAL	FAT (G)	% cal from fat	CHOL (mg)	SOD (mg)
Pudding, vanilla (Jell-O, Sugar Free Instant)	½ c	90	2	20	10	420

○◇◇

COMMENTS: Prepared with 2% low-fat milk, product has 80 fewer calories, 2 grams less fat, 5 milligrams less cholesterol, 20 milligrams less sodium than ½ cup regular Jell-O vanilla instant pudding made with whole milk. Very low in fat, but high in sodium. Sweetened with aspartame.

PRODUCT	SERV	CAL	FAT (G)	% cal from fat	CHOL (mg)	SOD (mg)
Pudding, vanilla (Royal, Sugar Free)	½ c	100	2	18	na	470

○

COMMENTS: Prepared with skim milk, product has 80 fewer calories, 3 grams less fat, 80 milligrams less sodium than ½ cup regular Royal sugar-free vanilla instant pudding made with whole milk. Very low in fat, but high in sodium. Sweetened with aspartame.

PRODUCT	SERV	CAL	FAT (G)	% cal from fat	CHOL (mg)	SOD (mg)
Pudding, vanilla (Weight Watchers)	½ c	90	0	0	na	510

○

COMMENTS: 87 fewer calories, 4 grams less fat than ½ cup regular instant vanilla pudding, but 88 milligrams *more* sodium. Fat free, but high in sodium. Sweetened with aspartame.

SNACKS

PRODUCT	SERV	CAL	FAT (G)	% cal from fat	CHOL (mg)	SOD (mg)
Chips, carrot (Health Valley, Carrot Lites)	1 oz	140	2	13	0	20

LITE PICK ○◇□□

COMMENTS: No direct comparison, but this product is very low in fat.

PRODUCT	SERV	CAL	FAT (G)	% cal from fat	CHOL (mg)	SOD (mg)
Chips, corn (Featherweight, Low Sodium)	1 oz	170	11	58	na	3

□

COMMENTS: Light only in sodium. 15 calories and 1 gram fat, *more* than 1 ounce regular corn chips, but 180 milligrams less sodium. Very high in fat.

PRODUCT	SERV	CAL	FAT (G)	% cal from fat	CHOL (mg)	SOD (mg)
Chips, corn (Health Valley, No Salt)	1 oz	160	11	62	0	1

◇□

COMMENTS: Light only in sodium. 5 calories and 1 gram fat *more* than 1 ounce regular corn chips, but 182 milligrams less sodium. Very high in fat.

PRODUCT	SERV	CAL	FAT (G)	% cal from fat	CHOL (mg)	SOD (mg)
Chips, nacho cheese (Featherweight)	1 oz	150	8	48	na	45

□□□

COMMENTS: Light only in sodium. 6 calories and 1 gram fat *more* than 1 ounce regular cheese flavor tortilla chips, but 121 milligrams less sodium. Very high in fat.

PRODUCT	SERV	CAL	FAT (G)	% cal from fat	CHOL (mg)	SOD (mg)
Chips, potato (Featherweight, Low Sodium)	1 oz	160	11	62	na	4

□

COMMENTS: Light only in sodium. 7 calories and 1 gram fat *more* than 1 ounce regular potato chips, but 203 milligrams less sodium. Very high in fat.

PRODUCT	SERV	CAL	FAT (G)	% cal from fat	CHOL (mg)	SOD (mg)
Chips, potato (Health Valley, Country Ripple No Salt)	1 oz	160	10	56	0	1

◇□

COMMENTS: Light only in sodium. 7 *more* calories than 1 ounce regular potato chips, but 206 milligrams less sodium. Very high in fat.

PRODUCT	SERV	CAL	FAT (G)	% cal from fat	CHOL (mg)	SOD (mg)
Chips, potato (Health Valley, Dip, No Salt)	1 oz	160	10	56	0	1

◇□

COMMENTS: Light only in sodium. 7 *more* calories than 1 ounce regular potato chips, but 206 milligrams less sodium. Very high in fat.

PRODUCT	SERV	CAL	FAT (G)	% cal from fat	CHOL (mg)	SOD (mg)
Chips, potato (Pringles, Light BBQ)	1 oz	150	8	48	na	125

□□□

COMMENTS: This product has 20 fewer calories, 5 grams less fat, 45 milligrams less sodium than 1 ounce regular Pringles, and is still very high in fat.

PRODUCT	SERV	CAL	FAT (G)	% cal from fat	CHOL (mg)	SOD (mg)
Chips, potato (Pringles, Light Ranch)	1 oz	150	8	48	na	135

□□□

COMMENTS: This product has 20 fewer calories, 5 grams less fat, 35 milligrams less sodium than 1 ounce regular Pringles, and is still very high in fat.

PRODUCT	SERV	CAL	FAT (G)	% cal from fat	CHOL (mg)	SOD (mg)
Chips, potato (Pringles, Light)	1 oz	150	8	48	na	120

□□□

COMMENTS: 20 fewer calories, 5 grams less fat, 50 milligrams less sodium than 1 ounce regular Pringles, and is still very high in fat.

PRODUCT	SERV	CAL	FAT (G)	% cal from fat	CHOL (mg)	SOD (mg)
Chips, tortilla (Dorito, Light Cool Ranch®)	1 oz	120	4	30	0	190

○◇

COMMENTS: 20 fewer calories, 3 grams less fat than 1 ounce regular Doritos.

PRODUCT	SERV	CAL	FAT (G)	% cal from fat	CHOL (mg)	SOD (mg)
Chips, tortilla (Dorito, Light Nacho Cheese)	1 oz	120	4	30	0	250

○◇

COMMENTS: 20 fewer calories, 3 grams less fat than 1 ounce regular Nacho Cheese Doritos.

PRODUCT	SERV	CAL	FAT (G)	% cal from fat	CHOL (mg)	SOD (mg)
Chips, tortilla (Featherweight)	1 oz	150	8	48	na	10

□□

COMMENTS: Light only in sodium. 11 calories and 1 gram fat *more* than 1 ounce regular tortilla chips, but 170 milligrams less sodium.

PRODUCT	SERV	CAL	FAT (G)	% cal from fat	CHOL (mg)	SOD (mg)
Chips, tortilla (Health Valley, Buenitos, No Salt)	1 oz	130	8	55	0	1

◇□

COMMENTS: 9 fewer calories, 165 milligrams less sodium than 1 ounce regular tortilla chips, but 1 gram *more* fat. Very high in fat.

PRODUCT	SERV	CAL	FAT (G)	% cal from fat	CHOL (mg)	SOD (mg)
Chips, tortilla (La Famous, No Salt Added)	1 oz	140	7	45	na	5

□□

COMMENTS: Light only in sodium. 161 milligrams less sodium than 1 ounce regular tortilla chips. Very high in fat.

PRODUCT	SERV	CAL	FAT (G)	% cal from fat	CHOL (mg)	SOD (mg)
Curls, cheese (Featherweight, Low Sodium)	1 oz	150	9	54	na	81

□□□

COMMENTS: No direct comparison, but this product is very high in fat.

PRODUCT	SERV	CAL	FAT (G)	% cal from fat	CHOL (mg)	SOD (mg)
Fruit snacks (Weight Watchers, all flavors)	1 oz	100	<1	<19	na	150

○

COMMENTS: No direct comparison, but this product is very low in fat.

PRODUCT	SERV	CAL	FAT (G)	% cal from fat	CHOL (mg)	SOD (mg)
Peanuts (Paul's, Partially Defatted Salt Free)	1 oz	156	10	57	0	0

◇□

COMMENTS: 14 fewer calories, 4 grams less fat, 138 milligrams less sodium than 1 ounce regular salted peanuts, but still very high in fat.

PRODUCT	SERV	CAL	FAT (G)	% cal from fat	CHOL (mg)	SOD (mg)
Peanuts (Weight Watchers, Partially Defatted)	.7 oz	100	7	63	na	5

□

COMMENTS: 19 fewer calories, 3 grams less fat, 92 milligrams less sodium than .7 ounce regular roasted, salted peanuts, but still very high in fat.

PRODUCT	SERV	CAL	FAT (G)	% cal from fat	CHOL (mg)	SOD (mg)
Popcorn (Boston Popcorn Co., Lite Gourmet No Salt Added)	1⅔ c	60	3	45	0	35

◇□□

COMMENTS: 30 fewer calories, but 2 grams *more* fat and 35 milligrams more sodium than 1⅔ cups regular unsalted popcorn.

PRODUCT	SERV	CAL	FAT (G)	% cal from fat	CHOL (mg)	SOD (mg)
Popcorn (Pillsbury, Microwave Salt Free)	3 c	170	7	37	na	0

□

COMMENTS: 40 fewer calories, 6 grams less fat, 420 milligrams less sodium than three cups regular Pillsbury Original Flavor Microwave Popcorn.

PRODUCT	SERV	CAL	FAT (G)	% cal from fat	CHOL (mg)	SOD (mg)
Popcorn (Weight Watchers, Microwave)	3 c	150	1.5	9	na	7.5

○□

COMMENTS: No direct comparison, but this product is much lower in fat and sodium than most microwave popcorn. Very low in fat.

PRODUCT	SERV	CAL	FAT (G)	% cal from fat	CHOL (mg)	SOD (mg)
Popcorn, cheese flavored (Boston Popcorn Co., Cheda Lite)	1⅔ c	70	4	51	na	100

□□□

COMMENTS: 20 fewer calories, but 3 grams fat and 100 milligrams *more* sodium than 1⅔ cups regular unsalted popcorn.

PRODUCT	SERV	CAL	FAT (G)	% cal from fat	CHOL (mg)	SOD (mg)
Pretzels (Estee, Unsalted) ◇□	5 pc	25	<1	<36	0	<5

COMMENTS: No direct comparison, but this product is much lower in sodium than regular pretzels.

PRODUCT	SERV	CAL	FAT (G)	% cal from fat	CHOL (mg)	SOD (mg)
Pretzels (Featherweight, Low Sodium) LITE PICK ○◇□	3 pc	20	0	0	0	5.2

COMMENTS: No direct comparison, but this product is fat free and much lower in sodium than regular pretzels.

PRODUCT	SERV	CAL	FAT (G)	% cal from fat	CHOL (mg)	SOD (mg)
Pretzels, whole wheat (Barbara's Bakery, No Salt Added Bavarian) LITE PICK ○◇□□	1 oz	120	4	30	0	10

COMMENTS: 190 milligrams less sodium than 1 ounce regular Barbara's Bakery Whole Wheat Bavarian Pretzels.

PRODUCT	SERV	CAL	FAT (G)	% cal from fat	CHOL (mg)	SOD (mg)
Puffs, barbecue (Lite Munchies)	½ oz	60	.2	3	.5	60

LITE PICK ○◇□□□

COMMENTS: No direct comparison, but very low in fat.

PRODUCT	SERV	CAL	FAT (G)	% cal from fat	CHOL (mg)	SOD (mg)
Puffs, barbecue (Weight Watchers, Great Snackers Barbecue)	1 oz	120	6	45	na	340

COMMENTS: No direct comparison, but this product is very high in fat and has *more* sodium than most potato chips.

PRODUCT	SERV	CAL	FAT (G)	% cal from fat	CHOL (mg)	SOD (mg)
Puffs, cheese (Health Valley, Cheddar Lites with Green Onion)	1 oz	160	4	23	0	140

LITE PICK ○◇□□□

COMMENTS: No direct comparison, but this product contains about the same calories and sodium as most chips, with less than half the fat.

PRODUCT	SERV	CAL	FAT (G)	% cal from fat	CHOL (mg)	SOD (mg)
Puffs, cheese (Health Valley, Cheddar Lites, No Salt)	1 oz	160	8	45	1.6	40

◇□□□

COMMENTS: No direct comparison, but this product has about the same fat and calories as most chips with about 75% less sodium. Very high in fat.

PRODUCT	SERV	CAL	FAT (G)	% cal from fat	CHOL (mg)	SOD (mg)
Puffs, cheese (Weight Watchers, Great Snackers Cheddar Cheese)	1 oz	120	6	45	na	340

COMMENTS: No direct comparison, but this product is very high in fat and has *more* sodium than most chips.

PRODUCT	SERV	CAL	FAT (G)	% cal from fat	CHOL (mg)	SOD (mg)
Puffs, chocolate (Lite Munchies, Rich Chocolate)	½ oz	60	2	30	.5	60

LITE PICK ○◇□□□

COMMENTS: No direct comparison, but low in fat.

PRODUCT	SERV	CAL	FAT (G)	% cal from fat	CHOL (mg)	SOD (mg)
Puffs, nacho cheese						
(Lite Munchies)	½ oz	60	2	30	.5	60

LITE PICK ○◇□□□

COMMENTS: No direct comparison, but low in fat.

PRODUCT	SERV	CAL	FAT (G)	% cal from fat	CHOL (mg)	SOD (mg)
Puffs, onion						
(Lite Munchies)	½ oz	60	2	30	.5	60

LITE PICK ○◇□□□

COMMENTS: No direct comparison, but low in fat.

PRODUCT	SERV	CAL	FAT (G)	% cal from fat	CHOL (mg)	SOD (mg)
Puffs, onion (Weight Watchers, Great Snackers Toasted Onion)	1 oz	120	6	45	na	240

COMMENTS: No direct comparison, but this product is very high in fat and high in sodium.

PRODUCT	SERV	CAL	FAT (G)	% cal from fat	CHOL (mg)	SOD (mg)
Puffs, wheat						
(Estee, Wheat Snax)	1 oz	110	1	8	0	35

LITE PICK ○◇□□

COMMENTS: No direct comparison, but this product is very low in fat.

PRODUCT	SERV	CAL	FAT (G)	% cal from fat	CHOL (mg)	SOD (mg)
Rice cakes						
(Pritikin, Sodium						
Free)	1 pc	35	0	0	0	0

LITE PICK ○◇□□

COMMENTS: About 10 milligrams sodium less than most regular rice cakes, or 30 milligrams less than regular Pritikin rice cakes. Fat free.

PRODUCT	SERV	CAL	FAT (G)	% cal from fat	CHOL (mg)	SOD (mg)
Rice cakes						
(Pritikin, Very Low						
Sodium)	1 pc	35	0	0	0	30

LITE PICK ○◇□□

COMMENTS: No direct comparison, but this product has about 20 milligrams *more* sodium than most regular rice cakes. Even so, it's still low enough to qualify as a LITE PICK. Fat free.

PRODUCT	SERV	CAL	FAT (G)	% cal from fat	CHOL (mg)	SOD (mg)
Rice cakes, 7-grain (Pritikin, Sodium Free)	1 pc	35	0	0	0	0

LITE PICK ○◇□

COMMENTS: 30 milligrams sodium less than regular Pritikin rice cakes; 5 milligrams less than Pritikin Very Low Sodium 7-Grain Rice Cakes. Fat free.

PRODUCT	SERV	CAL	FAT (G)	% cal from fat	CHOL (mg)	SOD (mg)
Rice cakes, 7-grain (Pritikin, Very Low Sodium)	1 pc	35	0	0	0	5

LITE PICK ○◇□□

COMMENTS: No direct comparison, but this product has about 5 milligrams less than most regular rice cakes. Fat free.

PRODUCT	SERV	CAL	FAT (G)	% cal from fat	CHOL (mg)	SOD (mg)
Rice cakes, sesame (Pritikin, Sodium Free)	1 pc	35	0	0	0	0

LITE PICK ○◇□

COMMENTS: 35 milligrams less sodium than one Pritikin Very Low Sodium Sesame Rice Cake. Fat free.

PRODUCT	SERV	CAL	FAT (G)	% cal from fat	CHOL (mg)	SOD (mg)
Rice cakes, sesame (Pritikin, Very Low Sodium)	1 pc	35	0	0	0	35

LITE PICK ○◇□□

COMMENTS: No direct comparison, but this product has about 25 milligrams *more* sodium than most regular rice cakes. Even so, it's still low enough to qualify as a LITE PICK. Fat free.

SOUP

PRODUCT	SERV	CAL	FAT (G)	% cal from fat	CHOL (mg)	SOD (mg)
Bean, canned (Health Valley, No Salt Black Bean)	7½ oz	160	4.3	24	0	20

LITE PICK ○◇□□

COMMENTS: 44 calories, 3 grams *more* fat than 8 ounces regular black bean soup, but 1,178 milligrams less sodium. Even with *more* fat and calories, this product still qualifies as a LITE PICK.

PRODUCT	SERV	CAL	FAT (G)	% cal from fat	CHOL (mg)	SOD (mg)
Bean, canned (Pritikin, Navy Bean)	7⅜ oz	130	<1	<7	0	170

LITE PICK ○◇□□□□

COMMENTS: 43 fewer calories, 3 milligrams less cholesterol, 782 milligrams less sodium than 8 ounces regular canned bean-with-bacon soup.

PRODUCT	SERV	CAL	FAT (G)	% cal from fat	CHOL (mg)	SOD (mg)
Bean w/bacon, canned (Campbell's, Special Request Bean with Bacon)	8 oz	120	4	30	na	540

○

COMMENTS: 310 milligrams less sodium than 8 ounces regular Campbell's Bean with Bacon Soup, but still high in sodium.

PRODUCT	SERV	CAL	FAT (G)	% cal from fat	CHOL (mg)	SOD (mg)
Beef broth, canned (Health Valley, No Salt)	7½ oz	8	.3	34	0	50

◇□□

COMMENTS: 8 fewer calories, 732 milligrams less sodium than 8 ounces regular canned beef broth. The high percentage of calories from fat is deceiving; since it contains less than 1 gram of fat per serving, this product is actually low in fat.

PRODUCT	SERV	CAL	FAT (G)	% cal from fat	CHOL (mg)	SOD (mg)
Beef broth, canned (Pritikin, Beef Broth)	6⅞ oz	20	<1	<45	<5	170

◇◇□□□□

COMMENTS: 6 *more* calories, but 514 milligrams less sodium than 7 ounces regular canned beef broth. The high percentage of calories from fat is deceiving; with less than 1 gram of fat per serving this product is actually low in fat.

PRODUCT	SERV	CAL	FAT (G)	% cal from fat	CHOL (mg)	SOD (mg)
Beef w/ vegetables, canned (Campbell's, Ready To Serve Low Sodium Chunky Beef and Mushroom)	10¾ oz	210	7	30	45	65

O☐☐☐

COMMENTS: No direct comparison, but this product is low in fat and much lower in sodium than regular soups.

PRODUCT	SERV	CAL	FAT (G)	% cal from fat	CHOL (mg)	SOD (mg)
Beef w/ vegetables, canned (Campbell's, Ready To Serve Low Sodium Chunky Vegetable Beef)	10¾ oz	170	5	26	50	60

O☐☐☐

COMMENTS: No direct comparison, but this product is low in fat and much lower in sodium than regular soups.

PRODUCT	SERV	CAL	FAT (G)	% cal from fat	CHOL (mg)	SOD (mg)
Beef w/ vegetables, canned (Featherweight, Low Sodium Vegetable Beef)	7½ oz	160	6	34	na	40

□□□

COMMENTS: 110 calories and 5 grams fat *more* than 7½ ounces regular vegetable beef soup, but 938 milligrams less sodium—much lower than regular soups.

PRODUCT	SERV	CAL	FAT (G)	% cal from fat	CHOL (mg)	SOD (mg)
Beef bouillon, instant (Featherweight, Instant Low Sodium Beef Bouillon)	1 tsp dry (equivalent 8 oz. recon- stituted)	18	1	50	na	10

□□

COMMENTS: 1 fewer calorie and 1,348 milligrams less sodium than 8 ounces regular beef bouillon. The high percentage of calories from fat is deceiving; since it contains only 1 gram of fat per serving, this product is actually low in fat.

PRODUCT	SERV	CAL	FAT (G)	% cal from fat	CHOL (mg)	SOD (mg)
Beef bouillon, instant (Wyler's LiteLine (R) Low Sodium)	1 tsp dry (equivalent 8 oz. recon- stituted)	12	<1	<75	na	5

□□

COMMENTS: 7 fewer calories, 1 gram less fat, 1,353 milligrams less sodium than 8 ounces regular beef bouillon.

PRODUCT	SERV	CAL	FAT (G)	% cal from fat	CHOL (mg)	SOD (mg)
Beef broth, instant (Weight Watchers, Beef Broth)	1 packet	8	0	0	na	930

○

COMMENTS: 11 fewer calories, 428 milligrams less sodium than 8 ounces regular reconstituted beef bouillon, but this product is still high in sodium. Fat free.

PRODUCT	SERV	CAL	FAT (G)	% cal from fat	CHOL (mg)	SOD (mg)
Beef w/noodles, instant (Estee, Beef Noodle)	6 oz	20	<1	<45	1	140

◇□□□

COMMENTS: 43 fewer calories, 574 milligrams less sodium than 6 ounces regular canned beef noodle soup. The high percentage of calories from fat is deceiving; since it contains less than 1 gram of fat per serving, this product is actually low in fat.

PRODUCT	SERV	CAL	FAT (G)	% cal from fat	CHOL (mg)	SOD (mg)
Broccoli, instant (Lipton, Lite Cup-a-Soup)	6 oz	50	1	18	na	470

○

COMMENTS: No direct comparison, but this product is very low in fat and high in sodium.

PRODUCT	SERV	CAL	FAT (G)	% cal from fat	CHOL (mg)	SOD (mg)
Chicken, canned (Campbell's, Special Request Cream of Chicken)	8 oz	110	7	57	na	520

COMMENTS: 290 milligrams less sodium than 8 ounces regular Campbell's Cream of Chicken Soup, but still high in sodium. Very high in fat.

PRODUCT	SERV	CAL	FAT (G)	% cal from fat	CHOL (mg)	SOD (mg)
Chicken, canned (Pritikin, Chicken Gumbo)	7⅜ oz	60	1	15	5	180

○◇◇

COMMENTS: No direct comparison, but this product is very low in fat, and lower in sodium than regular soups.

PRODUCT	SERV	CAL	FAT (G)	% cal from fat	CHOL (mg)	SOD (mg)
Chicken broth, canned (Campbell's, Ready To Serve Low Sodium Chicken Broth)	10½ oz	40	2	45	<5	70

◇◇☐☐☐

COMMENTS: 6 calories and 1 gram fat *more* than 10½ ounces regular Campbell's Chicken Broth, but 680 milligrams less sodium. The high percentage of calories from fat is deceiving; since it contains only 2 grams of fat per 10½ oz. serving, this product is actually low in fat.

PRODUCT	SERV	CAL	FAT (G)	% cal from fat	CHOL (mg)	SOD (mg)
Chicken broth, canned (Health Valley, No Salt)	7½ oz	34	2.3	61	1.8	0

◇☐

COMMENTS: 5 fewer calories, 1 gram less fat, 776 milligrams less sodium than 8 ounces regular canned chicken broth. The high percentage of calories from fat is deceiving. Since it contains only 2.3 grams of fat per 7½ oz. serving, this product is actually low in fat.

PRODUCT	SERV	CAL	FAT (G)	% cal from fat	CHOL (mg)	SOD (mg)
Chicken broth, canned						
(Pritikin)	6⅞ oz	14	0	0	0	175

○◇

COMMENTS: 20 fewer calories, 1 gram less fat, 570 milligrams less sodium than 7 ounces regular canned chicken broth. Fat free.

PRODUCT	SERV	CAL	FAT (G)	% cal from fat	CHOL (mg)	SOD (mg)
Chicken w/ noodles, canned						
(Campbell's, Ready To Serve Low Sodium Chicken Noodle)	10¾ oz	160	5	28	65	85

○□□□

COMMENTS: 66 calories and 2 grams fat *more* than 10¾ ounces regular Campbell's Chicken Noodle Soup, but 1,138 milligrams less sodium.

PRODUCT	SERV	CAL	FAT (G)	% cal from fat	CHOL (mg)	SOD (mg)
Chicken w/ noodles, canned						
(Campbell's, Special Request Chicken Noodle)	8 oz	70	2	26	na	560

○

COMMENTS: 350 milligrams less sodium than 8 ounces regular Campbell's Chicken Noodle Soup, but still high in sodium.

PRODUCT	SERV	CAL	FAT (G)	% cal from fat	CHOL (mg)	SOD (mg)
Chicken w/ noodles, canned (Featherweight, Low Sodium Chicken Noodle)	7½ oz	120	4	30	na	100

○□□□

COMMENTS: Light only in sodium, 70 calories and 3 grams fat *more* than 7½ ounces regular chicken noodle soup, but 1,391 milligrams less sodium.

PRODUCT	SERV	CAL	FAT (G)	% cal from fat	CHOL (mg)	SOD (mg)
Chicken w/pasta, canned (Pritikin, Chicken with Ribbon Pasta)	7¼ oz	60	<1	15	0	175

LITE PICK ○◇□□□□

COMMENTS: 8 fewer calories, 2 grams less fat, 828 milligrams less sodium than 7¼ ounces regular canned chicken noodle soup.

PRODUCT	SERV	CAL	FAT (G)	% cal from fat	CHOL (mg)	SOD (mg)
Chicken w/rice, canned (Campbell's, Special Request Chicken with Rice)	8 oz	60	2	30	na	520

○

COMMENTS: 280 milligrams less sodium than 8 ounces regular Campbell's Chicken with Rice Soup, but still high in sodium.

PRODUCT	SERV	CAL	FAT (G)	% cal from fat	CHOL (mg)	SOD (mg)
Chicken w/ vegetables, canned (Campbell's, Ready To Serve Low Sodium Chunky Chicken Vegetable)	10¾ oz	240	11	41	45	95

□□□

COMMENTS: No direct comparison, but this product is very high in fat. Much lower in sodium than most soups.

PRODUCT	SERV	CAL	FAT (G)	% cal from fat	CHOL (mg)	SOD (mg)
Chicken w/ vegetables, canned (Estee, Chunky Chicken)	7¼ oz	120	6	45	na	60

□□□

COMMENTS: 21 fewer calories, 745 milligrams less sodium than 7¼ ounces regular chunky chicken soup.

PRODUCT	SERV	CAL	FAT (G)	% cal from fat	CHOL (mg)	SOD (mg)
Chicken w/ vegetables, canned (Health Valley, No-Salt Chunky Chicken Vegetable)	8 oz	240	14	53	23	60

□□□

COMMENTS: No direct comparison, but this product is very high in fat, and much lower in sodium than regular soups.

PRODUCT	SERV	CAL	FAT (G)	% cal from fat	CHOL (mg)	SOD (mg)
Chicken w/ vegetables, canned (Pritikin, Chicken Vegetable)	7¼ oz	70	<1	<13	0	175

LITE PICK ○◇□□□□

COMMENTS: 2 grams fat, 9 milligrams cholesterol, 680 milligrams less sodium, but 3 calories *more* than 7¼ ounces regular canned chicken vegetable soup.

PRODUCT	SERV	CAL	FAT (G)	% cal from fat	CHOL (mg)	SOD (mg)
Chicken, instant (Lipton, Lite Cup-a-Soup Lemon Chicken)	6 oz	45	<1	<20	na	540

○

COMMENTS: No direct comparison, but this product is very high in sodium and very low in fat.

PRODUCT	SERV	CAL	FAT (G)	% cal from fat	CHOL (mg)	SOD (mg)
Chicken bouillon, instant (Featherweight, Instant Low Sodium Bouillon)	1 tsp dry (equivalent 8 oz reconstituted)	18	1	50	na	5

□□

COMMENTS: 3 fewer calories, 1,479 milligrams less sodium than one cup reconstituted chicken bouillon. The high percentage of calories from fat is deceiving; with only 1 gram of fat per 8 ounce serving, it is actually low in fat.

PRODUCT	SERV	CAL	FAT (G)	% cal from fat	CHOL (mg)	SOD (mg)

Chicken bouillon, instant
(Wyler's LiteLine®

Low Sodium)	1 tsp dry	12	<1	<75	na	5

□□

COMMENTS: 9 fewer calories, 1,479 milligrams less sodium than 8 ounces regular reconstituted chicken bouillon. The high percentage of calories from fat is deceiving; with less than 1 gram of fat per serving, the product is low in fat.

PRODUCT	SERV	CAL	FAT (G)	% cal from fat	CHOL (mg)	SOD (mg)

Chicken broth, instant
(Weight Watchers,

Chicken Broth)	1 packet	8	0	0	na	990

○

COMMENTS: 13 fewer calories, 1 gram less fat, 494 milligrams less sodium than 8 ounces regular reconstituted chicken broth. Fat free but high in sodium.

PRODUCT	SERV	CAL	FAT (G)	% cal from fat	CHOL (mg)	SOD (mg)
Chicken w/ noodles, instant (Estee, Chicken Noodle)	6 oz	25	<1	<36	4	135

◇◇□□□

COMMENTS: 15 fewer calories, 828 milligrams less sodium than 6 ounces regular chicken noodle soup from a mix. The high percentage of calories from fat is deceiving; since it contains less than 1 gram of fat per 6 ounce serving, this product is actually low in fat.

PRODUCT	SERV	CAL	FAT (G)	% cal from fat	CHOL (mg)	SOD (mg)
Chicken w/ noodles, instant (Weight Watchers, Chicken Noodle)	10½ oz	80	2	23	na	1230

○

COMMENTS: 10 fewer calories, 455 milligrams less sodium than 10½ ounces regular instant chicken noodle soup. Very high in sodium.

PRODUCT	SERV	CAL	FAT (G)	% cal from fat	CHOL (mg)	SOD (mg)
Chicken, instant (Lipton, Lite Cup-a-Soup Chicken Dijon Florentine)	6 oz	50	<1	18	na	540

○

COMMENTS: No direct comparison, but this product is very low in fat and high in sodium.

PRODUCT	SERV	CAL	FAT (G)	% cal from fat	CHOL (mg)	SOD (mg)
Clam chowder, canned (Health Valley, No Salt Manhattan Clam Chowder)	7½ oz	110	3.2	26	15.2	60

LITE PICK ○○◇◇□□□

COMMENTS: 37 calories, 1 gram fat, 13 milligrams *more* cholesterol than 7½ ounces regular canned Manhattan clam chowder, but 1,635 milligrams less sodium. Even so, this product still qualifies as a LITE PICK.

PRODUCT	SERV	CAL	FAT (G)	% cal from fat	CHOL (mg)	SOD (mg)
Clam chowder, canned (Pritikin, Manhattan Clam Chowder)	7⅜ oz	70	<1	<13	0	170

LITE PICK ○○◇□□□□

COMMENTS: 2 fewer calories, 1 gram less fat, 1,497 milligrams less sodium than 7⅜ ounces regular canned Manhattan clam chowder made with water, but 11 milligrams *more* cholesterol. Even so, this product still qualifies as a LITE PICK. Very low in fat.

PRODUCT	SERV	CAL	FAT (G)	% cal from fat	CHOL (mg)	SOD (mg)
Clam chowder, canned (Pritikin, New England)	7⅜ oz	118	<1	<8	0	170

LITE PICK ○◇□□□□

COMMENTS: 5 milligrams cholesterol, 744 milligrams sodium less than 8 ounces regular canned New England clam chowder made with water, but 23 *more* calories. Even so, this product still qualifies as a LITE PICK. Very low in fat. .

PRODUCT	SERV	CAL	FAT (G)	% cal from fat	CHOL (mg)	SOD (mg)
Lentil, canned (Pritikin)	7⅜ oz	100	0	0	0	170

LITE PICK ○◇□□□□

COMMENTS: 31 fewer calories, 2 grams less fat, 6 milligrams less cholesterol, 1,185 milligrams less sodium than 7⅜ ounces regular canned lentil soup with ham. Fat free.

PRODUCT	SERV	CAL	FAT (G)	% cal from fat	CHOL (mg)	SOD (mg)
Minestrone, canned (Estee, Chunky)	7½ oz	160	5	28	na	30

○□□

COMMENTS: 41 calories and 2 grams fat *more* than 7½ ounces regular chunky minestrone soup, but 834 milligrams less sodium, much less than regular soups.

PRODUCT	SERV	CAL	FAT (G)	% cal from fat	CHOL (mg)	SOD (mg)
Minestrone, canned (Health Valley, No Salt)	7½ oz	120	2.5	19	0	80

LITE PICK ○◇□□□

COMMENTS: 42 more calories than 7½ ounces regular minestrone soup, but 774 milligrams less sodium. Very low in fat and much lower in sodium than regular soups.

PRODUCT	SERV	CAL	FAT (G)	% cal from fat	CHOL (mg)	SOD (mg)
Minestrone, canned (Pritikin)	7⅜ oz	110	<1	<8	0	130

LITE PICK ○◇□□□

COMMENTS: 33 calories *more* than 7⅜ ounces regular canned minestrone soup made with water, but 1 gram fat, 710 milligrams less sodium. Even with *more* calories, this product still qualifies as a LITE PICK. Very low in fat.

PRODUCT	SERV	CAL	FAT (G)	% cal from fat	CHOL (mg)	SOD (mg)

Mushroom, canned
(Campbell's, Ready To Serve Low Sodium Cream of Mushroom)

	SERV	CAL	FAT (G)	% cal from fat	CHOL (mg)	SOD (mg)
	10½ oz	200	14	63	20	55

◇◇□□□

COMMENTS: 50 fewer calories, 5 grams less fat, 1,026 milligrams less sodium than 10½ ounces regular Campbell's cream of mushroom soup. Very high in fat but much lower in sodium than regular soups.

PRODUCT	SERV	CAL	FAT (G)	% cal from fat	CHOL (mg)	SOD (mg)

Mushroom, canned
(Campbell's, Special Request Cream of Mushroom)

	SERV	CAL	FAT (G)	% cal from fat	CHOL (mg)	SOD (mg)
	8 oz	100	7	63	na	530

COMMENTS: 290 milligrams less sodium than 8 ounces regular Campbell's cream of mushroom soup, but still high in sodium and very high in fat.

PRODUCT	SERV	CAL	FAT (G)	% cal from fat	CHOL (mg)	SOD (mg)

Mushroom, canned
(Featherweight, Low Sodium)

	SERV	CAL	FAT (G)	% cal from fat	CHOL (mg)	SOD (mg)
	7½ oz	100	2	18	na	30

○□□

COMMENTS: 20 fewer calories, 6 gram less fat, 937 milligrams less sodium than 7½ oz regular cream of mushroom soup made with water. Much lower in sodium than regular soups. Very low in fat.

PRODUCT	SERV	CAL	FAT (G)	% cal from fat	CHOL (mg)	SOD (mg)
Mushroom, canned (Pritikin)	7⅜ oz	60	<1	<15	0	170

LITE PICK ○◇□□□□□

COMMENTS: 59 fewer calories, 7 grams less fat, 2 milligrams less cholesterol, 780 milligrams less sodium than 7⅜ ounce regular canned mushroom soup made with water. Lower in sodium than regular soups and very low in fat.

PRODUCT	SERV	CAL	FAT (G)	% cal from fat	CHOL (mg)	SOD (mg)
Mushroom w/ barley, canned (Health Valley, No Salt Mushroom Barley)	7½ oz	110	3	25	0	20

LITE PICK ○◇□□

COMMENTS: No direct comparison, but this product is much lower in sodium than regular soups.

PRODUCT	SERV	CAL	FAT (G)	% cal from fat	CHOL (mg)	SOD (mg)
Mushroom, instant (Estee)	6 oz	40	2	45	1	115

◇□□□

COMMENTS: 32 fewer calories, 2 grams less fat, 649 milligrams less sodium than 6 ounces regular mushroom soup from a mix. Lower in sodium than regular soups. The high percentage of calories from fat is deceiving; since it contains only 2 grams of fat per 6 ounce serving, this product is actually low in fat.

PRODUCT	SERV	CAL	FAT (G)	% cal from fat	CHOL (mg)	SOD (mg)

Mushroom, instant

(Weight Watchers, Cream of Mushroom)

	SERV	CAL	FAT (G)	% cal from fat	CHOL (mg)	SOD (mg)
	10½ oz	90	2	20	na	1250

○

COMMENTS: No direct comparison. Very low in fat, but very high in sodium.

PRODUCT	SERV	CAL	FAT (G)	% cal from fat	CHOL (mg)	SOD (mg)

Onion, canned

(Campbell's, Ready To Serve Low Sodium French Onion)

	SERV	CAL	FAT (G)	% cal from fat	CHOL (mg)	SOD (mg)
	10½ oz	80	4	45	15	50

◇◇□□□

COMMENTS: 1 calorie and 1 gram fat *more* than 10½ ounces regular Campbell's French onion soup, but 1,131 milligrams less sodium. Very high in fat, but much lower in sodium than regular soups.

PRODUCT	SERV	CAL	FAT (G)	% cal from fat	CHOL (mg)	SOD (mg)

Onion, instant

(Estee)	SERV	CAL	FAT (G)	% cal from fat	CHOL (mg)	SOD (mg)
	6 oz	25	<1	<36	1	140

◇□□□

COMMENTS: 4 calories and 1 milligram cholesterol *more* than 6 ounces regular instant onion soup, but 496 milligrams less sodium. Lower in sodium than regular soups. The high percentage of calories from fat is deceiving; since it contains less than 1 gram of fat per 6 ounce serving, this product is actually low in fat.

PRODUCT	SERV	CAL	FAT (G)	% cal from fat	CHOL (mg)	SOD (mg)
Oriental, instant (Lipton, Lite Cup-a-Soup) ○	6 oz	30	<1	30	na	470

COMMENTS: No direct comparison, but this product is low in fat and high in sodium.

PRODUCT	SERV	CAL	FAT (G)	% cal from fat	CHOL (mg)	SOD (mg)
Pea, split, canned (Campbell's, Ready To Serve Low Sodium) LITE PICK ○□□	10¾ oz	240	5	19	na	25

COMMENTS: 38 calories *more* than 10¾ ounces regular Campbell's split pea soup, but 1,050 milligrams less sodium. Very low in fat and much lower in sodium than regular soups.

PRODUCT	SERV	CAL	FAT (G)	% cal from fat	CHOL (mg)	SOD (mg)
Pea split, canned (Health Valley, No Salt Green Split Pea) LITE PICK ○◇□□	7½ oz	160	1.7	10	0	25

COMMENTS: 6 calories *more* than 7½ ounces regular canned green pea soup, but 1 gram fat and 900 milligrams less sodium. Very low in fat and much lower in sodium than regular soups.

PRODUCT	SERV	CAL	FAT (G)	% cal from fat	CHOL (mg)	SOD (mg)
Pea, split, canned (Pritikin)	7½ oz	130	0	0	0	170

LITE PICK ○◇□□□□

COMMENTS: 24 fewer calories, 3 grams less fat, 755 milligrams less sodium than 7½ ounces regular canned green pea soup. Fat free and lower in sodium than regular soups.

PRODUCT	SERV	CAL	FAT (G)	% cal from fat	CHOL (mg)	SOD (mg)
Potato, canned (Health Valley, No Salt Potato Leek)	7½ oz	110	2.5	20	0	20

LITE PICK ○◇□□

COMMENTS: No direct comparison, but this product is low in fat and much lower in sodium than regular soups.

PRODUCT	SERV	CAL	FAT (G)	% cal from fat	CHOL (mg)	SOD (mg)
Tomato, canned (Campbell's, Ready To Serve Low Sodium Tomato with Tomato Pieces)	10½ oz	180	5	25	na	40

○□□□

COMMENTS: 62 calories and 2 grams *more* fat than 10½ ounces regular Campbell's tomato soup, but 839 milligrams less sodium—much lower than regular soups.

PRODUCT	SERV	CAL	FAT (G)	% cal from fat	CHOL (mg)	SOD (mg)
Tomato, canned (Campbell's, Special Request Tomato)	8 oz	90	2	20	na	470

○

COMMENTS: 200 milligrams less sodium than 8 ounces regular Campbell's tomato soup, but still high in sodium. Very low in fat.

PRODUCT	SERV	CAL	FAT (G)	% cal from fat	CHOL (mg)	SOD (mg)
Tomato, canned (Featherweight, Low Sodium Tomato)	7½ oz	120	0	0	na	52

○☐☐

COMMENTS: 24 fewer calories, 2 grams less fat, 832 milligrams less sodium than 7½ ounces regular canned tomato soup. Much lower in sodium than regular soups. Fat free.

PRODUCT	SERV	CAL	FAT (G)	% cal from fat	CHOL (mg)	SOD (mg)
Tomato, canned (Health Valley, No Salt)	7½ oz	110	2.8	23	0	40

LITE PICK ○◇☐☐

COMMENTS: 29 calories and 1 gram fat *more* than 7½ ounces regular canned tomato soup, but 778 milligrams less sodium—much lower than regular soups.

PRODUCT	SERV	CAL	FAT (G)	% cal from fat	CHOL (mg)	SOD (mg)
Tomato, canned (Pritikin, Tomato with Tomato Pieces)	7¼ oz	70	0	0	0	125

LITE PICK ○◇□□□

COMMENTS: 8 fewer calories, 2 grams less fat, 665 milligrams less sodium than 7¼ ounces regular canned tomato soup made with water. Fat free and lower in sodium than regular soups.

PRODUCT	SERV	CAL	FAT (G)	% cal from fat	CHOL (mg)	SOD (mg)
Tomato, instant (Estee)	6 oz	40	<1	23	0	95

LITE PICK ○◇□□□

COMMENTS: 36 fewer calories, 1 gram less fat, 1 milligram less cholesterol, 612 milligrams less sodium than 6 ounces regular tomato soup from a mix. Much lower in sodium than regular soups.

PRODUCT	SERV	CAL	FAT (G)	% cal from fat	CHOL (mg)	SOD (mg)
Tomato w/herbs, instant (Lipton, Lite Cup-a-Soup Creamy Tomato and Herb)	6 oz	70	<1	<13	na	370

○

COMMENTS: No direct comparison, but this product is very low in fat and high in sodium.

PRODUCT	SERV	CAL	FAT (G)	% cal from fat	CHOL (mg)	SOD (mg)
Turkey w/ vegetables and pasta, canned (Pritikin, Turkey Vegetable with Ribbon Pasta)	7⅜ oz	50	<1	<18	5	160

LITE PICK ○◇◇□□□□

COMMENTS: 13 fewer calories, 1 gram less fat, 751 milligrams less sodium than 7⅜ ounces regular canned turkey noodle soup. Very low in fat and lower in sodium than regular soups.

PRODUCT	SERV	CAL	FAT (G)	% cal from fat	CHOL (mg)	SOD (mg)
Turkey w/ vegetables, instant (Weight Watchers, Turkey Vegetable)	10½ oz	70	2	26	na	1020

○

COMMENTS: 27 fewer calories, 2 grams less fat, 168 milligrams less sodium than 10½ ounce regular turkey vegetable soup. Very high in sodium.

PRODUCT	SERV	CAL	FAT (G)	% cal from fat	CHOL (mg)	SOD (mg)
Vegetable, canned (Campbell's, Special Request Vegetable) ○	8 oz	80	2	23	na	520

COMMENTS: 280 milligrams less sodium than 8 ounces regular Campbell's vegetable soup, but still high in sodium.

PRODUCT	SERV	CAL	FAT (G)	% cal from fat	CHOL (mg)	SOD (mg)
Vegetable, canned (Health Valley, No Salt)	7½ oz	100	1	9	0	40

LITE PICK ○◇□□

COMMENTS: 32 *more* calories, but 1 gram fat and 1,080 milligrams less sodium than 7½ ounces regular vegetable soup. Very low in fat and much lower in sodium than regular soups.

PRODUCT	SERV	CAL	FAT (G)	% cal from fat	CHOL (mg)	SOD (mg)
Vegetable, canned (Pritikin)	7⅜ oz	70	0	0	0	150

LITE PICK ○◇□□□□

COMMENTS: 4 fewer calories, 2 grams less fat, 759 milligrams less sodium than 7⅜ ounces regular canned vegetable soup. Fat free and lower in sodium than regular soups.

PRODUCT	SERV	CAL	FAT (G)	% cal from fat	CHOL (mg)	SOD (mg)
Vegetable w/ beans, canned (Health Valley, No Salt Chunky 5-Bean)	7½ oz	100	2	18	0	60

LITE PICK ○◇□□□

COMMENTS: No direct comparison, but this product is very low in fat and much lower in sodium than regular soups.

PRODUCT	SERV	CAL	FAT (G)	% cal from fat	CHOL (mg)	SOD (mg)
Vegetable w/beef, canned (Campbell's, Special Request Vegetable Beef)	8 oz	70	2	26	na	480

○

COMMENTS: 270 milligrams less sodium than 8 ounces regular Campbell's vegetable beef soup, but still high in sodium.

PRODUCT	SERV	CAL	FAT (G)	% cal from fat	CHOL (mg)	SOD (mg)
Vegetable, w/ beef, canned (Estee, Chunky Vegetable Beef)	7½ oz	140	7	45	na	130

□□□

COMMENTS: 816 milligrams less sodium than 7½ ounces regular chunky beef soup, but 26 calories and 3 grams *more* fat. Very high in fat but lower in sodium than most soups.

PRODUCT	SERV	CAL	FAT (G)	% cal from fat	CHOL (mg)	SOD (mg)
Vegetable, instant (Weight Watchers, Vegetarian Vegetable)	10½ oz	100	2	18	na	1250

NO LITE BARGAIN ○

COMMENTS: 5 calories and 170 milligrams *more* sodium than 10½ ounces regular vegetarian vegetable soup, but very low in fat.

PRODUCT	SERV	CAL	FAT (G)	% cal from fat	CHOL (mg)	SOD (mg)
Vegetable w/beef, instant (Weight Watchers, Vegetable with Beef Stock)	10½ oz	90	2	20	na	1370

NO LITE BARGAIN ○

COMMENTS: 20 calories, 1 gram fat, 58 milligrams *more* sodium than 10½ ounces regular vegetable beef soup. Very low in fat, but high in sodium.

SPREADS

PRODUCT	SERV	CAL	FAT (G)	% cal from fat	CHOL (mg)	SOD (mg)
Butter blend (Blue Bonnet, Unsalted, stick)	1 T	90	11	100	5	0

◇◇□

COMMENTS: Same fat and calories, but 95 milligrams less sodium than 1 tablespoon regular Blue Bonnet Butter Blend stick.

PRODUCT	SERV	CAL	FAT (G)	% cal from fat	CHOL (mg)	SOD (mg)
Fruit spread (Smucker's, Low Sugar, all flavors)	1 tsp	8	0	0	0	<10

LITE PICK ○◇□□

COMMENTS: 10 fewer calories than 1 teaspoon regular Smucker's jams or jellies, but 10 milligrams *more* sodium.

PRODUCT	SERV	CAL	FAT (G)	% cal from fat	CHOL (mg)	SOD (mg)
Fruit spread (Smucker's, Simply Fruit)	1 tsp	16	0	0	0	0

LITE PICK ○◇□

COMMENTS: 2 calories fewer than 1 teaspoon regular Smucker's jams or jellies.

PRODUCT	SERV	CAL	FAT (G)	% cal from fat	CHOL (mg)	SOD (mg)
Jam (Smucker's, Slenderella Low Calorie Imitation, all flavors)	1 tsp	8	0	0	0	0

LITE PICK ○◇□

COMMENTS: 10 calories fewer than 1 teaspoon regular Smucker's jam. Sweetened with saccharin.

PRODUCT	SERV	CAL	FAT (G)	% cal from fat	CHOL (mg)	SOD (mg)
Jelly (Smucker's, Artificially Sweetened Imitation Grape)	1 tsp	2	0	0	0	1.5

LITE PICK ○◇□

COMMENTS: 16 calories less than 1 teaspoon regular Smucker's jelly, but only 1.5 milligrams *more* sodium. Sweetened with saccharin.

PRODUCT	SERV	CAL	FAT (G)	% cal from fat	CHOL (mg)	SOD (mg)
Margarine, soft						
(Blue Bonnet, Diet)	1 T	50	6	100	0	100

◇□□□

COMMENTS: 50 fewer calories, 5 grams less fat than 1 tablespoon regular soft Blue Bonnet margarine, but 5 milligrams *more* sodium. Very high in fat.

PRODUCT	SERV	CAL	FAT (G)	% cal from fat	CHOL (mg)	SOD (mg)
Margarine, soft						
(Blue Bonnet, Light Tasty Spread, 52% Vegetable Oil)	1 T	60	7	100	0	100

◇□□□

COMMENTS: 20 fewer calories, 1 gram less fat, 10 milligrams less sodium than 1 tablespoon regular Blue Bonnet spread. Very high in fat.

PRODUCT	SERV	CAL	FAT (G)	% cal from fat	CHOL (mg)	SOD (mg)
Margarine, soft						
(Country Morning Blend, Lightly Salted)	1 T	90	10	100	10	85

◇◇□□□

COMMENTS: 30 milligrams less sodium than 1 tablespoon Land O'Lakes soft margarine. Very high in fat.

PRODUCT	SERV	CAL	FAT (G)	% cal from fat	CHOL (mg)	SOD (mg)
Margarine, soft (Country Morning Blend, Unsalted)	1 T	90	10	100	10	1

◇◇□

COMMENTS: 84 milligrams less sodium than 1 tablespoon Lightly Salted Country Morning Blend. Very high in fat.

PRODUCT	SERV	CAL	FAT (G)	% cal from fat	CHOL (mg)	SOD (mg)
Margarine, soft (Fleischmann's, Diet with Lite Salt)	1 T	50	6	100	0	50

◇□□□

COMMENTS: 50 milligrams less sodium than 1 tablespoon regular Fleischmann's diet margarine. Very high in fat.

PRODUCT	SERV	CAL	FAT (G)	% cal from fat	CHOL (mg)	SOD (mg)
Margarine, soft (Fleischmann's, Diet)	1 T	50	6	100	0	100

◇□□□

COMMENTS: 50 fewer calories, 5 grams less fat than 1 tablespoon regular soft Fleischmann's margarine, but 5 milligrams *more* sodium. Very high in fat.

PRODUCT	SERV	CAL	FAT (G)	% cal from fat	CHOL (mg)	SOD (mg)
Margarine, soft (Fleischmann's, Lightly Salted Whipped)	1 T	70	7	90	0	60

◇□□□

COMMENTS: 30 fewer calories, 4 grams less fat, 35 milligrams less sodium than 1 tablespoon regular soft Fleischmann's margarine. Very high in fat.

PRODUCT	SERV	CAL	FAT (G)	% cal from fat	CHOL (mg)	SOD (mg)
Margarine, soft (Fleischmann's, Sweet Unsalted)	1 T	100	11	100	0	0

◇□

COMMENTS: Same fat and calories, but 95 milligrams less sodium than 1 tablespoon regular soft or stick Fleischmann's margarine. Very high in fat.

PRODUCT	SERV	CAL	FAT (G)	% cal from fat	CHOL (mg)	SOD (mg)
Margarine, soft (Fleischmann's, Unsalted Whipped)	1 T	70	7	90	0	0

◇□

COMMENTS: 30 fewer calories, 4 grams less fat, 95 milligrams less sodium than 1 tablespoon regular soft Fleischmann's margarine. Very high in fat.

PRODUCT	SERV	CAL	FAT (G)	% cal from fat	CHOL (mg)	SOD (mg)
Margarine, soft (Fleischmann's, Light Corn Oil Spread)	1 T	80	8	90	0	70

◇□□□

COMMENTS: 20 fewer calories, 3 grams less fat, 25 milligrams less sodium than 1 tablespoon regular Fleischmann's soft margarine. Very high in fat.

PRODUCT	SERV	CAL	FAT (G)	% cal from fat	CHOL (mg)	SOD (mg)
Margarine, soft (Fleischmann's, Light Corn Oil Spread)	1 T	80	8	90	0	70

◇□□□

COMMENTS: 20 fewer calories, 3 grams less fat, 25 milligrams less sodium than 1 tablespoon regular Fleischmann's stick margarine. Very high in fat.

PRODUCT	SERV	CAL	FAT (G)	% cal from fat	CHOL (mg)	SOD (mg)
Margarine, soft (Imperial, Diet)	1 T	50	2.5	45	0	136

◇□□□

COMMENTS: 50 fewer calories, 2.7 grams less fat than 1 tablespoon regular soft Imperial margarine, but 40 milligrams *more* sodium. The high percentage of calories from fat is deceiving; since it contains only 2.5 grams of fat per tablespoon, this product is actually low in fat.

PRODUCT	SERV	CAL	FAT (G)	% cal from fat	CHOL (mg)	SOD (mg)
Margarine, soft (Imperial, Light)	1 T	56	2.7	43	0	109

◇□□□

COMMENTS: 44 fewer calories, 2.5 grams less fat than 1 tablespoon regular soft Imperial margarine, but 13 milligrams *more* sodium. The high percentage of calories from fat is deceiving; since it contains only 2.7 grams of fat per tablespoon, this product is actually low in fat.

PRODUCT	SERV	CAL	FAT (G)	% cal from fat	CHOL (mg)	SOD (mg)
Margarine, soft (Kraft Parkay, Light Corn Oil Spread)	1 T	70	8	100	0	110

◇□□□

COMMENTS: 30 fewer calories, 3 grams less fat, 5 milligrams less sodium than 1 tablespoon regular soft Parkay corn oil margarine. Very high in fat.

PRODUCT	SERV	CAL	FAT (G)	% cal from fat	CHOL (mg)	SOD (mg)
Margarine, soft (Kraft Parkay, Reduced Calorie Diet)	1 T	50	6	100	0	110

◇□□□

COMMENTS: 50 fewer calories, 5 grams less fat, 5 milligrams less sodium than 1 tablespoon regular Kraft Soft Parkay margarine. Very high in fat.

PRODUCT	SERV	CAL	FAT (G)	% cal from fat	CHOL (mg)	SOD (mg)
Margarine, soft						
(Mazola, Diet)	1 T	50	6	100	0	130

◇□□□

COMMENTS: 50 fewer calories, 5 grams less fat than 1 tablespoon regular Mazola margarine. Very high in fat.

PRODUCT	SERV	CAL	FAT (G)	% cal from fat	CHOL (mg)	SOD (mg)
Margarine, soft						
(Mazola, Unsalted)	1 T	100	11	100	0	0

◇□

COMMENTS: 100 milligrams less sodium than 1 tablespoon regular Mazola margarine. Very high in fat.

PRODUCT	SERV	CAL	FAT (G)	% cal from fat	CHOL (mg)	SOD (mg)
Margarine, soft						
(Mazola, Light Corn						
Oil Spread)	1 T	50	6	100	0	100

◇□□□

COMMENTS: 50 fewer calories, 5 grams less fat than 1 tablespoon regular Mazola margarine. Very high in fat.

PRODUCT	SERV	CAL	FAT (G)	% cal from fat	CHOL (mg)	SOD (mg)
Margarine, soft (Promise, Extra Lite)	1 T	66	4	55	0	63

◇□□□

COMMENTS: 24 fewer calories, 3 grams less fat, 33 milligrams less sodium than 1 tablespoon regular soft Promise margarine. Very high in fat.

PRODUCT	SERV	CAL	FAT (G)	% cal from fat	CHOL (mg)	SOD (mg)
Margarine, soft (Weight Watchers, Reduced Calorie)	1 T	50	6	100	na	110

□□□

COMMENTS: 52 fewer calories, 5 grams less fat, 43 milligrams less sodium than 1 tablespoon regular soft margarine. Very high in fat.

PRODUCT	SERV	CAL	FAT (G)	% cal from fat	CHOL (mg)	SOD (mg)
Margarine, soft (Weight Watchers, Reduced Calorie Unsalted)	1 T	50	6	100	na	0

□

COMMENTS: 52 fewer calories, 5 grams less fat, 153 milligrams less sodium than 1 tablespoon regular soft margarine. Very high in fat.

PRODUCT	SERV	CAL	FAT (G)	% cal from fat	CHOL (mg)	SOD (mg)
Margarine, stick (Country Morning Blend, Lightly Salted)	1 T	100	11	99	10	115

◇◇□□□

COMMENTS: No difference between lightly salted and regular stick margarine. Very high in fat.

PRODUCT	SERV	CAL	FAT (G)	% cal from fat	CHOL (mg)	SOD (mg)
Margarine, stick (Country Morning Blend Unsalted)	1 T	100	11	99	10	1

◇◇□

COMMENTS: Same fat and calories, but 117 milligrams sodium less than 1 tablespoon lightly salted Country Morning Blend stick. Very high in fat.

PRODUCT	SERV	CAL	FAT (G)	% cal from fat	CHOL (mg)	SOD (mg)
Margarine, stick (Fleischmann's, Sweet Unsalted)	1 T	100	11	99	0	0

◇□

COMMENTS: Same fat and calories, but 95 milligrams less sodium than 1 tablespoon regular soft or stick Fleischmann's margarine. Very high in fat.

PRODUCT	SERV	CAL	FAT (G)	% cal from fat	CHOL (mg)	SOD (mg)
Margarine, stick (Imperial, Light)	1 T	75	5	60	0	109

◇☐☐

COMMENTS: 25 fewer calories, 4 grams less fat than 1 tablespoon regular Imperial stick margarine. Very high in fat.

PRODUCT	SERV	CAL	FAT (G)	% cal from fat	CHOL (mg)	SOD (mg)
Margarine, stick (Mazola, Unsalted)	1 T	100	11	99	0	0

◇☐

COMMENTS: Same fat and calories, but 100 milligrams less sodium than 1 tablespoon regular Mazola margarine. Very high in fat.

PRODUCT	SERV	CAL	FAT (G)	% cal from fat	CHOL (mg)	SOD (mg)
Margarine, stick (Promise, Extra Lite)	1 T	66	4	55	0	71

◇☐☐☐

COMMENTS: 24 fewer calories, 3 grams less fat, 41 milligrams less sodium than 1 tablespoon regular Promise stick margarine. Very high in fat.

PRODUCT	SERV	CAL	FAT (G)	% cal from fat	CHOL (mg)	SOD (mg)
Margarine, stick (Weight Watchers, Reduced Calorie)	1 T	60	7	100	na	110

□□□

COMMENTS: 42 fewer calories, 4 grams less fat, 22 milligrams less sodium than 1 tablespoon regular stick margarine. Very high in fat.

PRODUCT	SERV	CAL	FAT (G)	% cal from fat	CHOL (mg)	SOD (mg)
Peanut butter (Estee)	1 T	100	8	72	0	2

◇□

COMMENTS: 14 *more* calories than 1 tablespoon regular peanut butter, but 16 milligrams less sodium. Very high in fat.

PRODUCT	SERV	CAL	FAT (G)	% cal from fat	CHOL (mg)	SOD (mg)
Peanut butter (Featherweight, Low Sodium)	2 T	180	15	75	0	<3

◇□

COMMENTS: 8 calories and 1 gram *more* fat than 2 tablespoons regular peanut butter, but 15 milligrams less sodium. Very high in fat.

PRODUCT	SERV	CAL	FAT (G)	% cal from fat	CHOL (mg)	SOD (mg)
Peanut butter (Health Valley, No Salt Chunky)	1 T	83	7	76	0	1

◇□

COMMENTS: 10 fewer calories, 1 gram less fat, 65 milligrams less sodium than 1 tablespoon regular chunky peanut butter, but still very high in fat.

PRODUCT	SERV	CAL	FAT (G)	% cal from fat	CHOL (mg)	SOD (mg)
Peanut butter (Health Valley, No Salt Creamy)	1 T	83	7	76	0	1

◇□

COMMENTS: 3 fewer calories, 17 milligrams less sodium than 1 tablespoon regular creamy peanut butter, but still very high in fat.

PRODUCT	SERV	CAL	FAT (G)	% cal from fat	CHOL (mg)	SOD (mg)
Peanut butter (Smuckers, No-Salt-Added Natural)	1 T	100	9	81	0	0

◇□

COMMENTS: 14 calories and 2 grams *more* fat than 1 tablespoon regular peanut butter, but 18 milligrams less sodium. Very high in fat.

SWEETENERS
AND
SYRUPS

PRODUCT	SERV	CAL	FAT (G)	% cal from fat	CHOL (mg)	SOD (mg)
Fructose						
(Estee)	1 tsp	12	0	0	0	0

LITE PICK ○◇□

COMMENTS: 4 calories fewer than one teaspoon sugar.

PRODUCT	SERV	CAL	FAT (G)	% cal from fat	CHOL (mg)	SOD (mg)
Fructose (Sweet Lite, Granular)	1 tsp equivalent of 1 tsp sugar	15	0	0	0	0

LITE PICK ○◇□

COMMENTS: Because it is not as sweet in hot beverages as it is in cold beverages, twice as much is needed in hot beverages in order to get the same sweet taste.

PRODUCT	SERV	CAL	FAT (G)	% cal from fat	CHOL (mg)	SOD (mg)
Fructose (Sweet Lite, Liquid)	1 tsp sugar equivalent	22	0	0	0	0

○◇□

COMMENTS: Because it is not as sweet in hot beverages as it is in cold beverages, twice as much is needed in hot beverages in order to get the same sweet taste.

PRODUCT	SERV	CAL	FAT (G)	% cal from fat	CHOL (mg)	SOD (mg)
Molasses (Brer Rabbit, Light)	1 T	60	0	0	0	10

LITE PICK ○◇□□

COMMENTS: Lighter only in color. 5 milligrams *more* sodium than 1 tablespoon regular Brer Rabbit molasses.

PRODUCT	SERV	CAL	FAT (G)	% cal from fat	CHOL (mg)	SOD (mg)
Saccharin (Featherweight)	1 tablet	0	0	0	0	0

LITE PICK □◇○

COMMENTS: 16 calories fewer than 1 teaspoon sugar.

PRODUCT	SERV	CAL	FAT (G)	% cal from fat	CHOL (mg)	SOD (mg)
Sweetener (Equal)	1 packet equivalent of 2 tsp sugar	4	0	0	0	0

LITE PICK ○◇□

COMMENTS: 24 calories fewer than 2 teaspoons sugar.

PRODUCT	SERV	CAL	FAT (G)	% cal from fat	CHOL (mg)	SOD (mg)
Sweetener (Sweet 'n Low)	1 packet equivalent of 2 tsp. sugar	4	0	0	0	0

LITE PICK ○◇□

COMMENTS: 24 calories less than 2 teaspoons sugar.

PRODUCT	SERV	CAL	FAT (G)	% cal from fat	CHOL (mg)	SOD (mg)
Sweetener (Estee, Sweet'n It)	6 drops	0	0	0	0	1

○◇□

COMMENTS: 16 calories fewer than 1 teaspoon sugar, but 1 milligram *more* sodium.

PRODUCT	SERV	CAL	FAT (G)	% cal from fat	CHOL (mg)	SOD (mg)
Sweetener (Featherweight, Liquid)	3 drops	0	0	0	0	0

LITE PICK □◇○

COMMENTS: 16 calories fewer than 1 teaspoon sugar.

PRODUCT	SERV	CAL	FAT (G)	% cal from fat	CHOL (mg)	SOD (mg)
Sweetener (Sprinkle Sweet)	1 tsp equivalent of 1 tsp. sugar	2	0	0	0	1

LITE PICK ○◇□

COMMENTS: 14 calories fewer than 1 teaspoon sugar, but 1 milligram *more* sodium.

PRODUCT	SERV	CAL	FAT (G)	% cal from fat	CHOL (mg)	SOD (mg)
Sweetener (Sweet One)	1 packet equivalent of 2 tsp. sugar	4	0	0	0	0

LITE PICK ○◇□

COMMENTS: 24 calories fewer than 2 teaspoons sugar.

PRODUCT	SERV	CAL	FAT (G)	% cal from fat	CHOL (mg)	SOD (mg)
Sweetener (Sweet 10)	⅛ tsp equivalent of 1 tsp. sugar	0	0	0	0	2

LITE PICK ○◇□

COMMENTS: 16 calories fewer than 1 teaspoon sugar, but 2 milligrams *more* sodium.

PRODUCT	SERV	CAL	FAT (G)	% cal from fat	CHOL (mg)	SOD (mg)
Sweetener (Weight Watchers, Sweet'ner)	1 packet equivalent of 2 tsp. sugar	4	0	0	0	30

LITE PICK ○□□

COMMENTS: 12 calories fewer than 1 teaspoon sugar, but 30 milligrams *more* sodium.

PRODUCT	SERV	CAL	FAT (G)	% cal from fat	CHOL (mg)	SOD (mg)
Syrup, blueberry (Estee)	1 T	4	0	0	0	0

LITE PICK ○◇□

COMMENTS: No direct comparison, but this product has 46 fewer calories per tablespoon than 1 tablespoon regular pancake syrup. Sweetened with fructose and saccharin.

PRODUCT	SERV	CAL	FAT (G)	% cal from fat	CHOL (mg)	SOD (mg)
Syrup, blueberry (Featherweight)	1 T	16	0	0	0	35

LITE PICK ○◇□

COMMENTS: No direct comparison, but this product has 34 fewer calories per tablespoon than regular pancake syrup. Sweetened with fructose.

PRODUCT	SERV	CAL	FAT (G)	% cal from fat	CHOL (mg)	SOD (mg)
Syrup, chocolate (Estee)	1 T	6	0	0	0	3

LITE PICK ○◇□

COMMENTS: 30 calories, 21 milligrams less sodium than 1 tablespoon regular chocolate syrup. Fat free.

PRODUCT	SERV	CAL	FAT (G)	% cal from fat	CHOL (mg)	SOD (mg)
Syrup, corn (Karo, Light)	1 T	60	0	0	na	30

○◇□

COMMENTS: Lighter than regular Karo, only in color. Fat free.

PRODUCT	SERV	CAL	FAT (G)	% cal from fat	CHOL (mg)	SOD (mg)
Syrup, pancake (Aunt Jemima, Lite Reduced Calorie Syrup Product)	1 T	25	0	0	0	33
LITE PICK ○◇□□						

COMMENTS: 25 calories fewer than 1 tablespoon regular Aunt Jemima syrup, but 18 milligrams _more_ sodium. Even so, this product still qualifies as a LITE PICK. Fat free.

PRODUCT	SERV	CAL	FAT (G)	% cal from fat	CHOL (mg)	SOD (mg)
Syrup, pancake (Estee)	1 T	4	0	0	0	0
○◇□						

COMMENTS: 46 fewer calories than 1 tablespoon regular pancake syrup. Sweetened with fructose and saccharin. Fat free.

PRODUCT	SERV	CAL	FAT (G)	% cal from fat	CHOL (mg)	SOD (mg)
Syrup, pancake (Featherweight)	1 T	16	0	0	0	0
LITE PICK ○◇□						

COMMENTS: 54 fewer calories than 1 tablespoon regular pancake syrup. Fat free.

PRODUCT	SERV	CAL	FAT (G)	% cal from fat	CHOL (mg)	SOD (mg)
Syrup, pancake (Log Cabin®, Lite)	1 T	25	0	0	na	46

LITE PICK ○◇□□□

COMMENTS: 27 fewer calories but 40 milligrams *more* sodium than 1 tablespoon regular Log Cabin syrup. Fat free.

PRODUCT	SERV	CAL	FAT (G)	% cal from fat	CHOL (mg)	SOD (mg)
Syrup, pancake (Mrs. Butterworth's, Lite)	1 T	34	0	0	0	38

LITE PICK ○◇□□

COMMENTS: 18 fewer calories, 2 milligrams less sodium than 1 tablespoon regular Mrs. Butterworth's syrup. Fat free.

PRODUCT	SERV	CAL	FAT (G)	% cal from fat	CHOL (mg)	SOD (mg)
Syrup, pancake (Weight Watchers, Reduced Calorie)	1 T	20	0	0	0	20

○□□

COMMENTS: 30 fewer calories than 1 tablespoon regular pancake syrup, but 20 milligrams *more* sodium. Fat free.

VEGETABLES

PRODUCT	SERV	CAL	FAT (G)	% cal from fat	CHOL (mg)	SOD (mg)
Beans, baked, canned (Health Valley, No Salt Boston)	4 oz	110	1	8	0	25

LITE PICK ○◇□□

COMMENTS: No direct comparison, but this product is very low in fat and much lower in sodium than regular baked beans. Very low in fat.

PRODUCT	SERV	CAL	FAT (G)	% cal from fat	CHOL (mg)	SOD (mg)
Beans, green, canned (Del Monte, No Salt Added)	½ c	20	0	0	0	<10

LITE PICK ○◇□□

COMMENTS: Same calories, but 345 milligrams less sodium than ½ cup regular Del Monte green beans. Fat free.

PRODUCT	SERV	CAL	FAT (G)	% cal from fat	CHOL (mg)	SOD (mg)
Beans, green, canned (Featherweight, Low Sodium)	½ c	25	0	0	0	<10

LITE PICK ○◇□□

COMMENTS: 431 milligrams less sodium than ½ cup regular canned green beans, but 7 *more* calories. Fat free.

PRODUCT	SERV	CAL	FAT (G)	% cal from fat	CHOL (mg)	SOD (mg)
Beans, lima, canned (Featherweight, Low Sodium)	½ c	80	0	0	0	25

LITE PICK ○◇□□

COMMENTS: 239 milligrams less sodium than ½ cup regular canned lima beans, but 25 *more* calories. Fat free.

PRODUCT	SERV	CAL	FAT (G)	% cal from fat	CHOL (mg)	SOD (mg)
Beets, canned (Del Monte, No Salt Added)	½ c	35	0	0	0	100

LITE PICK ○◇□□□

COMMENTS: Same calories, but 190 milligrams less sodium than ½ cup regular Del Monte beets. Fat free.

PRODUCT	SERV	CAL	FAT (G)	% cal from fat	CHOL (mg)	SOD (mg)
Beets, canned (Featherweight, Low Sodium, Sliced)	½ c	45	0	0	0	55

LITE PICK ○◇□□□

COMMENTS: 180 milligrams less sodium than ½ cup regular sliced canned beets, but 23 *more* calories. Fat free.

PRODUCT	SERV	CAL	FAT (G)	% cal from fat	CHOL (mg)	SOD (mg)
Carrots, canned (Featherweight, Low Sodium)	½ c	30	0	0	0	30

LITE PICK ○◇□□

COMMENTS: 234 milligrams less sodium than ½ cup regular canned carrots, but 9 *more* calories. Fat free.

PRODUCT	SERV	CAL	FAT (G)	% cal from fat	CHOL (mg)	SOD (mg)
Corn, canned (Del Monte, No Salt Added Cream Style)	½ c	80	1	11	0	<10

LITE PICK ○◇□□

COMMENTS: Same calories but 345 milligrams less sodium than ½ cup regular Del Monte Cream Style Corn. Very low in fat.

PRODUCT	SERV	CAL	FAT (G)	% cal from fat	CHOL (mg)	SOD (mg)
Corn, canned (Del Monte, No Salt Added, Vacuum Packed)	½ c	90	1	10	0	<10

LITE PICK ○◇□□

COMMENTS: Same calories, but 345 milligrams less sodium than ½ cup regular Del Monte vacuum-packed corn. Very low in fat.

PRODUCT	SERV	CAL	FAT (G)	% cal from fat	CHOL (mg)	SOD (mg)
Corn, canned (Del Monte, No Salt Added, Whole)	½ c	80	1	11	0	<10

LITE PICK ○◇□□

COMMENTS: 10 *more* calories, but 345 milligrams less sodium than ½ cup regular Del Monte whole kernel corn. Very low in fat.

PRODUCT	SERV	CAL	FAT (G)	% cal from fat	CHOL (mg)	SOD (mg)
Corn, canned (Featherweight, Low Sodium Whole Kernel)	½ c	80	1	11	0	10

LITE PICK ○◇□□

COMMENTS: 20 fewer calories, 406 milligrams less sodium than ½ cup regular whole kernel corn. Very low in fat.

PRODUCT	SERV	CAL	FAT (G)	% cal from fat	CHOL (mg)	SOD (mg)
Peas, canned (Del Monte, No Salt added)	½ c	60	0	0	0	<10

LITE PICK ○◇□□

COMMENTS: Same calories, but 345 milligrams less sodium than ½ cup regular Del Monte peas. Fat free.

PRODUCT	SERV	CAL	FAT (G)	% cal from fat	CHOL (mg)	SOD (mg)
Peas, canned (Featherweight, Low Sodium)	½ c	70	0	0	0	<10

LITE PICK ○◇□□

COMMENTS: 233 milligrams less sodium than ½ cup regular canned peas, but 31 *more* calories. Fat free.

PRODUCT	SERV	CAL	FAT (G)	% cal from fat	CHOL (mg)	SOD (mg)
Potatoes, french fried, frozen (Ore-Ida, Lites)	3 oz	90	2	20	0	30

LITE PICK ○◇□□

COMMENTS: 30 fewer calories, 2 grams less fat and 5 milligrams less sodium than 3 ounces regular Ore-Ida Golden French Fries. Very low in fat.

PRODUCT	SERV	CAL	FAT (G)	% cal from fat	CHOL (mg)	SOD (mg)
Potatoes, french fried, frozen (Ore-Ida, Lites, Crinkle Cuts)	3 oz	90	2	20	0	35

LITE PICK ○◇□□

COMMENTS: 30 fewer calories and 2 grams less fat than 3 ounces regular Ore-Ida Golden Crinkles. Very low in fat.

PRODUCT	SERV	CAL	FAT (G)	% cal from fat	CHOL (mg)	SOD (mg)
Potatoes, shoestring, frozen (Ore-Ida, Lites)	3 oz	90	4	40	0	25

LITE PICK ○◇□□

COMMENTS: 50 fewer calories, 2 grams less fat, 5 milligrams less sodium than 3 ounces regular Ore-Ida shoestrings. Very low in fat.

PRODUCT	SERV	CAL	FAT (G)	% cal from fat	CHOL (mg)	SOD (mg)
Spinach, canned (Del Monte, No Salt Added)	½ c	25	0	0	0	35

LITE PICK ○◇□□

COMMENTS: Same calories, but 320 milligrams less sodium than ½ cup regular Del Monte spinach. Fat free.

PRODUCT	SERV	CAL	FAT (G)	% cal from fat	CHOL (mg)	SOD (mg)
Spinach, canned (Featherweight, Low Sodium)	½ c	35	1	26	0	30

LITE PICK ○◇□□

COMMENTS: 326 milligrams less sodium than ½ cup regular canned spinach, but 16 *more* calories.

PRODUCT	SERV	CAL	FAT (G)	% cal from fat	CHOL (mg)	SOD (mg)
Tomatoes, canned (Del Monte, No Salt Added)	½ c	35	0	0	0	45

LITE PICK ○◇□□□

COMMENTS: Same calories, but 310 milligrams less sodium than ½ cup regular Del Monte stewed tomatoes. Fat free.

PRODUCT	SERV	CAL	FAT (G)	% cal from fat	CHOL (mg)	SOD (mg)
Tomatoes, canned (Featherweight, Low Sodium)	½ c	20	0	0	0	<10

LITE PICK ○◇□□

COMMENTS: 4 fewer calories, 186 milligrams less sodium than ½ cup regular canned tomatoes. Fat free.

PRODUCT	SERV	CAL	FAT (G)	% cal from fat	CHOL (mg)	SOD (mg)
Vegetables, mixed, canned (Featherweight, Low Sodium)	½ c	40	0	0	0	25

LITE PICK ○◇□□

COMMENTS: 208 milligrams less sodium than ½ cup regular canned mixed vegetables, but 22 *more* calories. Fat free.

PRODUCT	SERV	CAL	FAT (G)	% cal from fat	CHOL (mg)	SOD (mg)
Zucchini sticks, frozen (Mrs. Paul's, Light Batter)	3 oz	200	12	54	na	440

NO LITE BARGAIN

COMMENTS: No direct comparison, but this product is very high in fat and high in sodium.

Lite Surprises

While researching lite foods, it was discovered that many foods qualify as lite foods, though they are not labeled as such. Though the list is far from complete, this section offers information on "regular" food items that are lighter in fat, sodium, and cholesterol than most regular products. By using the information provided in this book and by being an avid label reader, you'll be able to uncover some "lite surprises" of your own.

Light Surprise Baked Goods

PRODUCT	SERV	CAL	FAT (G)	% cal from fat	CHOL (mg)	SOD (mg)
Muffins, w/fruit (Health Valley, Oat Bran Fancy Fruit Blueberry)	2 oz	140	4	26	0	95

○◇□□□

PRODUCT	SERV	CAL	FAT (G)	% cal from fat	CHOL (mg)	SOD (mg)

Fruit bars, w/nuts
(Health Valley, Oat
Bran Jumbo Date &

| Almond) | 1½ oz | 150 | 4 | 24 | 0 | 5 |

○◇□□

PRODUCT	SERV	CAL	FAT (G)	% cal from fat	CHOL (mg)	SOD (mg)

Muffins, w/fruit
(Health Valley, Oat
Bran Fancy Fruit

| Raisin) | 1 pc | 140 | 3 | 19 | 0 | 100 |

○◇□□□

PRODUCT	SERV	CAL	FAT (G)	% cal from fat	CHOL (mg)	SOD (mg)

Cookies
(Health Valley, Oat

| Bran Animal Cookies) | 1 oz | 90 | 3 | 30 | 0 | 50 |

○◇□□□

PRODUCT	SERV	CAL	FAT (G)	% cal from fat	CHOL (mg)	SOD (mg)

Cookies
(Health Valley, Oat
Bran Fancy Fruit

| Chunks With Raisins) | 2 pc | 70 | 2 | 26 | 0 | 95 |

○◇□□□

PRODUCT	SERV	CAL	FAT (G)	% cal from fat	CHOL (mg)	SOD (mg)
Fruit bars (Health Valley, Oat Bran Jumbo Raisins & Cinnamon)	1½ oz	140	4	26	0	5

○◇□□

PRODUCT	SERV	CAL	FAT (G)	% cal from fat	CHOL (mg)	SOD (mg)
Cookies (Lance, Fig Bar)	1½ oz	150	2	12	0	85

○◇□□□

PRODUCT	SERV	CAL	FAT (G)	% cal from fat	CHOL (mg)	SOD (mg)
Fruit bars (Health Valley, Oat Bran Jumbo Fruit & Nut)	1½ oz	150	4	24	0	5

○◇□□

Light Surprise Crackers

PRODUCT	SERV	CAL	FAT (G)	% cal from fat	CHOL (mg)	SOD (mg)
Crackers (Barbara's Bakery, Cracklesnax)	2 pc	12	<1	na	na	17

□□

PRODUCT	SERV	CAL	FAT (G)	% cal from fat	CHOL (mg)	SOD (mg)
Crackers, sandwich						
(Lance, Lanchee)	1¼ oz	180	4	20	5	110

○◇□□□

Light Surprise Entree

PRODUCT	SERV	CAL	FAT (G)	% cal from fat	CHOL (mg)	SOD (mg)
Frozen entree, pizza						
(Celantano, Thick Crust)	4 oz	238	7	26	na	252

○

PRODUCT	SERV	CAL	FAT (G)	% cal from fat	CHOL (mg)	SOD (mg)
Frozen entree, chicken						
(Celantano, Chicken Primavera)	11½ oz	270	9	30	na	650

PRODUCT	SERV	CAL	FAT (G)	% cal from fat	CHOL (mg)	SOD (mg)
Chicken (Tyson, Chicken Originals Lemon Pepper)	3¾ oz	120	2	15	na	210

○

PRODUCT	SERV	CAL	FAT (G)	% cal from fat	CHOL (mg)	SOD (mg)
Chicken (Tyson, Gourmet Selection, Chicken à L'Orange)	9½ oz	300	9	27	na	670

○

PRODUCT	SERV	CAL	FAT (G)	% cal from fat	CHOL (mg)	SOD (mg)
Frozen entree, pizza (Celantano, 9-Slice)	1 sl	157	5	29	na	160

○

PRODUCT	SERV	CAL	FAT (G)	% cal from fat	CHOL (mg)	SOD (mg)
Chicken (Tyson, Chicken Originals, Teriyaki)	3¾ oz	130	2	14	na	290

○

PRODUCT	SERV	CAL	FAT (G)	% cal from fat	CHOL (mg)	SOD (mg)
Chicken (Armour Dinner Classics, Chicken Hawaiian) ○	10½ oz	280	5	16	na	670

PRODUCT	SERV	CAL	FAT (G)	% cal from fat	CHOL (mg)	SOD (mg)
Frozen entree, pasta (Celantano, Lasagna Primavera), ○	11 oz	300	9	27	na	500

PRODUCT	SERV	CAL	FAT (G)	% cal from fat	CHOL (mg)	SOD (mg)
Beef (Armour Dinner Classics, Sirloin Roast) ○	11 oz	300	10	30	na	760

Light Surprise Fish

PRODUCT	SERV	CAL	FAT (G)	% cal from fat	CHOL (mg)	SOD (mg)
Sole (Mrs. Paul's, Au Naturel) ○	5 oz	110	2	16	na	170

PRODUCT	SERV	CAL	FAT (G)	% cal from fat	CHOL (mg)	SOD (mg)
Perch (Mrs. Paul's, Au Naturel)	5 oz	110	2	16	na	200

○

PRODUCT	SERV	CAL	FAT (G)	% cal from fat	CHOL (mg)	SOD (mg)
Perch (Gorton's, Fishmarket Fresh)	5 oz	140	3	19	na	100

○□□□

PRODUCT	SERV	CAL	FAT (G)	% cal from fat	CHOL (mg)	SOD (mg)
Haddock (Mrs. Paul's, Au Naturel)	5 oz	100	2	18	na	230

○

PRODUCT	SERV	CAL	FAT (G)	% cal from fat	CHOL (mg)	SOD (mg)
Haddock (Gorton's, Fishmarket Fresh)	5 oz	110	1	8	na	120

○□□□

PRODUCT	SERV	CAL	FAT (G)	% cal from fat	CHOL (mg)	SOD (mg)
Sole (Gorton's, Fishmarket Fresh)	5 oz	110	1	8	na	140

○□□□

PRODUCT	SERV	CAL	FAT (G)	% cal from fat	CHOL (mg)	SOD (mg)
Flounder (Mrs. Paul's, Au Naturel)	5 oz	110	2	16	na	210

○

PRODUCT	SERV	CAL	FAT (G)	% cal from fat	CHOL (mg)	SOD (mg)
Cod (Mrs. Paul's, Au Naturel)	5 oz	110	2	16	na	200

○

PRODUCT	SERV	CAL	FAT (G)	% cal from fat	CHOL (mg)	SOD (mg)
Cod (Gorton's, Fishmarket Fresh)	5 oz	110	1	8	na	90

○□□□

Light Surprise Frozen Dessert

PRODUCT	SERV	CAL	FAT (G)	% cal from fat	CHOL (mg)	SOD (mg)
Frozen, non-dairy dessert (Vitari Soft Serve, all flavors)	4 oz	80	0	0	0	25

○◇□□

Light Surprise Pasta

PRODUCT	SERV	CAL	FAT (G)	% cal from fat	CHOL (mg)	SOD (mg)
Tortellini (Simply Natural)	2 oz	151	1.8	11	na	4.4

○

PRODUCT	SERV	CAL	FAT (G)	% cal from fat	CHOL (mg)	SOD (mg)
Stuffed Shells (Simply Natural)	2 oz	77	.8	9	0	302

○

PRODUCT	SERV	CAL	FAT (G)	% cal from fat	CHOL (mg)	SOD (mg)
Ravioli (Simply Natural)	2 oz	139	2.4	16	0	3.4

Light Surprise Snacks

PRODUCT	SERV	CAL	FAT (G)	% cal from fat	CHOL (mg)	SOD (mg)
Popcorn (Charles, Caramel Corn) ○◇	4 c	214	1.4	6	0	216

PRODUCT	SERV	CAL	FAT (G)	% cal from fat	CHOL (mg)	SOD (mg)
Popcorn (Bachman, Caramel Corn) ○◇	4 c	220	2	8	0	380

Appendix A

The following companies provided information on their food products. If you would like to request nutrition information on a particular company's products, be sure to address your correspondence to the Consumer Affairs Department.

All American Gourmet
1100 Town & Country Road
Orange, CA 92668

Allied Old English, Inc.
100 Markley Street
Port Reading, NJ 07064

American Glacé
10–34 47th Avenue
Long Island City, NY 11101

Angostura International Ltd.
1745 Elizabeth Avenue
Rahway, NJ 07065

Anheuser Busch, Inc.
One Busch Place
St. Louis, MO 62118

Armour Food Company
Con Agra Center
1 Central Park Plaza
Omaha, NE 68102

Barbara's Bakery, Inc.
3900 Cypress Drive
Petaluma, CA 94952

Baskin Robbins
P.O. Box 1200
Glendale, CA 91209

Batterlite Whitlock, Inc.
P.O. Box 3877
Springfield, IL 62708

Beatrice/Hunt-Wesson, Inc.
P.O. Box 4800
Fullerton, CA 92634–4800

Bernard Food Industries, Inc.
P.O. Box 1497
Evanston, IL 60204

Benihana Frozen Foods, Inc.
P.O. Box 661
Buffalo, NY 14240–0661

Best Foods
CPC International, Inc.
P.O. Box 8000
Englewood Cliffs, NJ 07632

Borden, Inc.
Corporate Nutrition
960 Kingsmill Parkway
Columbus, OH 43229–1142

Boston Popcorn Co.
246 Walnut Street
Newtonville, MA 02166

Campbell Soup Company
Consumer Nutrition Center
Campbell Place
Camden, NJ 08103–1799

Carnation
5045 Wilshire Boulevard
Los Angeles, CA 90036

Celantano
225 Bloomfield Avenue
Verona, NJ 07044

Coca-Cola USA
P.O. Drawer 1734
Atlanta, GA 30301

Colombo, Inc.
Frozen Products Division
3 Riverside Drive
Andover, MA 01810

ConAgra Frozen Food Company
P.O. Box 80
Ballwin, MO 63022–0070

Dannon
P.O. Box 593
White Plains, NY 10602–0593

Del Monte Corporation
P.O. Box 3575
San Francisco, CA 94119

Diamond Crystal Salt Company
916 South Riverside
St. Clair, MI 48079

Dole Packaged Foods Company
P.O. Box 7330
San Francisco, CA 94120–7330

Dorman-Roth Foods
14 Empire Blvd.
Moonachie, NJ 07074

Eagle Crest Foods
1925 Valley View Lane
Dallas, TX 75234

Edy's Grand Ice Cream
& Dreyer's Grand Ice Cream
8600 Bryn Mawr
Suite 220N
Chicago, IL 60631

Estee Corporation
169 Lackawanna Avenue
Parsippany, NJ 07054

Foodways National, Inc.
P.O. Box 10
Boise, ID 83707

Foulds, Inc.
520 East Church Street
Libertyville, IL 60048

Frito-Lay, Inc.
P.O. Box 660634
Dallas, TX 75266–0634

Frozfruit
14805 S. San Pedro Street
Gardena, CA 90248

Fruit a Freeze, Inc.
10504 Norwalk Blvd
Santa Fe Springs, CA 90670

Galaxy Cheese Customer Service
P.O. Box 5204
New Castle, PA 16105

General Foods
Consumer Center
250 North Street
White Plains, NY 10625

Gorton's of Gloucester
88 Rogers Street
Gloucester, MA 01930

Health Valley Foods, Inc.
16100 Foothill Boulevard
Irwindale, CA 91706–7811

Heinz
P.O. Box 57
Pittsburgh, PA 15230

The Hidden Valley Ranch Co.
1221 Broadway
Oakland, CA 94612

Hillshire Farm
Box 227
New London, WI 54961

Horace W. Longacre, Inc.
Div. of WLR Foods, Inc.
Ranconia, PA 18924–0008

Geo. A. Hormel & Co.
P.O. Box 800
Austin, MN 55912

Imagine Foods, Inc.
P.O. Box 298
Palo Alto, CA 94302

Jones Dairy Farm
Fort Atkinson, WI 53538

Kraft, Inc.
Nutrition and Health Information
Draft Technology Center
801 Waukegan Rd.
Glenview, IL 60025–9974

Land O'Lakes, Inc.
P.O. Box 116
Arden Hills, MN 55440

Legume, Inc.
170 Change Bridge Road
Montville, NJ 07045

Lever Brothers Co.
390 Park Avenue
New York, NY 10022

Thomas J. Lipton, Inc.
800 Sylvan Avenue
Englewood Cliffs, NJ 07632

Nabisco Brands, Inc.
Consumer Information Center
P.O. Box 1928
East Hanover, NJ 07936

Nestle Foods Corporation
100 Manhattanville Road
Purchase, NY 10577

Nutrition Industries Corporation
P.O. Box AE
Cresskill, NJ 07626–0330

Ocean Spray Cranberries, Inc.
1 Ocean Spray Drive
Lakeville-Middleboro, MA 02349

Ore-Ida Foods, Inc.
Consumer Communications
P.O. Box 10
Boise, ID 83707

Oscar Mayer
P.O. Box 7188
Madison, WI 53707

Parco Foods, Inc.
13153 S. Francisco
Blue Island, IL 60406–0267

Mrs. Paul's Kitchens, Inc.
5830 Henry Avenue
Philadelphia, PA 19128

Pepsi-Cola Company
Rt. 35 and 100
Purchase, NY 10577

Pet
P.O. Box 392
St. Louis, MO 63166

Pillsbury
200 South Sixth Street
Minneapolis, MN 55402

Pollio
120 Mineola Boulevard
Mineola, NY 11501

The Proctor & Gamble Company
P.O. Box 599
Cincinnati, OH 45201

The Pro-Mark Companies
P.O. Box 470231–74147
Tulsa, OK 74145

Quaker Oats Company
Consumer Affairs Center
P.O. Box 9001
Chicago, IL 60604–9003

Sandoz Nutrition Corporation
5320 West 23rd Street
P.O. Box 370
Minneapolis, MN 55440

Simply Natural Foods
3542 Conrad Street
Philadelphia, PA 191229

The J.M. Smucker Company
Strawberry Lane
Orrville, OH 44667–0280

Star-Kist Foods, Inc.
582 Tuna Street
Terminal Island, CA 90731

Stouffer Foods Corporation
Consumer Affairs Department
5750 Harper Road
Solon, OH 44139–1880

Swift-Eckrich, Inc.
1919 Swift Drive
Oak Brook, IL 60521

Superior Protein Products Co.
15612 New Century Drive
Gardena, CA 90248

Thompson Kitchens, Inc.
Pritikin Foods Division
2520 South Grand Avenue East
P.O. Box 3877
Springfield, IL 62708–3877

Tofutti Brands, Inc.
1098 Randolph Avenue
Rahway, NJ 07065

Tuscan
750 Union Avenue
Union City, NJ 07083

Tyson Foods, Inc.
2210 Oaklawn
Drawer E
Springdale, AR 72765-2020

Vitari
R.C. Auletta Co.
59 East 54th Street
New York, NY 10022

Walden Farms
P.O. Box 352
Linden, NJ 07036

Welch's
Main Street
Concord, MA 01742

Whitman's Chocolates
P.O. Box 6070
Philadelphia, PA 19114

Weight Watchers International,
   Inc.
The Jericho Atrium
500 North Broadway
Jericho, NY 11753

Appendix B

References

CBORD Diet Analyzer, 1987, using ESHA database.

Natow, Annette and Heslin, Jo-Ann, *The Cholesterol Counter,* New York, New York, Pocket Books, 1989.

Pennington, Jean A.T. and Church, Helen Nichols, *Food Values of Portions Commonly Used,* New York, New York, Harper & Row, 14th edition, 1985.

United States Department of Agriculture, *Agriculture Handbook No. 8,* Washington, D.C., U.S. Government Printing Office, 1975.

United States Department of Agriculture, *Handbook of the Nutritional Value of Foods in Common Units,* New York, New York, Dover Publications, Inc., 1986.

Appendix C

There are several excellent publications that will keep you updated on new lite foods in the market. A few are listed below:

Cooking Light Magazine—Published bimonthly, *Cooking Light* focuses on lighter eating. Although the focus is not specifically on new lite products on the market, lite products are advertised in the magazine and regular readers will learn about lighter ingredients and lighter cooking. For a year's subscription, send $12.00 to: *Cooking Light* Circulation Department, Box 1748, Birmingham, Alabama, 35201.

Environmental Nutrition Newsletter—An eight-page monthly nutrition newsletter for both consumers and nutrition professionals. The newsletter devotes two pages each month to a food comparison, which ranks foods from best to worst, usually by fat content. The food comparisons have in the past covered lite cheeses and lite frozen entrees. The newsletter also provides brief bulletins about new products in the supermarket. For a one-year introductory subscription, send $24.00 to: *Environmental Nutrition,* 2112 Broadway, Suite 200, New York, New York, 10023.

Nutrition Action—The sixteen-page monthly publication of Center for Science in the Public Interest (CSPI), a consumer advocacy group based in Washington, D.C. Most months, *Nutrition Action* features comparisons of foods ranging from packaged cakes to cold cereals. The last page provides CSPI's "Picks" and "Pans," a critical viewpoint of prepared foods. For a one-year subscription and membership in CSPI, send $19.95 to: Center for Science in the Public Interest, 1501 16th Street, N.W., Washington, D.C. 20036–1499.

Today's Gourmet—A bimonthly six-page newsletter devoted to the topic of lite foods. In each issue it addresses the questions of which foods are truly lite and how they taste. The food comparisons are brief and there are no feature articles, but you're likely to find out about a new lite product here first. For a one-year subscription, send $11.95 to: *Today's Gourmet*, 60 East 42nd Street, Suite 411, New York, New York 10165.

Tufts University Diet & Nutrition Letter—A monthly eight-page newsletter that covers a broad range of nutrition topics. Food comparisons are not a monthly feature, but Tufts has examined a variety of foods from lite frozen entrees to cookies. Each month, four pages of the newsletter—"The Special Report"—are devoted to a single topic. For a one-year subscription, send $20.00 to: *Tufts University Diet & Nutrition Letter*, P.O. Box 57857, Boulder, CO, 80322–7857.

Index

We Deliver!
And So Do These Bestsellers.